# DRIVER PASSENGER PEDESTRIAN

# WE LIVE IN A WORLD OF CARS

Behind the wheel, we are amplified. If we honk, we're louder. If we put our foot down, we are faster. The car bulks us out to encase us in claimed personal space. Our taste, lifestyle and personality - these find easy expression in the auto. People who would never shout instead beep, gesticulate, tailgate. Others who would struggle to be noticed assert their success or their style. We can control our speed and direction, and savour the sensation. But the car is at its best as a social space. Somewhere we can craft our environment - its sounds, climate, and cushioning. Somewhere we can be with others, a moving living room where we swap the television for the windscreen as a window on the world, and instead of merely watching it, venture into it. Or as a studio - a place to contemplate and mentally create. To others it is a temple - a shrine to mechanics and design - even a museum, an art exhibit. Or an office. A communications device, moving people and data. Its power to be what we want it to be places the car amongst our ultimate forms of expression.

Cars are about freedom. We all want a maximum of personal freedom, and the car offers itself as its symbol and facilitator. Yet freedom is balanced between one and the many. Your freedom creates my traffic jam, pollutes my air, disturbs my peace. In the case of the parking space, we compete with each other over this limited resource, and collude in our attempts to wrestle it from the authorities that want to charge us or clamp us, tow us away or crush us into cubes. In the next 20 years, cars will impress on all of us the attempts of ever-greater proportions of the world's population at claiming this freedom, throwing up huge challenges. Solutions are already being developed. Fossil fuels could be replaced by new energy sources like hydrogen. Sharing schemes could free city centres of congestion, as communally-owned, zero-emission cars silently hum us between destinations. Improved public transport could reduce reliance on cars, whilst taxes and tolls discourage their use further. Whatever happens, people will always want cars.

Why? Look at the unrepentant, resurgent global street-racing scene. Look at the Monaco Grand Prix - a beacon for anyone with a yacht to perch on. Ask yourself when was the last day that you did not see a single car. Look at bumper stickers, concept cars, car boot sales, car collectors, Jubilee parades, funeral processions, lowrider conventions, weddings. Look at sumptuous leather interiors with 16 speaker stereo systems. Look at fashion, design, literature, art, rock, hip hop, video games, films and TV. Look further afield and see the impression of cars on the landscape, on architecture, on the economy, on national boundaries. Personal and universal, the car is where the experiences and ideas that define our time intersect.

Rejecting a view of life as a route, rushing as fast as we can from one landmark to another without noticing what's in between, we're back on the road again, open to its distractions and discoveries, fiddling with the stereo, and enjoying the ride.

Dan Ross

# CONTENTS

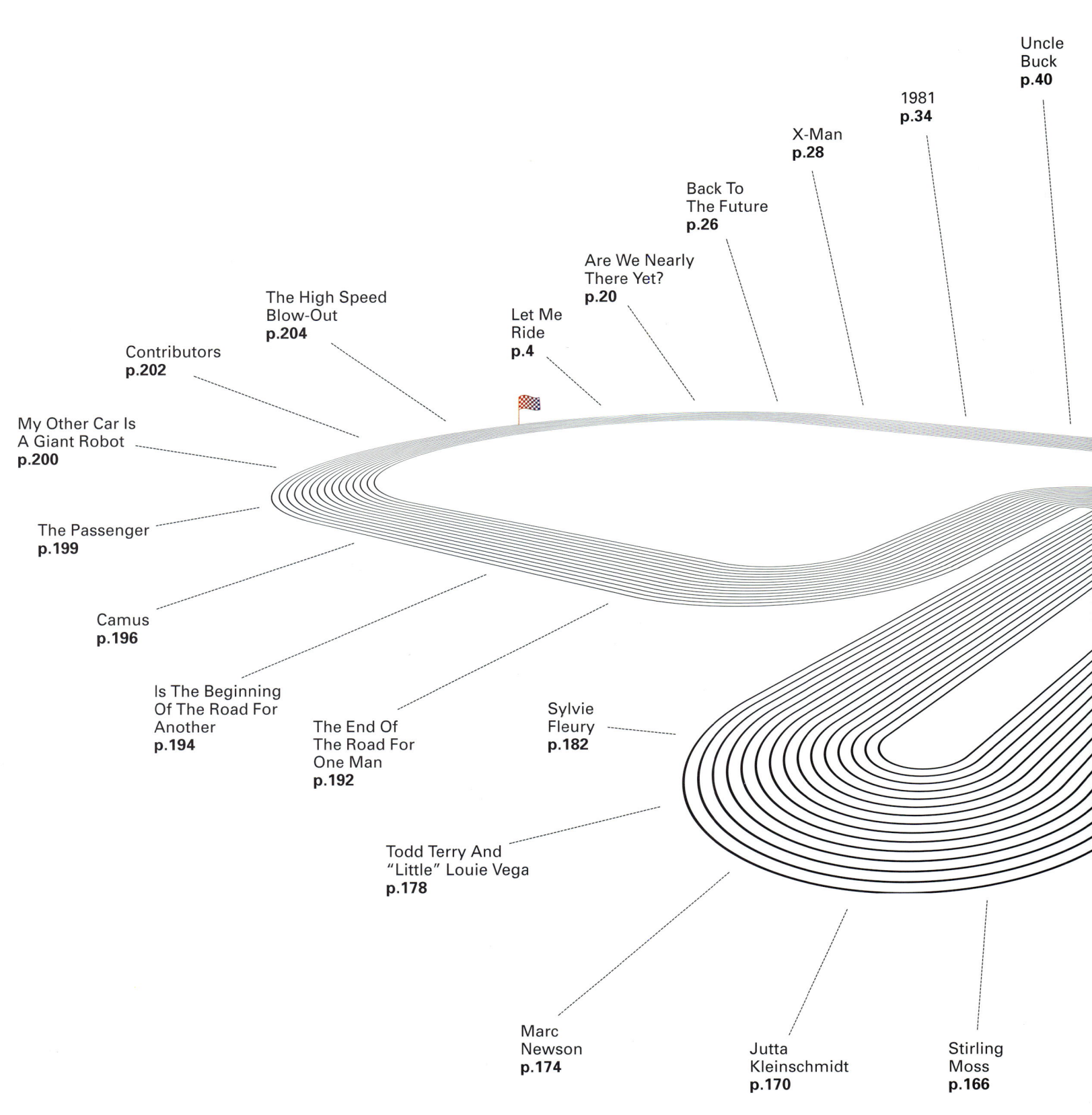

Uncle Buck **p.40**

1981 **p.34**

X-Man **p.28**

Back To The Future **p.26**

Are We Nearly There Yet? **p.20**

Let Me Ride **p.4**

The High Speed Blow-Out **p.204**

Contributors **p.202**

My Other Car Is A Giant Robot **p.200**

The Passenger **p.199**

Camus **p.196**

Is The Beginning Of The Road For Another **p.194**

The End Of The Road For One Man **p.192**

Sylvie Fleury **p.182**

Todd Terry And "Little" Louie Vega **p.178**

Marc Newson **p.174**

Jutta Kleinschmidt **p.170**

Stirling Moss **p.166**

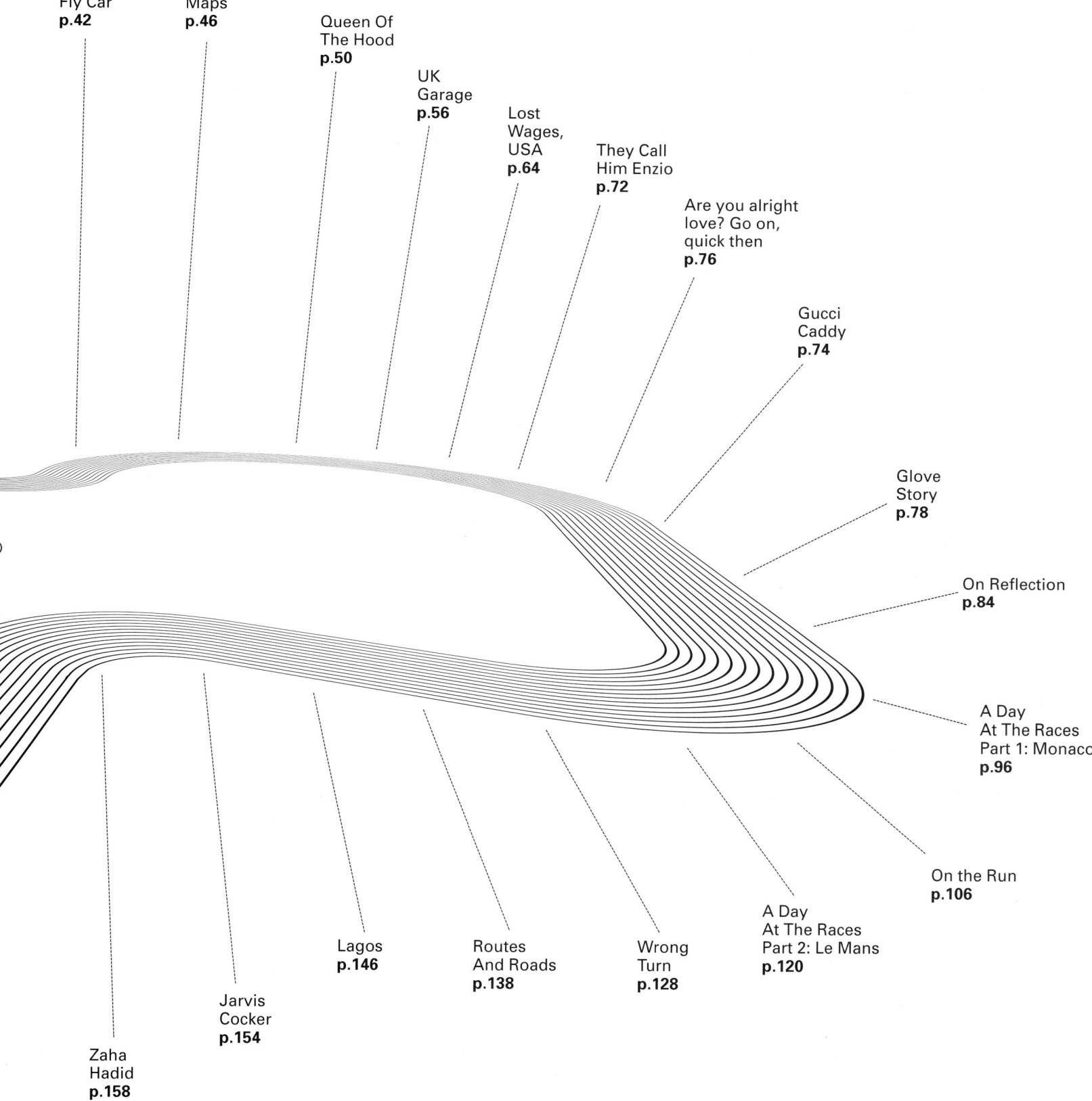

- Fly Car **p.42**
- Maps **p.46**
- Queen Of The Hood **p.50**
- UK Garage **p.56**
- Lost Wages, USA **p.64**
- They Call Him Enzio **p.72**
- Are you alright love? Go on, quick then **p.76**
- Gucci Caddy **p.74**
- Glove Story **p.78**
- On Reflection **p.84**
- A Day At The Races Part 1: Monaco **p.96**
- On the Run **p.106**
- A Day At The Races Part 2: Le Mans **p.120**
- Wrong Turn **p.128**
- Routes And Roads **p.138**
- Lagos **p.146**
- Jarvis Cocker **p.154**
- Zaha Hadid **p.158**

PHOTOGRAPHY
DANIEL HENNESSY

PHOTOGRAPHY
BRUNO BARBEY - MAGNUM

PHOTOGRAPHY
LUC DELAHAYE - MAGNUM

FUNERAL PROCESSION
GHANA
1997

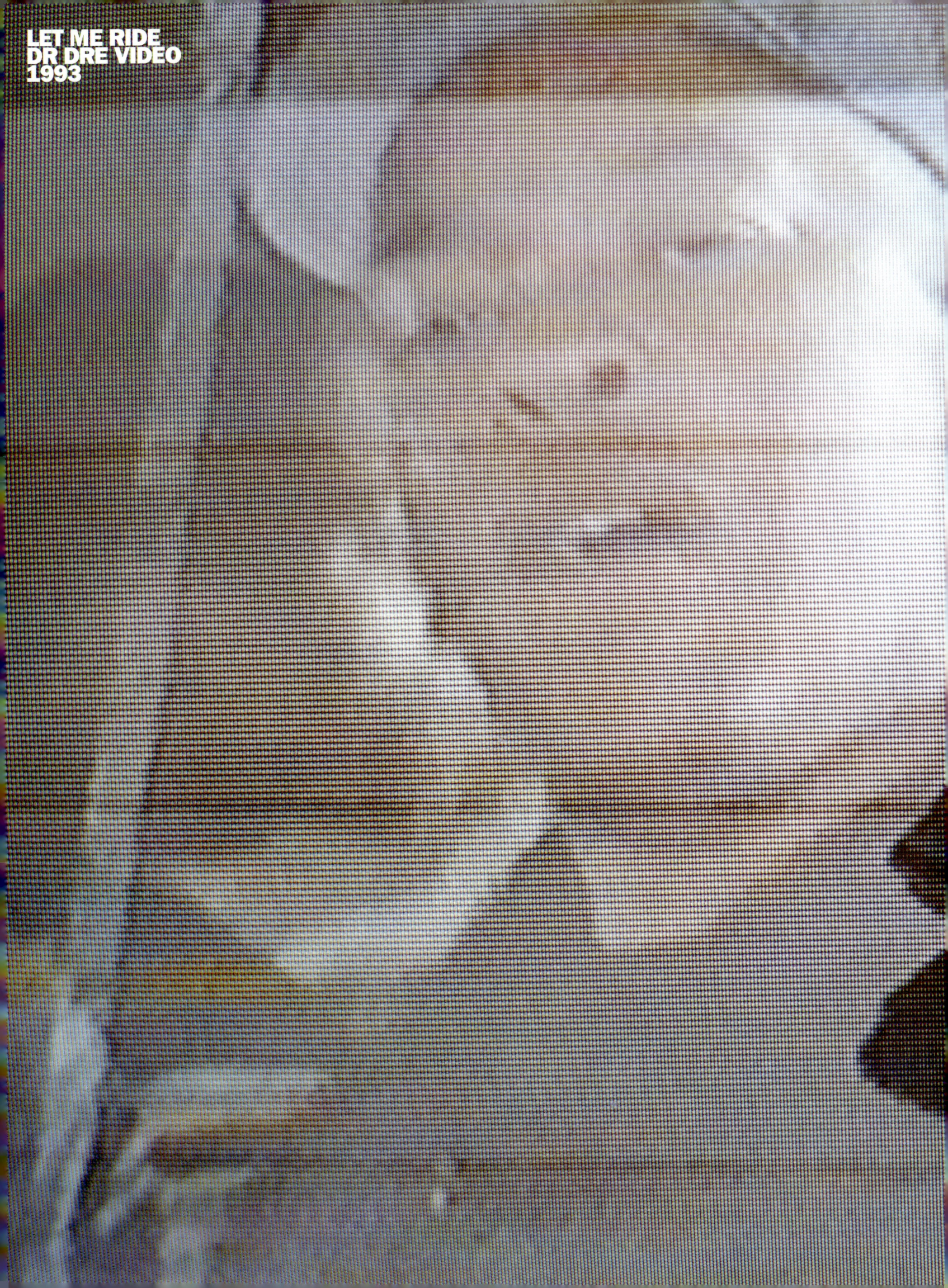

# ARE WE NEARLY

**SINCE HENRY FORD INTRODUCED MASS PRODUCTION TO MOTORING, CARS HAVE EVOLVED. BUT IN THE NEXT TWENTY YEARS THEY WILL BE REVOLUTIONISED ONCE AGAIN.**
**TEXT LIZZIE BAILEY**

## I. ELECTRONIC ORGANISERS

Cars are getting smarter. In the 1970s, the first ECUs (electronic control units) were introduced to reduce emissions and use fuel more efficiently. Today, you operate practically everything in your car using electronics - the luxury Mercedes S-class, for instance, has 40 ECUs. Between 10% and 20% of what you pay for a new car is actually the cost of its electronics. Their use has become universal, and their application is rapidly becoming more wide-ranging. Aside from the more obvious quality-of-life advances now taken for granted like electric windows, wing mirrors, and sunroofs, bip-bip alarm/lock remotes and digital stereos, electrical systems are moving to contol every aspect of the way a car works.

Drive-by-wire, which replaces mechanical parts with electronic systems to reduce the gap between command and action, is beginning to filter down, often from Formula One, to luxury and even entry level cars. For example, you may soon be able to entirely stop using hydraulics, pumps, hoses, belts and fluid to steer your car. A firm in Michigan has built E-Steer, where a sensor detects the movement of your hand on the steering wheel and then gets an electric motor to do all the work. E-Steer makes your car even lighter and easier to handle, and should be on the road by 2003.

Smarter technology can also mean safer. We no longer measure a new car's safety on whether it has an airbag to protect the driver but on how many it has in total. Electronics that sense and stop skids by controlling the braking of selective wheels are starting to be more regular features of new cars. Your distance from other cars can also be controlled intelligently. Adaptive cruise control available on luxury cars like the Jaguar XKR and Mercedes S-class senses cars in your proximity, and automatically slows and speeds in response to the environment. You can, of course, override it.

## II. ROBOCOP 2

Your smarter car will also most likely be a connected car, through what is called telematics - blending computers and wireless telecoms technologies, particularly GPS (global positioning system) satellites, to bring you automatic roadside assistance, remote diagnostics and a host of value-added services.

Getting lost or stuck unexpectedly in traffic will become harder. The Satellite Navigation (satnav) systems that are currently available are based on plotting your movement using GPS against a static map, but they are unable to weave in live traffic data to inform you of hold-ups caused by accidents, roadworks or heavy

**IN FRANCE, CHEATING HUSBANDS CAUGHT OUT BY FRONT-SHOT TRAFFIC CAMERAS SUCCESSFULLY LOBBIED FOR THE INCRIMINATING IMAGES NOT TO BE SENT TO THEIR HOMES**

congestion. The next stage satnav - already available in Germany - allows Traffic Message Channel (TMC) compatible systems to link this pre-stored cartographic information to live updates on road conditions. Real time data, collated from sources like Trafficmaster, the AA and RAC in the UK, will be broadcast on a national FM radio station and then be picked up by the TMC satnav system in your car and interpreted for your route. It will then prompt you with re-route options around the problems. It could be in the UK and beyond sometime next year.

The road network, too, is becoming more intelligent. The cat's eyes on the motorway might soon begin to oversee your road use. UK firm Astucia has created intelligent road studs that photograph your number plate and monitor your speed, but they might also warn you of hazardous conditions. They're solar powered, using a radio-frequency network to transmit information. Combined with existing cameras, sensors and media reports, it will mean you'll be able to forecast journey times, select the quickest route, and navigate it more safely.

Losing your car is also made harder by GPS. It's not a huge leap of the imagination to link your mobile phone to your car's GPS to remind you where you parked in that 3,000 capacity car park. Car thieves already have to contend with satellite tracking devices as they make their escape. Mercedes and Lexus have keyless locks and ignition, and more mainstream cars like the new Renault Laguna have similar systems, increasing the requisite skill-set for a successful car criminal further.

It will be harder to get lost even if you want to. The system that follows stolen cars will be able to track you when you drive too. If recent attempts by the British and American governments to gain access to, and archive, personal electronic information are anything to go by, car criminals will not be the only ones apprehended thanks to new technology. In France, cheating husbands caught out by front-shot traffic cameras successfully lobbied for the incriminating images not to be sent in marked envelopes to their homes. Forthcoming examples of automotive technology intruding into the private lives of drivers are likely to raise questions about civil liberty, no doubt to be answered by cries of: "If you're not doing anything wrong then why complain?" But few drivers can honestly claim to follow the Highway Code to the letter, and for the driver who enjoys the challenge of outfoxing the system to escape parking or speeding tickets, the bar is being raised considerably. Digital speed cameras that never run out of film; intelligent road-studs; systems being tested to automatically slow your car down to obey the speed-limit; traffic and parking cameras that are able to scan for specific registration numbers - are all in the pipeline or already being implemented. Mechanisms exist which could be easily adapted to police the roads more rigorously, for example in countries with toll systems

# THERE YET?

by calculating the time taken to cover the distance between two booths. If you cover 100 miles in an hour, the maths already leave no doubt that you've been speeding. It is therefore a social or political issue, technology just makes it harder to ignore.

As cars have insulated us from the sensation of speed, we go faster before we feel our movement. Better brakes mean we adapt to new limits to push our vehicles to. This doesn't imply blame - we're not necessarily doing anything wrong in doing so. We're just getting used to what our cars can do. New technology promises to make our cars safer, but human nature suggests that these new parameters of performance will cause a reaction that is unpredictable and, no doubt, unwanted by those running the roads.

### III. DO YOU WANT FRIES WITH THAT?

As all brands become lifestyle brands, and all personal information becomes commodified, the cultural impact of networked, satellite-pinpointed cars will be to wire the car deeper into culture, communication and commerce. Writer William Gibson insists that all cultural change is caused by technology. Marx thinks that economics are responsible. In the car, we will see the two hypotheses play out as chicken and egg.

Between high streets, out of town malls, drive-ins and car boot sales, the transformation will be completed from shopper's car into shopping cart. GPS, for example, means that the market knows where you are too. That valuable information will allow it to offer you prompts to stop at service stations, attractions and events along your way. Satnav maps already have cultural data - tourist sites, hotels, service stations - programmed in. With telematics, driving is only a voice command away from shopping. Will your car's manufacturer become gatekeeper to the media portal embedded in your dashboard, or will it be a telecommunications company? As corporations continue to merge and the "attention" economy increasingly values access to the consumer's mind over physical goods, the sectors will converge, or at least co-exist in close harmony. The potential synergy between the group purchasing power of a marque and its drivers with the marketing impetus of the retail chain will offer the potential to create new allegiances. Will buying a BMW mean cheaper rooms at the nearby hotels your GPS-informed onboard system recommends? Will purchasers make decisions based on the services the car delivers, beyond the way it drives, the way it looks? They already are. In the way that some car companies moved from just offering finance to including free insurance with their new cars, they are branching out into networked services and elite ownership privileges. Extrapolating, these could even extend to where you can take your car - will luxury cars come bundled with access to congestion-free shortcuts? The only limiting factors are what you are prepared to pay for, and what society will allow.

Closer to reality, imagine a button that allows you to purchase the song that you are listening to on the radio, but can't catch who it's by and don't have time to go to the shop to pick

**BETWEEN HIGH STREETS, OUT-OF-TOWN MALLS, DRIVE-INS AND CAR BOOT SALES, THE TRANSFORMATION WILL BE COMPLETED FROM SHOPPER'S CAR INTO SHOPPING CART**

up. Record companies already are. Now imagine hearing an announcement for a Madonna concert, and pressing that button to connect to the ticket line before the price soars into four figures. Now imagine programming your car to alert you when opportunities like that arise. The idea of "permission-based" marketing may be taken to further extremes. As television-screening devices (like TiVO) and viewers work together to skip advertising messages, outdoor advertising has benefited. An American sci-fi television programme floated the idea a few years ago that an alternative to the toll-road could be the ad-way, where we swap rights to bombard us with advertising in exchange for not having to pay for our passage. Companies are already sponsoring clean-up schemes along highways. In the UK a local golf course has turned a weed-infested roundabout into a cultivated flowerbed in exchange for spelling its name in daffodils in a relatively innocuous example of a worldwide trend. Wait until the pattern repeats itself everywhere.

Road signs are changing and so could billboards. Rolls-Royce is working as a manufacturer with Transport Research Labs on new Variable Message Signs - think Steve Martin in LA Story - to be rolled out in 2003. They'll be visible from much greater distances than the signs out there now; they'll have three colours - red, white and off-white - use a much clearer typeface, and be able to display images (of congestion ahead, say) and text. Will these signs eventually be sponsored too? What will determine how technology and economics alter the driving experience will be what the culture itself demands, these demands amplified and accelerated in turn. McDonalds may offer special meal deals to passing family-sized cars, but cars did not create the Big Mac. Yet the drive-in brings us one step closer to eating a Happy Meal. Telematics will bring exponentially more purchases within our impulsive reach, meaning that we're more likely to buy what we already want. And that we're more likely to want what we can now buy.

### IV. CARS THAT TELL JOKES

Emerging technology also offers new opportunities for personalising the driving experience. Telematics might mean that on a road trip from Berlin you tune into your favourite German radio station as you drive through France, whilst catching weather bulletins from the resort you're driving to in Spain. Nissan's Chappo concept offers a vision of the car as a mobile living room. In urban areas of Japan, shortage of space means that the car is often treated as an extra room, as much a part of the home as the kitchen. Glass that can instantly change from transparent to opaque could turn the cabin into a private bedroom. Inflatable architecture could expand it into a temporary abode. If traffic slows much further, we could be spending more waking time in our cars than in our living rooms; the car will become even more a space we use to relax, to be entertained, to catch up with friends in. It will adapt to this function, and be marketed on the basis of how well it fulfils it. The recently announced, top-of-the-range Mercedes Maybach limousine parallels this with a mobile boardroom. Neither will seem new to a generation growing up watching DVDs and playing games on their own, personalised in-car-entertainment systems. Tomorrow, time spent in the car needn't be vastly different from being at the desk or on the sofa. If this can apply to drivers, for passengers it is doubly so. The modern successor to the model T is beginning to offer the option of atomising each of us in our own media bubble, complete with its own air-conditioned microclimate, making where we physically are and who we are with virtually irrelevant, should we want it to be.

BMW's recently updated 7-series employs their new iDrive system, based around a relative of the gaming joystick, designed to reduce dashboard clutter and make communications and computer navigation as integral and intuitive to using the car as the stereo. Ford's 24-7 concept car also strives to streamline communications between driver and car. Designed by Laurens Van Den Acker, chief designer at Ford Motor Company's California design studio, the 24-7 combines telematics with voice-activated controls. "When you step into your car and close the door," says Van Den Acker, "you're isolated, fumbling in a dangerous situation. Car interiors today are about as sophisticated as a typewriter. They were never designed to house 200-plus functions. Every function has a button; whenever a new function gets added, you get a new button." Ford put voice control in the 24-7 instead, as it makes both interaction and information display flexible: the 24-7 shows only the instrumentation you need, only when you ask for it, on a state-of-the art rear-projection dashboard screen. For instance, "If the GPS is in the middle of the console and down, that's the last place I'd look if I'm lost and stressed; if I'm not lost, I don't need it," says Van Den Acker. The 24-7 will "Call Mum", "show GPS" and respond appropriately to "I'm hot" by tweaking your climate control system. Some Jaguars and Mercedes already offer similar voice commands for aircon, radio and carphone, and when voice becomes cheaper it should also go mainstream, fast. Voice may become increasingly necessary if the various bodies lobbying the UK government to make it illegal to drive while talking on your handheld phone succeed. The latest research questions whether it is too distracting to speak whilst driving even on hands-free. Whether talking to others from our cars differs greatly to talking to our cars, or talking to others in our cars, remains to be explored. But, excluding situations we consider relatively hazardous or exotic, driving is certainly an activity most of us do with only part of our minds engaged.

This problem is being addressed too. Retinal detectors will be able to tell from your eyes whether you are tired and need a break. Within five years, your car may know you well enough to keep you company on the road. A patented system developed by IBM dubbed the Artificial Passenger attempts to keep you alert by interacting with you, asking questions to gauge whether you need a burst of fresh air, a spritz of water, or just someone to talk to on a long, solo trip. With the potential to build a highly personal driver profile, a dash-mounted camera will then be able to read your lips, and learn how you speak. Start to flag, and it'll play your preferred type of uplifting music, or sound a buzzer. If you get a simple question wrong, say, "Who was your first lover?" or give it the silent treatment, it will assume something is wrong, and key into the car's systems to wake you up. It might advise taking a break, then defuse the tension caused by it ordering you to pull over by telling you a joke. It's conceivable that such a system might develop into entertaining, informing and even counseling you. Will your car become a tamagochi-style pet, which demands attention and offers affection? Again, the personal information and access the machine holds will be valuable, and will need to be guarded carefully to avoid excessive commercial exploitation.

In the age of attention deficit disorders, slow-moving traffic and time pressure, driving may, however augmented, still be unable to hold our attention, and the answer could ultimately be to separate driving for necessity and driving for pleasure entirely. Experiments don't give hope for it anytime soon, but the future already points to driving being far too important to be left to humans.

## THE FUTURE ALREADY POINTS TO DRIVING BEING FAR TOO IMPORTANT TO BE LEFT TO HUMANS

It is only a matter of time before the car takes over on motorways, and eventually driving may become just a hobby, which a minority engage in solely for fun. In such a future, manually driven cars might not be allowed to endanger the computer-controlled vehicles that transport people between A and B, immersed in their interactive business/entertainment environments. If we want to drive, we'll have to visit dedicated tracks, or escape the system in remote areas.

### V. THE HOMERMOBILE

Nicholas Negroponte, new media guru at the Massachusetts Institute of Technology, argues that people don't want technology, they want what the technology can deliver them. He uses the example of power-tools to show that what we want is not a brand new Black & Decker, but the holes in walls it produces. Or, better still, the picture hanging on the wall that we needed the hole to put the pin in to keep it from falling on the floor. What do we want from our cars? We certainly want to be as safe, comfortable, and mobile as possible. We also want to express our style and individuality. In the past, that meant choosing from the range offered by a large number of independent, state and conglomerate-owned car manufacturers, or building or customising our own vehicles. However, new technology will enable today's multi-branded, mega manufacturers to respond quicker to more niche demands.

Ford's Chief Executive, Jac Nasser, foresees that, thanks to the internet, "direct customer choice will 'pull' the perfect vehicle from the system [integrating customers, dealers, manufacturers and suppliers] for each individual order. Customers will tell us exactly what to build - and when to build it." Range Rover already does this on a limited level with its Autobiography range, as does Mercedes and Volvo. The bespoke approach could allow you to decorate the inside of your car as you would your home, choosing from materials, designs and features supplied by your favourite designers, or even submitting your own patterns for manufacture, like Nike's customisable slogan shoe. And, like Niketown, car showrooms are becoming "brand experiences".

Cadillac have called on French interior designer Andree Putman to create their new dealer showrooms; sub-brands, like MINI, owned by BMW, and Smart, part of DaimlerChrysler, are sold in distinctive, marque-specific showrooms. Lexus has been given its own showrooms, whereas in the past the cars were sold along with parent company Toyota's lower value cars. The VW group has built a town around its products called Autostadt next to their factory and HQ in Wolfsburg, Germany, dedicated to their various brands from Skoda to Audi and Bentley, replete with a museum and hotel. Mercedes are moving towards a strategy of "experience centres", as new competition regulations loom which threaten manufacturers' control of where, by whom, and for how much, their cars are sold. Buying a car offline is therefore becoming more involving, and, like other forms of luxury retail, more of a leisure activity. If, by 2008, the car salesman is supplanted by information technology and car-buying theme parks, then an automotive revolution will have truly occurred.

### VI. IT'S NOT EASY BEING GREEN

Nasser also cites growing demand for corporate social responsibility as a reason why the automotive industry is undergoing great change. So, with any luck your new smarter car will also be a greener car. Conventional wisdom holds that we've got a maximum of another 50 years left in fossil fuels and we'll have to start using alternatives before then. Most big car companies are

Ford 24-7 concept

Nissan Chappo concept

aware that they can no longer wait around for oil and petrol to run dry, and are working on finding a sustainable successor.

The most likely long-term solution is hydrogen, to be used either powering fuel cells, or burning in internal combustion engines. Hydrogen can be easily extracted from water through electrolysis - splitting $H_2O$ into its constituent parts, hydrogen and oxygen. Hydrogen can also be extracted from methanol (marsh gas) and converted onboard to hydrogen, as in DaimlerChrysler's Necar 5 concept. To date most of the major car manufacturers are working to develop fuel cells that use enormous amounts of platinum - an expensive metal and in very short supply - to work. They can currently cost around £300,000 each. Smaller firms are investigating other types of fuel cells. London's Westminster Council already uses a van to service some of its parks that runs using a ZeTek AFC (alkaline fuel cell). Honda, Ford, DaimlerChrysler and Renault will, they say, have commercially available (if not commercially viable) fuel cells by 2003 or soon thereafter. Texaco, Shell, BP Amoco and Exxon Mobil are all working on hydrogen infrastructure projects. However, until we have a refueling infrastructure for hydrogen and electricity that can rival that for petrol, change will be slow. Pure hydrogen fuel cell vehicles are unlikely to become widespread before 2020.

In the meantime we're likely to see more hybrid electric-petrol cars, such as Honda's Insight and Toyota's Prius, though let's hope they get more attractive. The Prius uses a battery-powered electric engine to start up and drive at slow speeds, then automatically senses when it is more efficient to swap over to the petrol engine. The Insight uses an electric motor to supplement the petrol engine when needed, and assists it sufficiently to increase fuel economy to as high as 83mpg (an average petrol Ford Focus manages 40mpg). Ford recently announced plans to build a hybrid version of its Escape SUV (known as the Maverick in Europe) in early 2004 and Ford, DaimlerChrysler and GM all plan within the year to market different hybrid fuel cell vehicles to dramatically reduce emissions.
Another option has been developed by Formula One engineer Guy Nègre and his son Cyril, who have designed a car that runs on compressed air. And the KAZ, a concept SUV designed by the Faculty of Environmental Information at Keio University in Japan, not only uses a zero-emissions motor but also a reduction-gear system that decreases the transmission loss between the motor and a wheel, and reduces the total weight of the vehicle.

Of course, alternative fuel sources don't entirely solve the problem. The power for huge hybrid batteries still has to be generated elsewhere. Onboard solar power is unlikely to become a viable mass alternative, even where the sun shines brightest. Apart from a small amount of electricty generated through wind or water (hydroelectric) power, most of the world's electricity still tends to be generated by burning fossil fuels, harming the environment by producing the global warming gas carbon dioxide again. Creating and decommissioning batteries can also damage the environment. But electric hybrids at least transfer local air pollutants like nitrous oxide, hydrocarbons and particulates associated with petrol and diesel engines away from crowded urban areas. The beneficial health implications make the electric hybrid a good medium term bridge between conventional combustion engines and hydrogen power.

Consumers aren't yet willing to create the impetus for change with their wallets, leaving government with the initiative to spur industrial change. European Union countries and other developed nations already impose strict emissions restrictions on new cars before they can be sold. In the uncertain wake of the aborted Kyoto treaty, however, there are few signs of a unified approach. The UK has put in place a new road and company car tax scheme based around the carbon dioxide your car emits (the

**THE DESIGNERS OF THE FORD PUMA DELIBERATELY PUMPED THE NOISE OF THE ENGINE INTO THE INTERIOR TO GIVE THE DRIVER THAT GO-FASTER FEELING**

lower the $CO_2$ emissions - the less tax you pay) which is being looked at by other European nations. California has lead in the US by pushing the auto industry into developing zero-emission cars as a prerequisite for the biggest car-makers to sell their vehicles in its state. But after low take-up from the public the focus has moved towards petrol/electric hybrids. Other states lag behind. Eastern Europe, the former Soviet Union, China and almost all of the developing world offer little incentive for carmakers to do likewise. As it is widely predicted that China will become a huge market for cars within the coming decades, this issue has moved to the foreground. In the meantime, the more local and national authorities that, like Westminster Council, encourage change, the faster we will see it occur.

Whatever the fuel of the future, and the efforts or lack thereof by government, the complex mire of deliverability and desirability looks set to keep petrol burning in our engines until the last drops are running dry, if not in the developed world than elsewhere. Technology will answer society's demands for cleaner, more environmentally friendly energy solutions only when the average driver can be convinced that a fuel cell Ferrari is as attractive as a petrol-powered version. Again, technology may provide an answer. Manufacturers are known for spending millions perfecting the clunk of a closing door. On the popular Ford Puma coupe, the designers deliberately pumped the noise of the engine into the interior to give the driver that go-faster feeling, while actively reducing it outside for the benefit of pedestrians and other road users. Maybe on future fuel cell cars, in the absence of actual engine noises they'll follow the video game makers' lead and sample the varying whine and roar of old style engines, to give the illusion that our zero-emission, silent, telematic transporters still have street appeal.

# BACK THE F

**CAN LOOKING BACKWARDS
BE FORWARD THINKING?
TEXT UMA JONES**

Borrowing the concept of sampling the past to create something new from fashion, music and film, Intersection examines the motor industry's retro fixation.

In 1989, Nissan's Figaro introduced the idea of nouveau-vieux, a new car that was deliberately styled to look old. New concepts from Chrysler and Ford also play the retro card, with designs either inspired by or based on cars from the past. Part of the alternative school of futurists, Renault's head designer Patrick le Quement says, "the biggest risk for us is to not take risks," begging the question whether the retro option is capable of being a groundbreaking, risk taking strategy, or is just a cynical attempt to tug on sentimental strings. According to Sjoerd Dijkstra of DaimlerChysler's Design&Technology division, the PT Cruiser has proved popular because "heritage design touches customers emotionally. It makes them feel good, even customers too young to remember original designs. Quality and performance are a given for any vehicle, as are value and versatility. An emotional bond is the added bonus that makes the Chrysler PT Cruiser stand apart from its competition."

Growth of these niche models is attributable to a new breed of affluent, style-guided consumers who approach the purchase of a car unburdened by the previous generation's concern over those "given" factors. Bold, original contemporary designs like the Audi TT do take risks - the Renault Avantime is a big risk, but one that anyone who intuitively sides with originality will appreciate. Retro is less risky, although it hasn't always been so. Ten years ago, the MG RV8, a relaunched version of the 1969 MGB, was looked upon as eccentric in the extreme. Yet just a few years later in 1994, Volkswagen stunned the world by unveiling its Concept 1. With customer chequebooks waving frantically before VW's eyes, the "New Beetle" just couldn't be thrust into showrooms quick enough. In the States, the new Bug whipped up a flurry of Beetle-mania - not only in terms of sales but also culture. It has been adopted by the rich and famous, appeared in numerous R&B videos and simultaneously revitalised the VW brand. A generation transported to school on the vinyl back seat of ma's old Volkswagen has been emotionally swept away by the chocolate-box charm of this Golf-based retro exercise. Says J Mays, the Concept 1's designer: "We took on the role not so much as designers of a new vehicle but rather as curators of an idea". Elsewhere, the story is not quite so rosy. In the UK the New Beetle was stifled initially by left-hand-drive status and inflated prices and it seems as if the car's moment has now passed by. In Germany the situation was worse, as the original was always seen as utilitarian and not particularly loveable, a feeling that has done the new version no favours at all. Perhaps the most significant impact of the Concept 1 was to revive the notion that a small car can be as desirable as a much more expensive, bigger model, helping to pave the way, for example, for the Smart.

Retro rebirth is, however, generally a promotion - perhaps to help justify their resurrection - updated models carry much higher specifications than their loveable, flawed ancestors, and are priced into a higher bracket accordingly. The change from '60s "Mini" to the new, all-capitalised, 21st Century "MINI" is apt - the new machine feels much more solid, and its size has bulked out accordingly. Accompanied by hype that makes *Big Brother* appear low-key, the MINI is the branded launch pad from which BMW will offer us a whole new range of compact cars. An overwhelmingly

# TO JTURE

cute go-kart, both inside and out, to question whether it is a cynical pastiche of the '59 original is unfair and irrelevant. Back then, Alec Issigonis, who had no concept of "active lifestyles" or "premium compact product positioning", created the smallest possible car that could carry four people. The shape was purely form following function, which is why it aged so well. The new car reflects a different society, where, even in the lower priced products, function is subordinate to style. The original Mini lasted 40 years. The new version is already planned to be replaced in four. Styles change faster now, perhaps even more so for retro designs.

This is the one major problem with retro. By their very nature, these reinvented cars will never be as brilliantly new as the original, as they are automotive actors. They almost play the part too well, removing the quirks and challenges that are warmly recalled from their less reliable, more sparsely specified predecessors. Part of the joy of owning an old Volkswagen, for example, is that it is so noisy. When it breaks down, when something falls off, it is all part of the charm and the thing is forgiven and cherished further. A polished New Beetle with a three year warranty and smooth 16-valve engine cannot compete with this sort of relationship. Indeed, "real" Beetle owners rarely extend their customary friendly fellow-Bug-driver wave to those piloting the new version. To them, it's like buying a new pair of '70s-look Levi's rather than the authentic item from a charity shop. But the argument doesn't really ring true. We like the quirks of the original but most of us wouldn't put up with them, especially not in a new car that doesn't share the original's rock-bottom pricing. In a sense, retro is a rose-tinted view of the past. Under J Mays, the designer responsible for the New Beetle whilst at VW, Ford has developed the new Thunderbird model and the Forty-Nine concept, alluringly sympathetic updates of famous Ford classics. The company describes the Forty-Nine as a "sentimental drag-race" down memory lane, while the Thunderbird "has a strong emotional connection to early versions", and is painted in a pallet that evokes memories of the original, yet is in fact entirely new. An alternative approach is exemplified by Chrysler's highly successful PT Cruiser, which captured the appeal of retro without being based on a specific old car, but rather on a general genre - the hot rod. As a consequence, it has an aura all of its own, yet is still a powerful representation of a time gone by. Plymouth's Prowler, another Chrysler creation, is also a retro exercise based on no particular car, like the Nissan Figaro. For manufacturers with iconic models steeped in pop cultural significance, the temptation to revive them is greater. VW's stylish Microbus will test whether a further icon can be reintroduced. Harking back to the hippy-connoting Combi van, the Microbus will be another revival equipped and priced into a higher bracket. In the meantime, the MINI has quickly supplanted the old version in the aspirations of a new generation, which didn't realise or care that, until last year, the original Mini was still on sale.

1 Nissan Figaro

2 Ford Forty-Nine concept car

Illustrations by Yorgo Tloupas

# X-MAN

**THE X-COUPE IS BMW'S MOST IMPORTANT DESIGN CONCEPT FOR A DECADE. WE SPOKE TO CHRIS BANGLE, BMW'S CHIEF DESIGNER, ON THE NEW FACE OF THE MUNICH MARQUE.**
**TEXT JOHN ARLIDGE**
**PHOTOGRAPHY MICHAEL DANNER**

**BMW has been criticised by some for producing sober-looking cars. The X-Coupé is a radical new departure. Is it time for a dramatic change?**
I don't agree with the criticism. In the Z8, we maybe made the most beautiful car in the world. Not a Ferrari, a BMW. But, yes, we have decided we need to make a big jump. That's hard because people don't expect to be surprised by BMW. In fact, they're probably positively happy not to be surprised. But we want to get away from this idea that BMW is only a safe, limited little thing that does not scare people or refresh them. This is what the X-Coupé is all about. It's authentic and in-your-face. It's not what you would expect from a BMW in the past.

**Are you changing design philosophy?**
Yes. In the past we used this 'wedge' concept as the major way to signify the dynamic, with a line sloping from the rear of the car down towards the front. But there are many different types of shapes that create a dynamic, shapes that have no fixed start and finish point. Think about falling water, a flag in the wind, or flames. We want to use those softer shapes in future. You can see them in the X-Coupé. It

The X-Coupe

casts off the traditional wedge in favour of cantilevered forms and sculpture. The car is much more three-dimensional.

**Is the interior as radical?**
Absolutely. We are challenging pre-conceptions with this vehicle - getting rid of pillars, creating new curves. What we have come up with is this wonderful asymmetrical design. When you open up the back it's like looking inside a baby grand piano. The new approach creates more space and more engagement for passengers. On the surfaces, we are using new materials - nubuck leather, neoprene, different types of rubber. We also want to let more light in, so it is very airy.

**What about the driver?**
We want to get away from the philosophy that every function has a switch and the switches are wrapped around the driver. There are now 700 or 800 different functions in modern cars and they are starting to look like an Apollo cockpit. So a few years ago the electrical engineers, body engineers and our design ergonomists got together to come up with an alternative. We want to put the essential controls on the steering wheel and make sure there are hard switches for those functions for which you need immediate feedback - heaters, blowers, defrosters and sound. All the other functions will be controlled by the iDrive system - a multi-function computer that the driver operates using a single rotary knob. This new approach keeps the fascia clean and helps the driver to concentrate his or her eyes forward. You know people often say, 'Why can't driving be simple like it used to be?' They miss that; it has been lost in the clutter of those 800 functions. iDrive is about giving it back.

**On the inside of the car, are you saying less is more?**
To a certain extent, but in the luxury goods market 'less is more' can easily become 'less is a bore' and that is wrong. If you reflect on any luxury product, you can see that what they have developed is a style that allows multiple depths of reading. You can read as deep as you like. If you want simplicity, you don't have to look very deep but if you take time to really look at the design then you realise the complexity of the product. This is the opposite of the past when there was one viewing plane and everything that was simple was brutally simple. Take a wallet or handbag. When you see it you may think, 'Oh yes. What a great simple design, what elegant lines.' And you can leave it at that. But, if you want,

## WHEN I GOT TO BMW, I WAS TOLD CUSTOMERS BUY OUR MOTORS AND YOU GET TO DO THE PACKAGING

you can take a closer look and you will see, 'Oh yes. They have wrapped the leather surfaces under each-other, used the clasp in a particular way, and stitched it this way or that way.' We want to make sure you can do that with a BMW - that the cars have simplicity but also follow-up.
If you look at the X-Coupé it has this multi-layered effect - first you are engaged by the rhythm of its energy but once it has got your attention and you look closer, you extract from it some major bold statements and fine details.

**But when you first showed off the X-Coupé in Detroit in January critics declared it the 'dog of the show'.**
Well, the *New York Times* called it 'brilliant', *Auto & Design* wrote 'by far the best showcar' and *Autocar* labelled it the 'Detroit Show Star'. But we fuelled our share of outrage too, I will admit. We have a new animal, a new species and there are a lot of dogmas out there in the world of car design that people don't feel comfortable about challenging. When you plan as far ahead as we are planning, you have to be three jumps ahead of everybody else, so it's no wonder that you will shock people. Almost any endeavour that is not conservative or is more creative is criticised at the beginning and then years later everybody looks back and says it was the fundamental defining moment for the whole genre. I was just in Paris and I was looking at Manet's 'Olympia'. Somebody sent me cuttings from that time showing how he was ostracised and publicly ridiculed and yet that painting today is seen as the defining movement into modernism. We have the same situation here. The X-Coupé is way too much for a lot of people to take right now but over time they will look back and say this car played a leading role in the way cars took a jump to expressionism.

**However much you change your approach what are the elements that make a BMW a BMW, which you can never lose?**
We want cars that look alert, powerful, dynamic, authentic, with harmonious tension - a wound-up spring effect. They're not just any old cars but passionate cars driven by passionate people. They have to seem like they want to be driven, not parked. We are a wheel-orientated company and like to show off the big wheels with the brake calipers visible. We want to keep the kidney grille and the double eyes but they can't just be repetitiously applied. They are all

The Z9 is another futuristic concept car from BMW featuring the iDrive system

under new interpretation provided we keep a certain amount of face and look that's awake, that has a bird-of-prey type of feel to it.

**Observers say designers and concept cars like the X-Coupé are becoming more and more important because most people buy cars because they like how they look, rather than how they drive? Do you agree?**

If I did, I would be asking for more money. Are designers the most important people? No. Design is too important to leave to the designers; it needs to be balanced with a strong engineering team. If you don't have that, the designers run off at the mouth and have fun and lose sight of what is the heart and soul of the machine. And the heart and soul of a BMW is that it is a driving machine, not a parking-and-looking-at machine. This is the Bayerische Motoren Werke, not the Bayerische Design Werke. When I got to BMW, I was told customers buy our motors and you get to do the packaging - which is true. I worked at Fiat before and they had a completely different approach. There, it was important who designed the car. Here it's important that the car is a BMW. There I was paid to do Chris Bangle cars and here I'm paid to run a team that does BMWs.

**Fiat sounds more fun.**

Are you kidding? Stravinsky said the artist cannot operate in a vacuum. If he does, he creates waste. He has to operate within the context that defines his art and, here, the BMW board, my engineer colleagues and the ethos of this great marque define my art. Art and commerce will never be on the same side of the street but they can be on the same journey - with some help from folks like me.

**Okay, but some critics say that big**

### A LOT OF PEOPLE ARE HAPPY WITH THOSE OLD BOXES THAT GO FROM A TO B JUST THE SAME AS A LOT OF PEOPLE ARE HAPPY WITH CEILINGS PAINTED WHITE BUT EVERY ONCE IN A WHILE I WANT A SISTINE CHAPEL, DAMN IT

**car firms, including BMW, are turning out cars that are all the same, dull even? That things aren't what they used to be?**

Dull? The X-Coupé? Sure, the industry has changed. Look at car shows, these days. They are more sanitised, more politically correct. Not so many dancing girls. But, you know, it would be a disaster if we all thought these changes were for the worse and we were boring ourselves to tears with what we do. What is important is to learn from the past and not feel that we are a lost generation of designers with no future because they did it all before. Like all the great stuff has already been done. That can't be. I do not accept that as a premise for my profession or for my own future or that of my team. I believe if we do it right, people will collect our cars just like we collect cars from the past. And they will do it for the same reason. There is this emotional connection to passionate artwork, where you can see that a craftsman has been at work and gave his all. And, my god, he created something beautiful. 'Wow! The hand of man did that.' The most wonderful thing about this profession is that it gives us a chance to still do that. A lot of people are happy with those old boxes that go from A to B just the same as a lot of people are happy with ceilings painted white but every once in a while I want a Sistine Chapel, damn it. I want to know that somewhere we have a Michelangelo among us. Wouldn't it be great if he was in our team and BMW were the ones that did that? That's what I live for.

# 1981

**LIKE SCIENCE FICTION, CONCEPT CARS REFLECT THE SPIRIT OF THE DAY TRANSPOSED ONTO AN IMAGINARY FUTURE. MORE HISTORY LESSON THAN FUTURE SHOCK, INTERSECTION PICKS OUT ITS FAVOURITES FROM TWENTY YEARS AGO.
TEXT DAN ROSS**

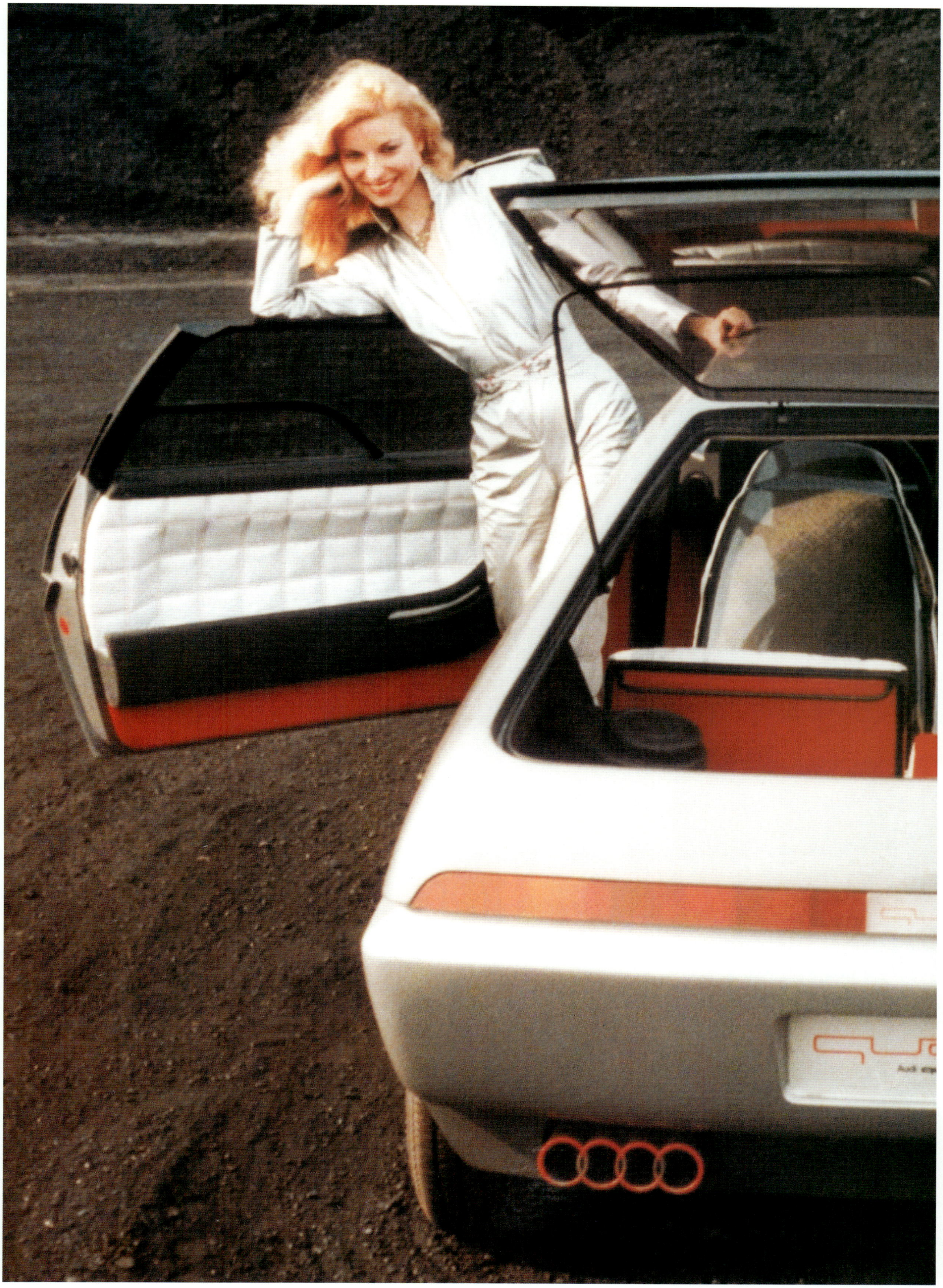

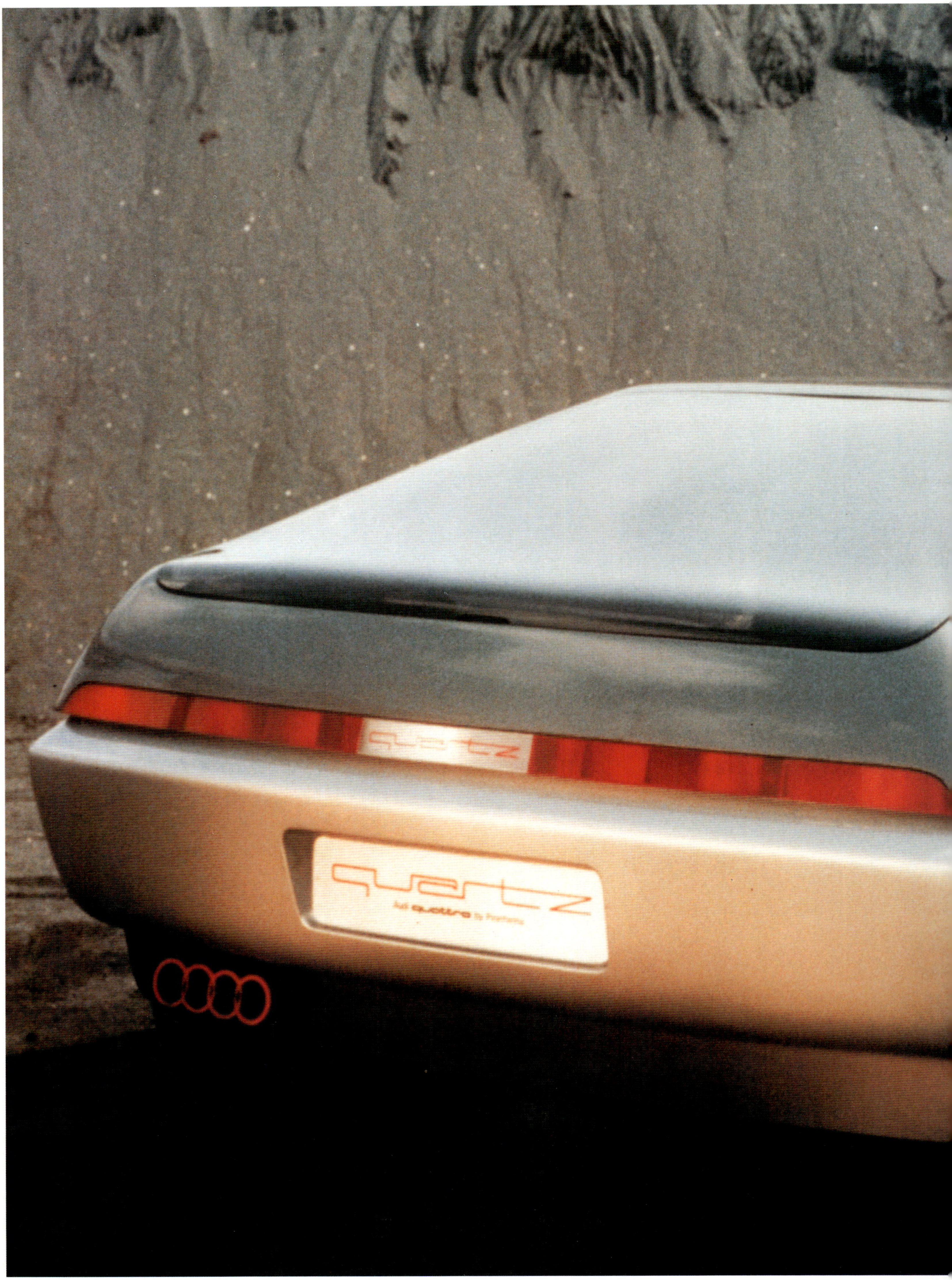
quartz

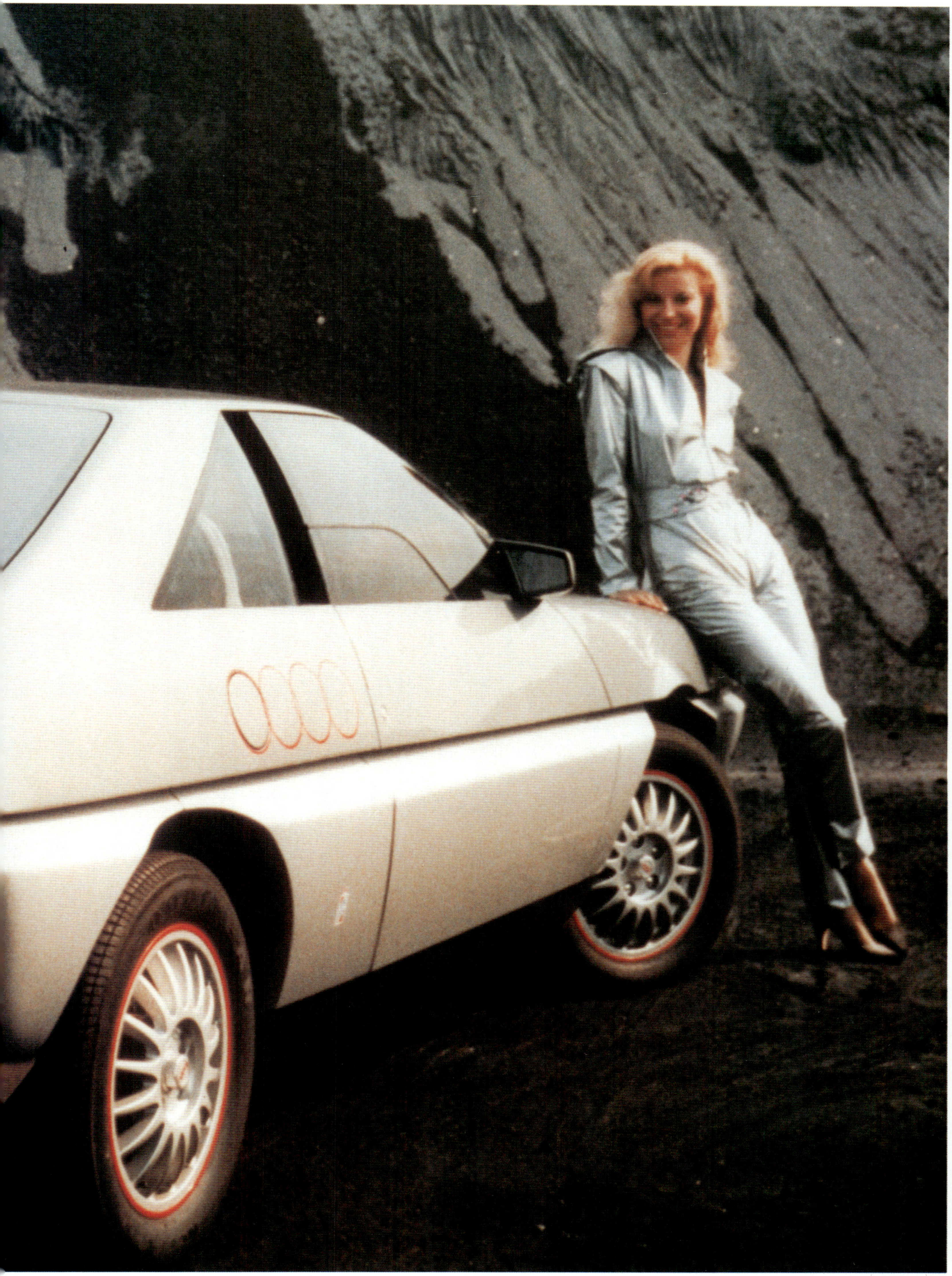

# 1981

The year the Space Shuttle makes its maiden voyage, Ronald Reagan is in the White House and on the other side of the iron curtain Leonid Breznev is in the Kremlin. France welcomes its new President, Francois Mitterand. Margaret Thatcher rules Britannia, and *Chariots Of Fire* wins the Academy Award for best picture. Whilst it will be years before film makes the swift transition to tape, Betamax looks sure to become the dominant video format of the future. Glamour-soap *Dallas* tops the US television ratings, and down-to-earth darts-based game show *Bullseye* begins its long run in the UK. Pope John Paul II is shot twice, leading to a redesign of the Popemobile. Reagan also survives an assassination attempt. No one has yet made a serious attempt to kill Thatcher.
Chrysler introduces the K-car line, restoring the company's good fortunes and establishing chairman Lee Iacoca as the definitive management guru of the '80s. Doomed supercar manufacturer DeLorean starts production in Ireland with millions of pounds taxpayers' money. Alain Prost secures his first Grand Prix victory. Mercedes offer the world's first commercially available airbag in their 500SEL model. John "you can not be serious" McEnroe is the year's Wimbledon champion. Atari launch their popular 2600 model (dispensing with a wood finish in favour of moulded plastic), allowing home gamers to play a rudimentary form of virtual tennis using a paddle control and a collusive measure of imagination. IBM launch the personal computer.

*Previous pages*:
Pininfarina Audi concept
*Left*: Ford Probe III
*Above near right*: Probe III
*Right*: Ford Pockar

In the last days of disco, MTV begins broadcasting music videos, promising to kill the radio star. Blondie's "Rapture" popularises rap, breakdance and graffiti art, by topping the charts.

Electronic fuel injection and turbochargers are the new go-faster buzzwords, and all the major carmakers of the day are exhibiting cars fitted with them at the Tokyo Motor Show, reviewed dramatically as "the arrival of a turbo age". Recreational vehicles with more distinct functions, such as minivans and 4x4s, increase in number. At the time they are geared towards people who actually require such features, rather than appreciating them for their stylistic qualities. In the UK, the Ford Cortina is the best selling car. Looking to the future,

## THE TOKYO MOTOR SHOW HERALDS THE ARRIVAL OF THE TURBO AGE

Ford suggests the innovative storage compartments of the Pockar concept. *The Fall Guy* debuts, joining *Hart To Hart*, *The Dukes Of Hazard*, *Hill St Blues*, *CHiPs* and *Magnum PI* on television, all of which are shot in the fashionable brown hues that Ford observantly pick out for their neatly-stowed luggage. Italian design house Pininfarina shows its space-age design concept loosely based on the latest sportscar sensation - the new Audi Quattro - catching the imagination of a generation following the television exploits of *Buck Rogers In The 25th Century*. Neither become production models.

# UNCLE BUCK

**AERODYNAMICALLY DESIGNED AND JET-PROPELLED, THE CAR OF THE FUTURE IS A HIGH-PERFORMANCE BUG-SHAPED PEOPLE MOVER WITH ECONOMICAL FUEL CONSUMPTION.**
**TEXT CHRIS CAMPION**

So believed Buckminster Fuller, the visionary thinker, designer and engineer better known as the inventor of the geodesic dome, who designed and built such a vehicle in 1933. In an era when the Ford motor car had only just evolved from the jalopy-like Model T, Fuller's sleek, space-age "Dymaxion" car caused a sensation. HG Wells, who rode in it, was inspired to include a Dymaxion-like vehicle in the '36 film version of his novel *The Shape Of Things To Come*.

But the car's production was so beset by problems that within two years it was consigned to the garbage heap of great ideas that almost made it. As some sort of consolation it acquired the status of a design classic.

Buckminster Fuller was a colourful character. After flunking Harvard twice and almost sinking his father-in-law's family firm with his poor business acumen that was to doom many future projects, in '27 he retreated into silence for a full year and reinvented himself as a visionary thinker, having taught himself architecture and engineering from first principles. It was during this "year of silence" that Fuller came up with his concept of 4-D design - four-dimensional thinking that operated in time as well as space, considering the consequences of inventions for humanity instead of just immediate personal gain. Fuller possessed an irrepressible energy and would electrify audiences at public-speaking engagements with his radical ideas for mankind - in 1975, at the age of 80, he gave a series of lectures on his philosophical world-view that lasted a total of 42 hours. He devised the idea of a global electricity grid that would standardise the units of energy and production worldwide, and once proposed the construction of a see-through climate-controlled dome to cover Manhattan.

The word "Dymaxion" was coined as a compound of the words "dynamic", "maximum" and "ions", to represent the core of Fuller's synergistic concept of obtaining the maximum performance from the minimum of raw materials. It was also a neat futuristic-sounding brand name for Fuller's all-encompassing design for life. The diminutive chrome-domed inventor was also responsible for designing the first energy self-sufficient, prefabricated dwelling: the Dymaxion house.

The initial drawings Fuller made of the car in '27 - the same year that Ford motor company unveiled the Model A after spending $43 million on its development - looked like a streamlined, three-wheeled seaplane. It had inflatable wings attached to its aircraft-like fuselage and was driven by three liquid air turbines; more of a road-worthy aeroplane than a motor vehicle, this was exactly the point. While Ford was selling the newly-cast Model A on the basis of its simple reliability and endurance, Fuller was aiming higher, much higher. His dream was to realise the mass production of an omni-medium wingless transport vehicle, propelled and manoeuvred by twin rockets and jet stilts and capable of travel in the air, on land and at sea. He refined his ideas in '33, hiring his lifelong friend, the Japanese sculptor Isamu Noguchi, to mould small-scale plaster models of the car.

Fuller's car designs attracted the attention of a Philadelphia stock broker named Philip Pearson, who had a fervent belief that a radical

**IN 1927 HE RETREATED INTO SILENCE FOR A FULL YEAR AND REINVENTED HIMSELF AS A VISIONARY THINKER**

design breakthrough in the fledgling motor industry could raise America out of the depression precipitated by the Wall Street crash of '29. Fuller had, in turn, been swept away by the ideas of William Stout, one of Pearson's advisers and the designer of Ford's Trimotor aircraft. Stout believed that car designers should look towards the standards set by the aviation industry; in short, a mass-produced vehicle with a large, luxurious interior space, near-silent functioning, effortless steering and economical fuel consumption. With a backer in place, Fuller brought on board Stirling Burgess, designer of the '30s Americas Cup winning yacht, as his partner. They fitted out a disused autoplant in Bridgeport, Connecticut, and employed coach builders recently laid-off from Rolls-Royce. Just four months later, the first Dymaxion prototype was ready. It featured an aerodynamic teardrop-shaped aluminium fuselage and removable canvas roof on an ash wood frame. With rear-wheel steering and front-wheel drive (powered by an 80hp V8 engine), the Dymaxion car mimicked the behaviour of birds and fish rather than established design principles for motor vehicles. A single steering wheel towards the back of the chassis (that was operated by a steering column like a boat) could turn all of 160 degrees, allowing an unprecedented amount of manoeuvrability. The 19.5ft, 11-seater vehicle could slip sideways in and out parking spots and turn 180 degrees in seconds. A retractable periscope acted as a panoramic rear-view mirror.

The car was immediately sold to Gulf Oil who exhibited it at the '33 World's Fair two months later. But while being tested by a British auto enthusiast interested in placing an order, it was involved in a crash that killed the driver. Newspapers rounded on Fuller's invention, branding the Dymaxion a "freak car", and although it was eventually exonerated from blame, its reputation was damaged beyond repair. To add to the car's problems, high-speed testing revealed a potentially catastrophic design fault. An unorthodox weight distribution (75% at the front) caused the tail end of the car to levitate off the road at speeds over 50mph. Fuller had intended to correct this by attaching an air rudder, but it was never incorporated into the final design. Undeterred, Fuller immediately began work on a new model, despite an argument with Pearson over the returns on his investment that forced him to finance its construction himself. A third prototype was completed just before Fuller's funds ran dry in '34, at which point the company was wound up and its production facility closed down. The final Dymaxion car was that year still proudly exhibited at Chicago's "Century Of Progress" World's Fair, where Fuller himself welcomed passengers in and out of the vehicle.

**IT DISAPPEARED FROM VIEW FOR MANY YEARS AND WAS REDISCOVERED IN CALIFORNIA IN THE '60S WHERE THE FUSELAGE WAS BEING USED AS A CHICKEN COOP**

But the story of the Dymaxion car did not end there. Buffeted by circumstance, each car had a peculiar history following retirement from public service. Car number one, which continued to be used as a promotional vehicle by its owners Gulf Oil, was destroyed in an accidental garage fire while in storage at the National Bureau of Standards in Washington DC. Model number two was given to the Dymaxion plant labour force in lieu of unpaid wages just before the liquidation sale. It disappeared from view for many years and was rediscovered in California in the '60s. Its interior had been ripped out and the fuselage was being used as a chicken coop. Bought and restored by the National Auto Museum in Reno, it remains on display there to this day. Car number three was briefly owned by the conductor and car enthusiast Leopold Stokowski. But on the few occasions he took it out on the road, Stokowski was terrified by the way it handled and its tendency to veer off erratically in the slightest wind. The car turned up again in New York in the '40s, where it was briefly used as a mobile advertising hoarding before being abruptly abandoned in Brooklyn. At this point, with over 300,000 miles on its clock, Fuller bought it back for restoration and exhibition at the Beech Aircraft Plant in Wichita, Kansas. In the '50s it came into the possession of a junkyard owner who broke it down and sold it for scrap.

One final attempt was made to revitalise interest in the Dymaxion car in '43. Fuller designed the Kaiser D45 (named after industrialist Henry Kaiser who funded the project), solving the levitation problem by mounting the back wheel on an extendable boom. He returned to his original triple-engine design. The car's frame was squeezed so that it was just ten feet long but could sit four abreast. Kaiser continued to employ engineers to refine the design but eventually abandoned the project in '46. At that time, Fuller, whose ardent mindset was such that repeated failure did not dim his enthusiasm for realising new (and ever-more ambitious) dreams, had already begun working on the blueprints for his low-cost, prefabricated Dymaxion house. By 1950, the failures of the past would all be forgiven. Fuller invented his world-changing Geodesic Dome, the less-is-more structure that fulfiled his dymaxion vision, finally cementing his reputation as a radical thinker, way ahead of his time.

*For more information visit the Buckminster Fuller Institute website at www.bfi.org*

*Image courtesy of the National Automobile Museum, Reno, Nevada.*

# FLY CAR

**FIRST, IMAGINE A CAR THAT CAN FLY. NOW IMAGINE IT AS PART OF EVERYDAY LIFE. FINALLY, AS NOBODY ELSE SEEMS TO HAVE MADE ONE YET, IMAGINE DECIDING TO BUILD IT YOURSELF. ALMOST 40 YEARS AGO, PAUL MOLLER DID ALL THREE, AND BEGAN A LIFE'S WORK THAT MAY YET SEE THE IMAGINARY SKYCAR REALISED.**
**TEXT LIZZIE BAILEY**

Ridley Scott's *Bladerunner* opens with a shot of an insalubrious future Los Angeles, a future we most profoundly hope never comes to pass. Yet one of the film's most enduring images is of something most westerners born in the 20th century have only dreamed of: Rick Deckert's squad car launching into the air in a gentle, curved ascent. The squad car is a vehicle that takes off and lands like a helicopter, flies like an aeroplane but is, in fact, a mere automobile. Luc Besson's *The Fifth Element* plays with the idea of a commonplace flying vehicle in the satirical form of Bruce Willis' New York taxicab.

A car that flies is no longer merely the stuff of dystopian science fiction; just outside the Californian capital of Sacramento, Canadian-born Paul Moller is building the real thing. The Moller M400 Skycar or "volantor" is a vertical take-off and landing (VTOL) device that uses Moller's own Rotapower engine. The Skycar prototype, with its lipstick-red, curvaceous carapace is a more promising venture than any of its numerous predecessors. We're not quite there yet though: Moller first took the Rotapower engine up in 1965 but the Skycar has yet to make its maiden flight.

The early 20th century saw the automobile usher in an era of unprecedented personal freedom, first in the US and then further afield, and the Skycar would be the ultimate expansion of that freedom. "As a consequence of the car being used widely," says Moller, "at some point, highways came to America. Roads became the limiting factor, then we saw highways."

But we've expanded almost as much as we can in two dimensions and our driving space is now wildly overcrowded. The average speed on a Los Angeles freeway, for instance, is expected to slow to a mere 17mph by early this century. Elsewhere, especially in older cities built with pedestrians, not cars, in mind that modest velocity is already out of reach for much of the day.

Anticipating that this situation can only get worse, Moller is designing the Skycar for a tomorrow he foresees as inevitably gridlocked unless radical solutions are found. If all goes to plan, the Skycar could tap into one of the world's relatively underused resources - the open sky - providing mass transport for the 21st century and becoming the natural successor to the street-bound car.

Dr Moller has his own personal reasons for wanting to move the Skycar from the drawing board to realisation. "I grew up on a farm in Canada on the side of a hill," he says, from where he would trek through two feet of snow to get to school in winter. "From what I can gather, from the time I was born I was interested in the mechanical and then aeronautical worlds. I designed my first helicopter at 14.

"I wanted to be like the hummingbird. I guess the hummingbird was not an inspiration but symbolic of what I was trying to achieve. If you look at it, it's wondrous, and it faces very similar problems to those we face with the Skycar: you need a very high metabolism for hovering."

The Skycar's own high metabolism is found in the powerful, lightweight Rotapower engine Moller and his colleagues designed. "We're engine designers as much as aircraft designers," Moller says. "My constructions always centred round the engine and this engine, which we did in the '90s, meant we could have a vehicle that was practical."

**IN ORDER FOR CESSNAS TO PARTICIPATE IN SAFER OPERATION OF EXISTING AIRSPACE YOU'D HAVE TO BUILD EQUIPMENT THE SIZE OF A CIGARETTE PACKET, POWERED BY TWO AA BATTERIES, AND SELL IT FOR THE PRICE OF A MOBILE PHONE**

"It's a vehicle that flies in the entire airspace," says Moller. "Airplanes work more efficiently at higher altitudes, but the Skycar will go short distances at no higher than about 5,000ft. Once it goes from hovering mode, like a helicopter, it's really an airplane."

The plan is that they'll be completely computer controlled - like having HAL from *2001: A space Odessey* in your cockpit, only hopefully a more balanced version. "You don't control direction or speed - if I go from London to Liverpool, I'm taken there almost like a package."

During the first phase, anyone with a pilot's licence will be able to fly a Skycar. Elsewhere, new systems are already being tested which streamline aircraft controls into a simple joystick, with one screen replacing the hundreds of dials and monitors of current cockpits. "The vehicle will go out there and be used like an aeroplane or helicopter" explains Moller. "There's no skill required. In the second phase we'll take even that very limited skill completely out of the hands of the pilot, so there'll be no more drunk drivers."

Moller predicts that the machine will be controlled by GPS (global positioning system) satellites, advanced computerised transponder signal relays, pre-programmed flight plans and sensors to detect other vehicles, all of which will go towards ensuring "you're safely delivered to your home or site. We know it's all do-able." The Skycar, says Moller, won't even provide the illusion of control. From take-off to set-down, the journey will be completely automated.

The US authorities would like to deploy something similar for motorways. "They are talking about making highways totally automated," says Moller, "but the problem with that is though it could be successful at increasing traffic capacity by 50 or 75%, we're looking at ten times as much traffic if things don't improve - it would only delay the problem."

"The technology is applicable in the air but debatable on the ground," he adds. "The Skycar is not going to replace the car; we'll see [an integrated transport system made up of] electric cars and the Skycar, which is perfect for journeys of 50 miles or more and less appropriate for around town."

The Skycar is pretty green too. According to the results of a study undertaken at Vanderbilt University last autumn, its engine is ten times less polluting than a car engine and achieved 18 to 20 miles to the gallon, with the crucial difference being that these are miles as the crow flies. On ground the distance covered might double. Moller's Rotapower engine uses petrol far more efficiently than a car motor, burning less and burning it more completely. The project concluded that if the population chose to use a Skycar for destinations over 60 miles instead of a personal automobile, pollution could be significantly reduced.

Currently the Skycar is just that little bit too noisy to fly over residential areas, but Moller is unworried. "In experimental mode it's higher than 85dbs," he says. The issue is "how do you get to 70dbs at 50ft? We know we can get it down to 85dbs at 50ft. It has to be done." The solution to this is appropriately futuristic. "The technology is available today," Moller assures me. "It's called Mutual Noise Cancellation. What you do is analyse a noise that exists and then generate a noise and phase-shift it so it wipes out the existing noise. It's

*Main picture*: An early prototype of Moller's Skycar.
*Above*: The latest version

the only way to see this in the 70 to 60db level. But it's fairly expensive, so we're dependent on other people developing these technologies."

No one, at this point, is anticipating the Skycar landing and taking off from a Tesco's supermarket parking lot - for one thing it creates too much heat. Prototype Russian VTOLs melted the decks of the aircraft carriers they launched from. The Skycar will, Moller believes, simply dictate a solution: "They'll probably land at some cylindrical building and you'll take an elevator down.

"This really is paradigm-shifting technology," says Moller. "Whether we did this or we didn't, the technology is coming. Traffic is stopping at airports and on highways. What's it going to look like in ten years time if this doesn't happen? Just look around.

"I've just been to San Francisco and it's not an experience I'd care to repeat." Since the technology boom began, San Francisco traffic has been growing ever more dense and Moller's tale of recently being gridlocked on the Golden Gate Bridge perfectly illustrates his fundamental point that traffic congestion diminishes our enjoyment of urban environments. "We have to utilise the largest natural resource we have in the world today. You can fly across the US and never see another plane - it's totally unused." Certainly the space looks available. Surface area increases as the radius of a globe gets bigger, and the Earth's airspace is multi-dimensional, so flying vehicles could increase travel space not arithmetically but geometrically. As the Vanderbilt project report puts it, "Even if there were the same number of Skycars in the sky tomorrow as there are cars on the roads today, each Skycar in the sky would be over a mile away (in all directions) from any other Skycar in the sky."

Moller is not alone in wanting to exploit this natural resource. In the US, the FAA (Federal Aviation Authority) and NASA are cooperating to develop Small Aircraft Transport Systems (see its website at www.hq.nasa.gov/office/aero/library/nasao/). This includes an exploration of the viability of "sky taxis" - airborne vehicles that would transport passengers from regional aerodromes to international airports.

One of the technologies currently being developed for small aircraft is the Airborne Collision Avoidance System (ACAS). Martin Robinson, chief executive of the UK's Aircraft Owners and Pilots Association (AOPA), explains: "ACAS replaces controllers in towers with an imaginary 'bubble' between 50 and 150 nautical miles in diameter around each aeroplane. When the bubbles begin to overlap, the system alerts the pilots that another aircraft at X heading and Y height is approaching their air space.

But ACAS isn't appearing in a Skycar near you any time soon. ACAS, says Robinson, isn't currently fit for small aircraft: "It's very expensive, and it uses lots and lots and lots of power." In order for Cessnas to participate in safer operation of existing airspace using this technology, he says, "You'd have to build equipment the size of a cigarette packet, powered by two AA batteries, and sell it for the price of a mobile phone."

Robinson foresees two major hurdles to the Skycar's arrival in our skies. Firstly, it has yet to receive official safety approval from national aviation authorities; and second, it would, in its first phase at least, need qualified pilots to fly it. This would entail more rigorous health checks and testing than are currently required for driving a car and there are currently 25,000 licensed pilots in the UK as compared to around 33 million licensed drivers.

Robinson acknowledges another problem which could prevent the Skycar taking off: "The airlines are talking about doubling the current level of air traffic by 2012," so that empty, untapped natural resource - even taking advantage of ACAS - is already looking more congested. Richard Wright of National Air Traffic Services (NATS), which provides the UK's air traffic control, states that, "If the thing is flying you're going to need to maintain a safe distance from your neighbour - above and below, back and front and sideways."

Moller doesn't yet know how much clearance the Skycar will require but thinks it will be "pretty much like an airplane. We've done some analysis and we expect to be able to fly them

**I WANTED TO BE LIKE THE HUMMINGBIRD IF I COULD. IF YOU LOOK AT IT, IT'S WONDROUS, AND IT FACES VERY SIMILAR PROBLEMS TO THOSE WE FACE WITH THE SKYCAR: YOU NEED A VERY HIGH METABOLISM FOR HOVERING**

a few hundred feet apart if adequately controlled at all times".

Wright continues, "You still have to stay out of main air corridors reserved for commercial flights." The system in the UK works slightly differently than in the US: "Very broadly speaking, not all air space is controlled," he explains. "Private, prop-driven Cessnas do not occupy the same airspace in the UK they do in the US - they can fly where they like outside controlled airspace in the UK and it's the pilot's responsibility to see and avoid other traffic."

In the US, says Robinson, all airspace is controlled above 18,000ft, while in the UK it's controlled over 12,000ft only above populated areas, meaning there are more areas in the UK and Europe where it's not controlled at all. A Skycar, he points out, still couldn't fly lower than 500ft in built-up areas, and couldn't go higher than about 10,000ft without extras such as oxygen, pressurisation, de-icing and the like.

Dr Moller isn't suggesting, however, we should use the Skycar for journeys under 50 miles or above 5,000ft - he's a firm believer in vehicles such as ZeTek's AFC cars (see Are We Nearly There Yet?, pages 20-25) to get us short distances. His vision of hummingbird like vehicles occupying empty space remains a compelling one.

*Below*: Police Skycar

The UK landmass occupies 242,910 km$^2$. Conversely, just the volume of airspace above the UK controlled by NATS, which extends halfway across the North Sea to Dutch airspace, halfway across the Atlantic to Canadian-controlled airspace and halfway down the Channel to French airspace, and up to 27,000ft, is over one million square miles (2,589,998 km$^2$).

And the Skycar does tap into our collective yearning for freedom and space - our desire to be independent of noisy, smelly combustion engines and equally of mismanaged, overcrowded, hot and perpetually late public transport.

Other unconventional, experimental solutions are available to those of us impatient with being stuck in traffic. If you've more money than sense, you can opt for a Backpak Helicopter (£25,000), a Solo Trek jetpack (£59,995), a Sub Bob underwater scooter (£10,000) or even invest in your own submarine (from £400,000), all from www.gadgetmasters.com. None of these, however James Bond-like, quite realises our fantasy of a future where flying cars are as commonplace (and grimy) as battered old autos, primarily because none quite offers such a degree of self-determination. The thought of having your own, self-contained means of getting from London to Liverpool, of giving two fingers to the Strategic Rail Authority and the Department of Transport, well, it's an almost irresistible fantasy. Let's most devoutly hope Dr Moller gets the Skycar off the ground sooner rather than later.

Skycar at www.moller.com

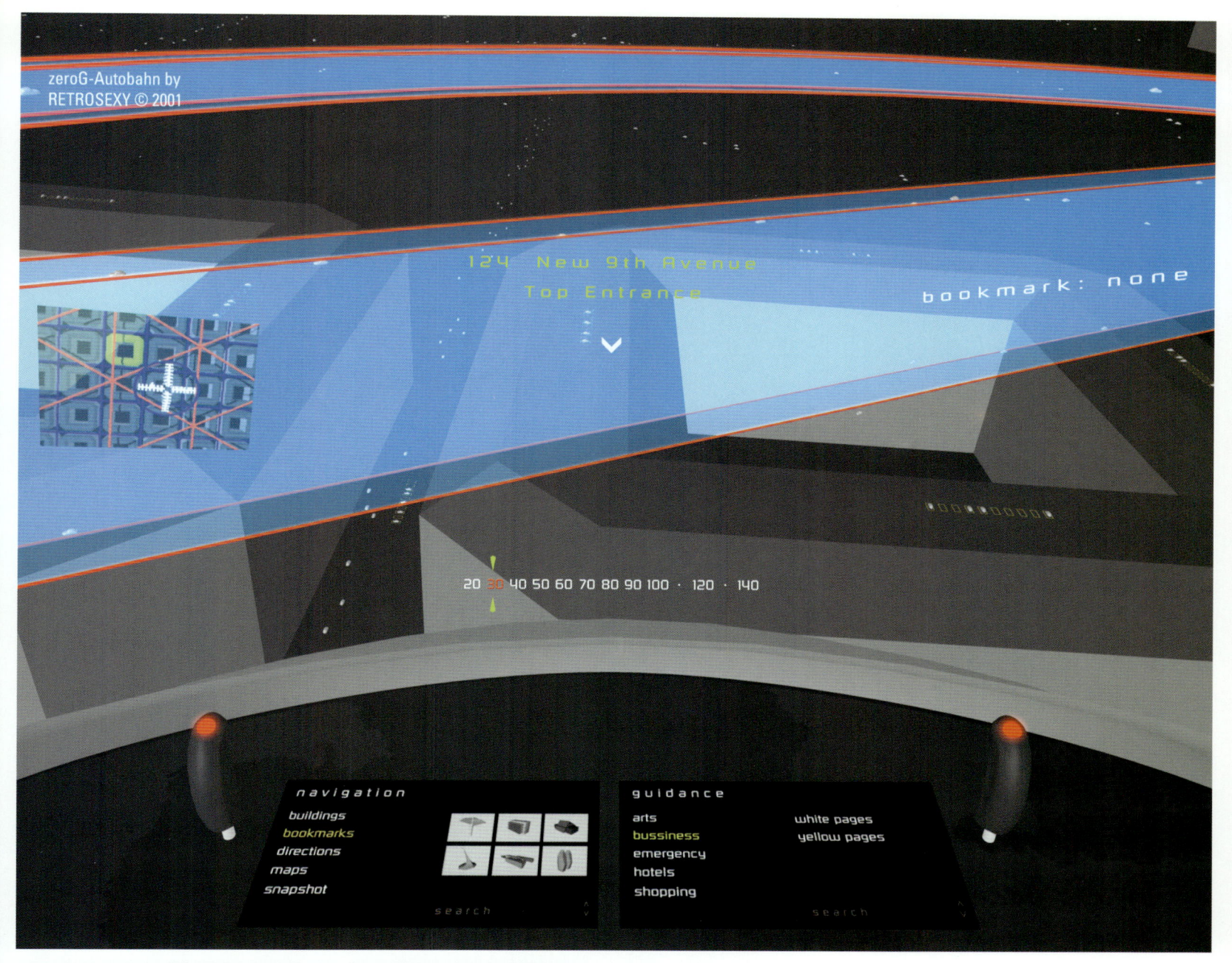

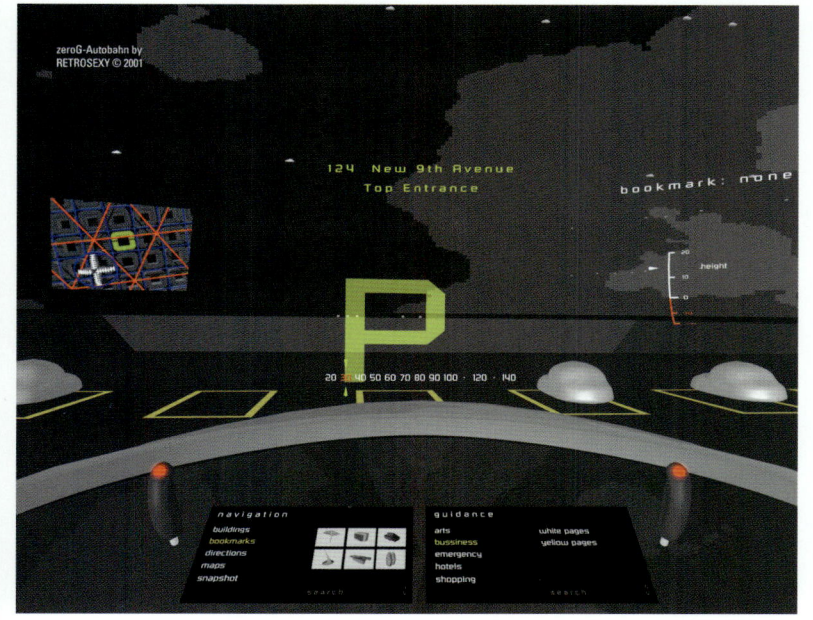

*Above:*
images from Zero-G Autobahn, a theoretical traffic and navigation system for flying cars

### ZERO-G AUTOBAHN

Christian Frey is a 28-year-old graphic designer based in Berlin. "Zero-G Autobahn" is his captivating computer-animated study in spatial perception and augmented reality. Based on a hypothetical flying traffic system, and using a head's up display (HUD) and graphical user interface (GUI), in theory it works like the internet - for example, allowing the bookmarking of a chosen skyscraper for reference next time you're looking for a parking space. Research fed in ideas gleaned from sources as varied as NASA, British architectural theorist Bill Hillier, MIT, and the US Airforce, to Moller himself and, of course, science fiction. Following screenings in Berlin and at last year's Sonar Festival in Barcelona, enthusiastic input has flowed in from "artists, specialists and nerds from different backgrounds", encouraging him to pursue the idea further. "The way any person who travels perceives their environment is influenced by motion, and differs from a static observation of that environment" says Frey, the statement's simplicity belying the elegant complexity of his animation. Under his system, a degree of autonomy is allowed to the driver/pilot. The technology polices safety regulations, meshing traffic into a flowing stream, whilst the viewer experiences the engaging sensations of navigation. The communications and guidance software needed is already technically possible. It is the hardware that's currently missing. Maybe he and Moller should talk more often.

# WORLD POPULATION 2001

TOTAL : 6,082,966,429
SOURCE : U.S. CENSUS BUREAU, INTERNATIONAL DATABASE AND THE WORLD FACTBOOK.

RUSSIA 145470197

NLAND 5175783
053
ESTONIA 1423316
LATVIA 2385231
UANIA 3610535
52815  BELARUS 10350194
S 15981472  UKRAINE 48760474  KAZAKHSTAN 16731303
ND 38633912  UZBEKISTAN 25155064  KYRGYZSTAN 4753003  MONGOLIA 2,654,999
36  BULGARIA 7707495  AZERBAIJAN 7771092
50835  ROMANIA 2364022  TURKMENISTAN 4603244  TAJIKISTAN 6578681  NORTH KOREA 21968228
H REPUBLIC 10264212  GEORGIA 4989285  SOUTH KOREA 47904370
HUNGARY 10106017  ARMENIA 3336100
AVIA 10677290  MOLDOVA 4431570  AFGHANISTAN 26813057  JAPAN 126771662
OATIA 4334142  PAKISTAN 144616639
SLOVAKIA 5414937
RZEGOVINA 3522205
623835  BHUTAN 2049412  **CHINA 1273111290**
MACEDONIA 2046209
TURKEY 66493970  IRAN 66128965  NEPAL 25,284,463
762867  IRAQ 23331985  TAIWAN 22370461
JORDAN 5153378  BANGLADESH 131,269,860
SYRIA 16728808  **INDIA 1029991145**
LEBANON 3627774
ISRAEL 5938093  THAILAND 61797751  LAOS 5635967
KUWAIT 2041961  BURMA 41994678  VIETNAM 79939014
536644  UNITED ARAB EMIRATES 2407460  CAMBODIA 12491501
SAUDI ARABIA 22757092  BAHRAIN 645361
QATAR 769132  PHILIPPINES 82841518
OMAN 2622198
707078  YEMEN 18078035
UDAN 36080373  ERITREA 4298269
DJIBOUTI 460700
3576884  SOMALIA 7488773  SRI LANKA 19408635  BRUNEI 343653
ETHIOPIA 65891874  MALAYSIA 22229040
MALDIVES 310764  SINGAPORE 4300419
UGANDA 23985712
393221  KENYA 30765916
26635626  COMOROS 596202  **INDONESIA 228437870**
4 RWANDA 7312756
3220 BURUNDI 6223897  PAPUA NEW GUINEA 5049055
ONGO 2894336
4718  SOLOMON ISLANDS 480442
ALAWI 10548250
366031
MAURITIUS 1189825
IA 36232074
MBIQUE 19371057  SEYCHELLES 79715
WE 11365366
BIA 9770199
SWANA 1586119  MADAGASCAR 15982563  AUSTRALIA 19357594
97677  SWAZILAND 1104343
LESOTHO 2177062
AFRICA 43586097
NEW ZEALAND 3864129

# WORLD CAR OWNERSHIP 2001

TOTAL : 535,748,400
SOURCE : MOTORSAT
MAPS YORGO TLOUPAS

ICELAND 151400
NORW...
SWE...
DENM...
NETHERLANDS 6...
BELGI...
UK 27539100
LUXEMBOURG 257800
PO...
CANADA 14150000
IRISH REP. 1270000
GERMANY 4...
MONACO 17000
FRANCE 2696400...
ITALY 3220...
ANDORRE 37000  SAN MARIN...
SPAIN 1684740...
USA 133000000
PORTUGAL 3350000  GIBRALTAR 2100...
ALGERIA
MOROCCO 1035000...
MAURITANIA 10000
MEXICO 9000000
BELIZE 7000
BAHAMAS 75000  ST. KITTS 5000
CUBA 19000
PUERTO RICO 1510000
HAITI 33000  ST. LUCIA 9500
ST. VINCENT 6100
MALI 2100...
DOMINICAN REP. 3500  JAMAICA 115000  MARTINIQUE 198000
GAMBIA 7000
DOMINICAN REP. 160000   NETHERLANDS ANTILLES 75000
SENEGAL 93000
HONDURAS 40000  ANTIGUA 15500  BERMUDA 26000
CAPE VERDE ISLANDS 3500  BURK...
GUATEMALA 140000  ARUBA 41000
GUINEA BISSAU 4500
SALVADOR 95000  NICARAGUA 53000  BARBADOS 46000
GUINEA 17000
COSTA-RICA 190000
SIERRA LEONE 35000  GHANA 9...
PANAMA 190000  VENEZUELA 1850000
LIBERIA 10000
GUYANA 25000
TOGO
FRENCH GUYANA 31000
IVORY COAST 1...
COLOMBIA 980000
ECUADOR 105000
BRAZIL 15300000
PERU 550000
TRINIDAD & TOBAGO 235000
BOLIVIA 130000
FRENCH POLYNESIA 43000   CAYMAN ISLANDS 11000
PARAGUAY 85000
SAMOA 3600   TONGA 5300
FIJI 48000
URUGUAY 300000
VANUATU 4000
ARGENTINA 5150000
CHILE 1050000
FALKLAND ISLANDS 1000

...LAND 2069200
...9900
ESTONIA 451000
LATVIA 520000
...700 LITHUANIA 980000
BELARUS 1150000
...00 UKRAINE 4900000
47200 CZECH REP. 3700000
8000000 SLOVAKIA 1246900
23200 AUSTRIA 4009600
BULGARIA 1750000 MOLDAVIA 170000
ROUMANIA 2300000
...VITZERLAND 3467200 HUNGARY 2365000
...ENSTEIN 20500
KIRGIZISTAN 140000 ARMENIA 2000
...00 SLOVENIA 800000 AZERBAIDJAN 270000
BOSNIA-HERZEGOVINA 120000 GEORGIA 400000 AZERBAIJAN 125000
...OSLAVIA 2250000 CROATIA 950000 TURKEY 4072300
...ACEDONIA 285000 ALBANIA 90000 SYRIA 155000 AFGHANISTAN 35000
...GREECE 2610000 JORDAN 180000
...TA 170000 CYPRUS 200000 LEBANON 700000 IRAN 1630000
ISRAEL 1200000 IRAQ 670000
KUWAIT 640000
...YBIA 480000 ARAB EMIRATES 380000
EGYPT 1325000 SAUDI ARABIA 1900000
BAHRAIN 150000
QATAR 145000 INDIA 4700000

SUDAN 80000 YEMEN 190000
ERITREA 5000
DJIBUTI 11000
SOMALIA 10500
775000 CENTRAL AFRICAN REP. 9000 ETHIOPIA 45000
SRI LANKA 220000
...ON 100000 UGANDA 26000
...UINEA 3500 RWANDA 9000 KENYA 180000
CONGO 26000
...IRE 100000 BURUNDI 10000
...AM 52000 TANZANIA 49000
SEYCHELLES 6600
COMOROS 9000 MAURITIUS 47000
...NGOLA 122000 MALAWI 18000 LA REUNION 141000
ZAMBIA 100000 MOZAMBIQUE 80000
ZIMBABWE 210000
MADAGASCAR 57000
BOTSWANA 27000
NAMIBIA 58000 SWAZILAND 24000
LESOTHO 6000
**TH AFRICA 4060000**

**RUSSIA 16000000**

MONGOLIA 25000

**SOUTH KOREA 7837000**
**JAPAN 51164000**

CHINA 3500000
PAKISTAN 900000

**TAIWAN 4800000**

BANGLADESH 50000
LAOS 10000
BURMA 38000 HONG KONG 363000
KAMPUCHEA 17000 VIET-NAM 141000
OMAN 200000
**THAILAND 1700000** PHILIPPINES 700000
MACAO 47000
GUAM 110000
BRUNEI 140000
SINGAPORE 400000 **MALAYSIA 3852000**
**INDONESIA 2500000**
PAPUA NEW GUINEA 36000

NEW CALEDONIA 64000

**AUSTRALIA 9700000**

NEW ZEALAND 1920000

# QUEEN OF THE HOOD

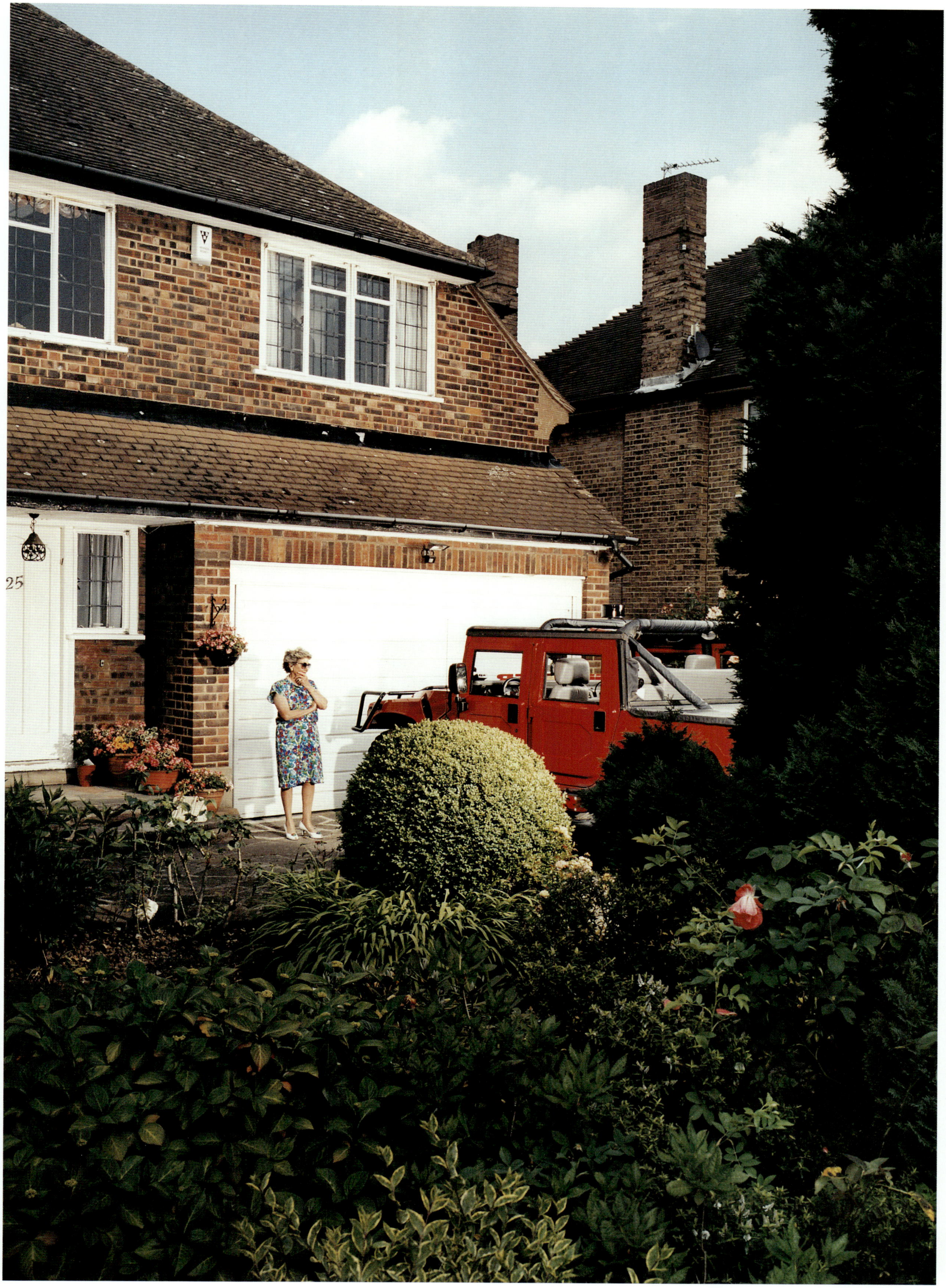
25

# JILL EVANS TEST DRIVES THE HUMMER
## TEXT GUY BIRD
## PHOTOGRAPHY EWEN SPENCER

How secure and threatening does your car make you feel? Are you comfortable at the traffic lights when the local hoodlums draw up beside your worryingly small and inferior vehicle and stare menacingly? Even if you don't imagine your local neighbourhood as a potential war zone, it doesn't hurt to take vehicular precautions. And there is no bigger vehicular precaution than a Hummer pickup. The Hummer is the civilian version of the US Army's vehicle of choice during the 1991 Gulf War, nicknamed the "Humvee" after its technical title, the HMMWV - or High Mobility Multipurpose Wheeled Vehicle. Its manufacturer, AM General, decided to sell to the public in the same year the war ended, "to allow non-military personnel to experience the exceptional off-road performance and problem-solving abilities of a military-base utility vehicle". The civilian-adjusted Hummer doesn't come with such "problem-solving" options as the roof rack-mounted machine gun, available on the military Humvee, but does benefit from a more car-like interior with carpets, leather seats, stereo and cupholders. It's still extremely tough though. Schwartzenegger tough. According to Hummer legend, Arnie bought the first one off the production line. The Hummer suggests itself to those who cast themselves as action heroes.

But can it survive on the suburban streets of North London? Civilian grandmother Jill Evans, 74, put a '95 Hummer through its paces to see if it can really deliver. First impressions of its bright red exterior are positive. Although Jill is not a big fan of 4x4s, she is immediately impressed by the size of the Hummer's tyres and drawn towards its bold styling. "My grandson would love it. The cow-catcher on the front - or should that be tank catcher - is pretty super." Is it Jill's kind of style statement? "I'm all for the attention on the road but I think the Hummer looks a bit a threatening. I'm not a threatening person, but I can be quite aggressive, so perhaps I'd like to have a front row of lights like that on my Renault Clio, that I could suddenly flash up." Driving along the superficially calm streets Jill doesn't have her normal trouble getting let out of side turnings. Lines of traffic tend to part like the biblical Red Sea when the Hummer's in town. It is a feel-good intimidation factor compact cars can't deliver. But despite its huge presence, its dimensions are akin to the bigger conventional off-roaders on the market. Both the Range Rover and Toyota Landcruiser are actually longer and around the same height, but the Hummer is a set of wing mirrors wider than the Range Rover - a significant width when manoeuvring through narrow London streets full of parked cars. Jill negotiates one such situation by raising one wheel onto a parked Renault 5. Momentarily caught out by the powering, she corrects herself and tilts off of the bonnet of the smaller car, managing to avoid shattering its windscreen or buckling its roof.

Getting in and out of the vehicle is easy for Jill, despite the step up and height: "It's fine, even in a tight skirt. It's a bit bigger than I'm used to driving. I've only done a little offroading before on Dartmoor with an old Land Rover." A decent driving position is also easy to attain with the help of a travelling cushion (test driver's own), used to gain additional height. Aside from the two conventional seats front and back, a pair of extra raised-up rear seats in the centre look particularly throne-like, allowing four passengers to sit side-by-side in the back. Behind this is a large covered pickup space with a fold down flap for easy access where you could fit a couple of bicycles, plus a tent for a trip to the country. For a vehicle some people might say is impractical for civilian use, Jill observes, the Hummer certainly has its practical moments.

Steering is easy, even a little light, as Jill comments: "Driving something as big as this I like to be feeling more in control and I didn't really feel the steering was that direct." The automatic box is simple and clear though. Due to weight and auto gearing the Hummer feels like it has its own momentum, crawling along by itself. But the brakes were solid. Acceleration takes a while to kick in, (flooring it, 0-60mph is eventually achieved by Jill in 18 seconds) but the 6.5-litre diesel engine feels incredibly quiet and refined, supplying a pleasant hum appropriate to its name.

Fuel consumption, according to its confectionary salesman owner Patrick Kear, founder of the Hummer Owners Club, is about six miles per gallon around town, although it can reach 18mpg on open roads. "A bit too expensive for me to run," says Jill, "but I don't do many miles a year now, so maybe that's not too prohibitive." However, an $80,000 price tag and an effective ban on selling them in the UK help to explain the paltry dozen registered. Should Jill want to buy one, her only current European option is a French Hummer dealer (Passion for USA, enquiries: passion@starnet.fr). General Motors acquired exclusive ownership of the Hummer brand globally in '99. GM has already unveiled a smaller and updated version - with aesthetics as well as utility in mind - called the H2. The "baby Hummer" could make production by 2003 and some could reach the UK, although they won't be imported officially. But don't worry, the H2 isn't for wimps. As Ron Zarella, GM's executive vice president, puts it: "The H2 vision demonstrates how GM plans to uphold a tradition based on aggressiveness and toughness." Good news for sweet salesmen, grandmothers and film stars everywhere.

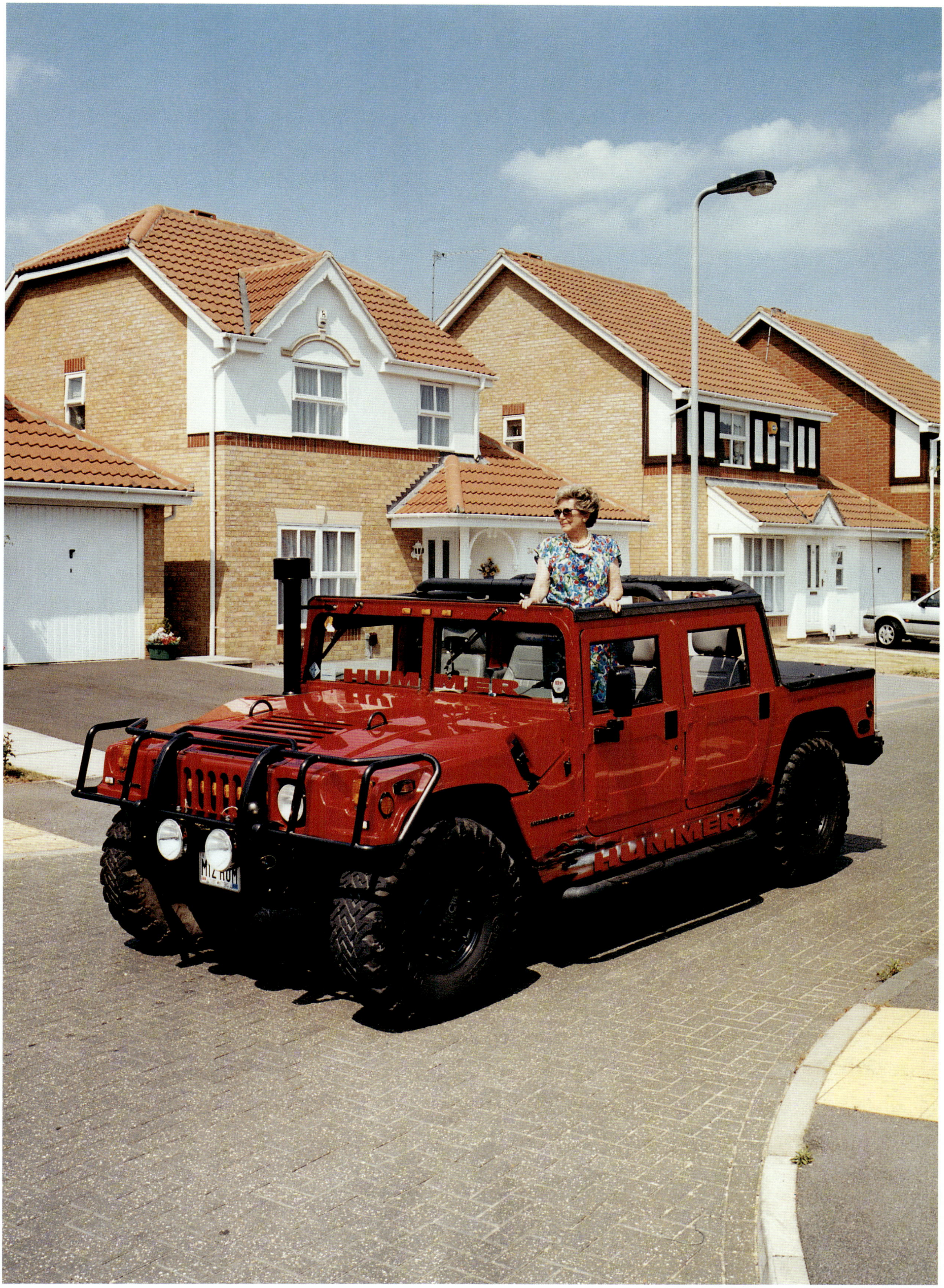
HUMMER
HUMMER

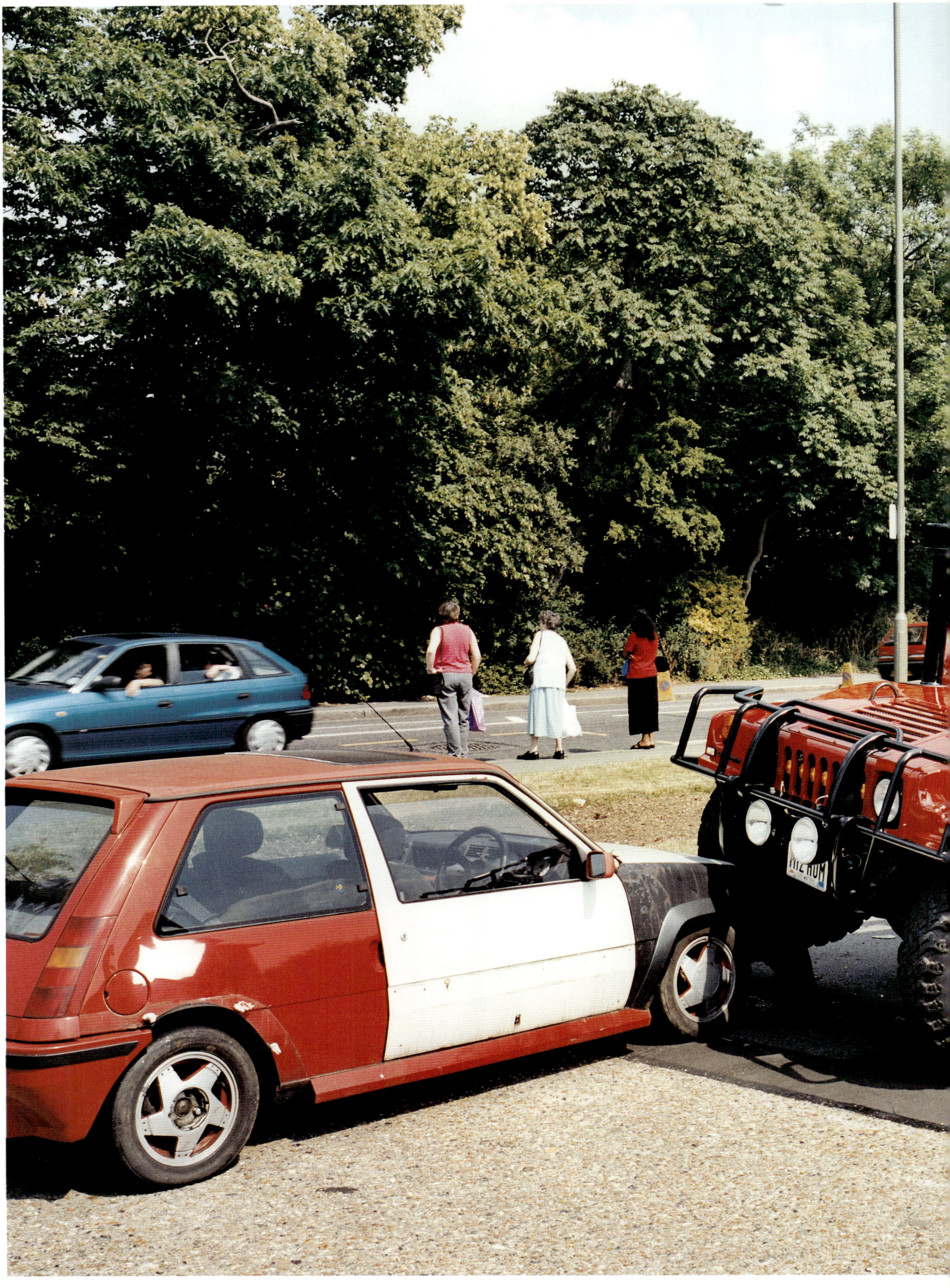

**SPECIFICATION**
Hummer 6.5 L V8 auto (1995 model)
On test **Diesel 4dr soft-top pickup**
Price **$83,733 (where sold)**
Horsepower **150**
Torque **393Nm@1700rpm**
0-60 **18secs**
Top speed **100mph***
Economy
**6mpg (urban cycle)***
**18mpg (extra urban)***
**12mpg (combined)***
Width(without mirrors) **2197mm**
Length **4686mm**
Height **1905mm**
*owner's figures

**Equipment**
leather seats, aircon, runflat tyres, underbody protection guard, armoured plating (landmine proof), water wading kit up to 6ft or top of windscreen, side steps, bull bars

Thanks to Patrick Kear for loan of the vehicle. Contact him at www.specialist-leisure.co.uk

Amid the two-step whirlwind of bad beats and hype rhymes, the general perception of UK garage music is that it's all about the dough. In a material-obsessed world where you are what you drive, the impression conveyed to those outside a close-knit scene is, "show up in the wrong car and you're not coming in". But wade through the veneer of pretentiousness and you'll find the real two-steppers are moving to a different beat. Amid the "Beemer and Benz" bravado there lurks a steadily-grafting hardcore who've been there since day one. These kids are rich. They have nice cars (some of them), but they speak of practicality and function as the main priority when choosing their motors. And in a business where your car becomes your second home, what else would you really expect? For every headrest-mounted TV with DVD player and Sony PlayStation, there's a mind-numbing five-hour drive to play a (storming) two-hour set. Finishing work at five in the morning with 300 miles between you and your bed, why wouldn't you insist on cruise control and a leather interior? But where does the misconception that garage is just as much about your choice of car as your DJing stem from? The name itself is taken from '70s New York gay club the Paradise Garage - located in a former garage. Since the concept of speed was added to garage in 1996 - bringing with it a fusion of drum & bass-style beat patterns and soulful R&B vocals, your car has been seen as a direct index of "where you at". But somewhere along the way, the distinction between a materialism that is universal and a bunch of hard-working people wanting the best for their money has become indeterminately blurred.

**WHAT DO LONDON'S GARAGE DJS DRIVE? WE ASK A SELECTION WHY THEY BOUGHT THEIR CARS. TEXT MATT CARROLL PHOTOGRAPHY DAVID BURTON**

# UK GARAGE

DJ NAME: MASTERSTEPZ
REAL NAME: "THAT'S EXCLUSIVE"
LIVES: EAST LONDON
CAR: BMW X5

This is my company car really, it represents the whole Sound Base Crew. Me and my boys travel round in this car when we do gigs, so space is really important. I chose this car 'cos of that and 'cos of the comfort factor - we drive about 1000 miles a weekend sometimes. It's definitely not a status thing, it handles well and holds the road, you know? It does look good, though, don't get me wrong! But really, this car is for all my company. I've got a little daytime car - you really want the taxman to get me, don't you - my other car is a C-class Mercedes - that is me. I haven't put any tricks on it, just lowered it. I'm getting a glass roof fitted, but that's standard on some models, so it doesn't really count. Oh yeah, and I'll get a TV put in it when I get a bit more money. My car is very important to me. If you haven't got a car in this game, you're finished. I remember back in the days when I used to DJ and I didn't have a car. My friends had to pick me up and they'd be late, or you'd have to get a train or a bus. I went to the Colliseum one time on the train - I'm not ashamed to admit that. You know, I've driven some real bangers, man. But then you step up. It's so good to have a new car - no one else has driven it, you own it, it's your car. If you drive a shit car, it means untold hassle. With the business I'm in, I haven't got time to go to the garage on a Saturday and get my car fixed. A brand new car means less hassle.

Masterstepz wears Nike Air Boing trainers, £130; trousers by Gianfranco Ferre, £90; shirt by Dolce & Gabbana, £70; hat, £25, bracelet, $700 from US; watch by Rolex, £1,700

**DJ NAME: LADY SPIRIT**
**REAL NAME: TRISH**
**LIVES: EDGWARE, NW LONDON**
**CAR: FORD FIESTA SRI**

I bought my car about 18 months ago, it's just a standard Fiesta SRi - 1.4-litre, 16-valve. I chose it because it's small, convenient for parking and it gets me from A to B. I wouldn't say cars are that important to the garage scene. Obviously you'll always get individuals who take it to an extreme, but I think people who splash out money on expensive cars and obviously have an admiration for cars will always buy a nice car, you know what I mean, regardless of whether they happen to be involved with garage. I see cars as a big part of life, not necessarily the garage scene. But as a DJ, a car is very important. I always drive everywhere and could never ask someone else to drive me. I love driving. I think my nature's quite placid behind the wheel, even though you always find a few idiots on the road.

Lady Spirit wears shoes by Barbara Dossi; jeans and t-shirt by Miss Selfridge; jacket from Portobello market

**DJ NAME: JOLIE**
**REAL NAME: JOLIE ("I'M NOT TELLING YOU MY SURNAME")**
**LIVES: BRENTWOOD, ESSEX**
**CAR: NEW MINI**

I first saw the new Mini when I was DJing up in Manchester. They were giving people a preview, so I test drove it. It handled really well, and I've never had a brand new car before, so I bought one. I was looking for something primarily that got me from A to B. I know it sounds stupid but I know it's reliable, which is important to me. And it's pretty nippy too, which is good because I'm a bit of a Speedy Gonzales on the road! I haven't had anything done to it - it's all pretty standard. Just a sunroof and chrome bumpers, but they're optional extras when you get the car anyway. Even the stereo is standard. I could have had a mini-disc player fitted, but I wasn't really that bothered. I listen to the radio a lot anyway, especially pirate stations at weekends. At the moment I'm listening to an album from [San Francisco-based record label] Naked Music - it's called *New Dimensions*. I love listening to that in the car. When it's turned up loud people are looking at me thinking, 'What's she listening to?' - it's quite different. Having said that, I do listen to garage when I'm driving too. Sometimes people say you can tell what a person's like from their car, but I don't know if that's true. I mean, the car looks good and I don't look bad, so maybe...? I suppose this car for me is an independence thing in a way. I don't see cars as massively important to my scene. I think it's all down to money. I mean, if you're a millionaire, you won't be driving round in a Lada, will you? If you've got money to spend on a car then you're obviously going to go and buy something you can afford. I think people on the outside of the garage scene see cars as more important to this culture than it is. People are told garage is sexy and stylish, that it's all about the clothes you're wearing, the drink you're drinking and the car you're driving. But personally I don't see it like that...

Jolie wears adidas Allstars trainers, £30, from Germany; trousers by Onyx, £12, from Italy; top £4, from Spain; jacket from Gap, £20; necklace from Top Shop, £4

**DJ NAME: PSG**
**REAL NAME: PAUL SIMON GABRIEL**
**LIVES: LIMEHOUSE, E LONDON**
**CAR: BMW 330Ci**

My car's in the garage right now. I've got a BMW 330Ci - it's got a DVD and a TV and all that - but it's being adjusted so I've got a courtesy car, a 325 convertible. For me, having a BMW isn't about being flash. Yeah, it's important that I look nice, but it's never really about that. It can't be about that. I want a car that holds the road well, holds its value. German cars are strong - I'm keeping it German at the moment 'cos I've had no problems. I wasn't born with a silver spoon in my mouth, you know? Everything in this car is there 'cos I need it. The amount of driving I do means my car almost has to drive me sometimes. The navigation system helps when you're in a town and it says, 'Next left, next right', you know? I've changed quite a lot on it since I bought it. I've got black leather interior, chrome, sports drive, Switchtronic gearbox. But I got it from abroad so I'm paying nowhere near what people are paying over here. I drive about 40,000 miles a year. I live in my car - I'm in it more than I am in my house. Although from the outside looking in this scene seems pretty glamorous, I don't think there's a big relationship between cars and garage. When people come out of the clubs and they see certain cars, they add it up together and that's where this reputation all comes from. But a lot of the people who like this kind of music are working and so they have money, that's all. From the outside looking in, Hollywood's glamorous, footballers' lives are glamorous - I don't really know what 'glamorous' is. I think trying to be flash is when you haven't got the money and you're busting your balls to get this or that thing. I'm not trying to get myself an Aston Martin because that's way out of my bracket, you know what I mean?

PSG wears Nike Shox trainers, £110; jeans from mate's shop, £40; t-shirt by Nike, £20; white gold bracelet and silver necklace from Aiya Napa

**DJ NAME: MATT JAM LAMONT**
**REAL NAME: MATT LAMONTAGNE**
**LIVES: MUSWELL HILL, N LONDON**
**CAR: BMW 330I SPORT**

I've always had BMWs. I bought this one in September 2000 and it's the most reliable car I could ever think of buying. I used to be a designer in the building trade and a BMW was what I always had in those days too. Doing all the mileage I do in this job, you need something reliable. To me, the car needs to be as reliable as I am - and I like to think I'm quite reliable. It's comfortable too. I would only ever buy a Mercedes or a BMW. It's not a flash thing. I could have bought a two-door and lowered it, or flashed it out in a convertible, but when I'm parking outside a club, I don't want it turning heads. It looks perfect as it is. I've gone for function here, as well as good looks. Mind you, the M3 is what I really want… Rather than being about showing off, a car is about what you've achieved personally. You know, you've got the car, you've got the house, you've got respect from your public - you want to feel you've achieved something. I feel that by driving my car I've achieved something I set out to do ten years ago. In terms of outside image - the fact people buy my records is good enough recognition for me. I suppose where some of garage's reputation stems from is a form of camaraderie between various DJs. You know, you can see Norris [Windross] is doing well, Spoonie [from the Dreem Teem] is doing well and it's respected between us. But it's not showing off. Everybody just wants to see everyone else doing well. I think your car says a lot about who you are. I mean, this car says 'stability' and I like to think I'm quite a stable person. It's thoughtful: BMW as a company think ahead - and I always think ahead. Style - I also like to think I'm quite stylish in whatever I do. Yeah, I think the BMW suits me to a tee.

Matt Jam Lamont wears Nike Air Max trainers, £110; trousers by Gap, $20 (from US); t-shirt from Sound Design (Todd Terry's record label), free; watch by Tag Heuer, £750 (from Singapore); bracelet £500

**DJ NAME: DEED**
**REAL NAME: DANIELLE YOUNG**
**LIVES: WEST LONDON**
**CAR: MERCEDES SLK**

Working in a male-dominated business, my car is about status. It's nice pulling up in a smart car - there's an immediate respect thing happening. Even driving here today, with the roof down, we had loads of men shouting to us, 'Yeah, you are too hot!' And if I'm going to a meeting in a Merc, I think I'm likely to be taken more seriously. The thing about this business is you're almost expected to have a nice car. Garage is quite a showy culture - quite 'blingy' - it's about the clothes you're wearing and the car you're driving. The two kind of go hand in hand. This car has got quite a few extras. The colour isn't standard - it's a special midnight blue. And the number plate obviously. That's actually a bit of a family heirloom: it belonged to my grandmother who got it in the '60s. She was a bit of a flash lady. She paid about £100 back then but I think it's worth about £10-15k now. The other thing I like about my car is the brakes, they are amazing.

The anti-skid [function] is great for avoiding accidents. I nearly totalled it on the way here. I went to get it waxed and pulled out afterwards, and I don't know where this woman came from. I still don't know how I didn't hit her - there must have been a guardian angel looking out for me. Imagine that, showing up here with the car all smashed up, my insurance premium rising...

I like the fact I get a lot of attention in my car, though people often think, 'Fucking rich bitch'. But it's not always negative attention - it's nice when people turn around and are like, 'Wicked!', and realise there's a bit of humour involved. I'm not driving round trying to be cool. I've worked really hard at my music and I've been doing it for a long time. I'm just beginning to reap the rewards - I've got a chrome BMX at home which I've waited ten years to get.

Deed wears shoes by M&S, £28; skirt, $5 and belt, $5, both by Canal from US; top by Mango, £13; sunglasses by River Island, £12; necklace and bracelet, custom-made by Guillamo, £200; earrings by Hennes, £2

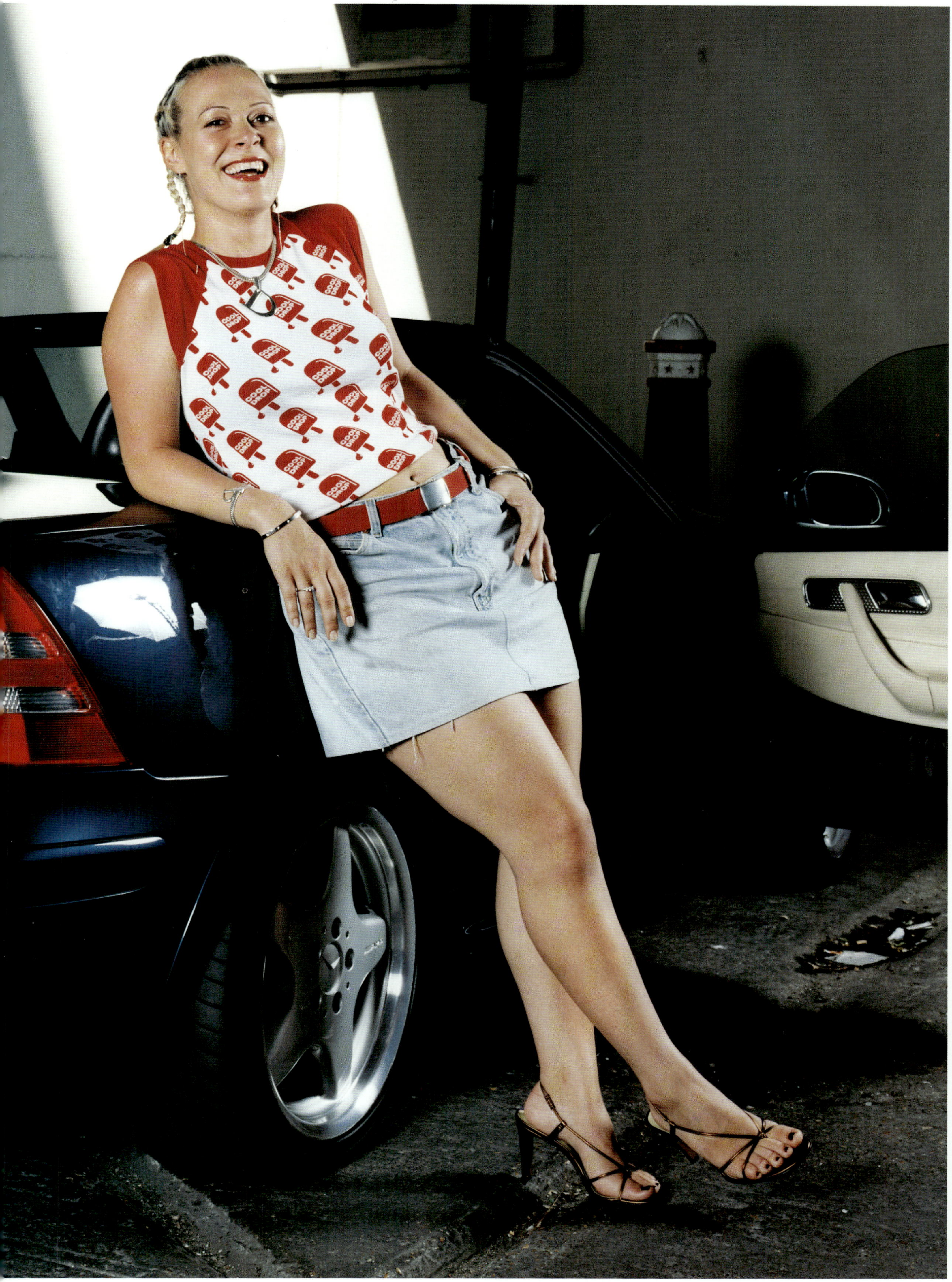
COOL DROP!

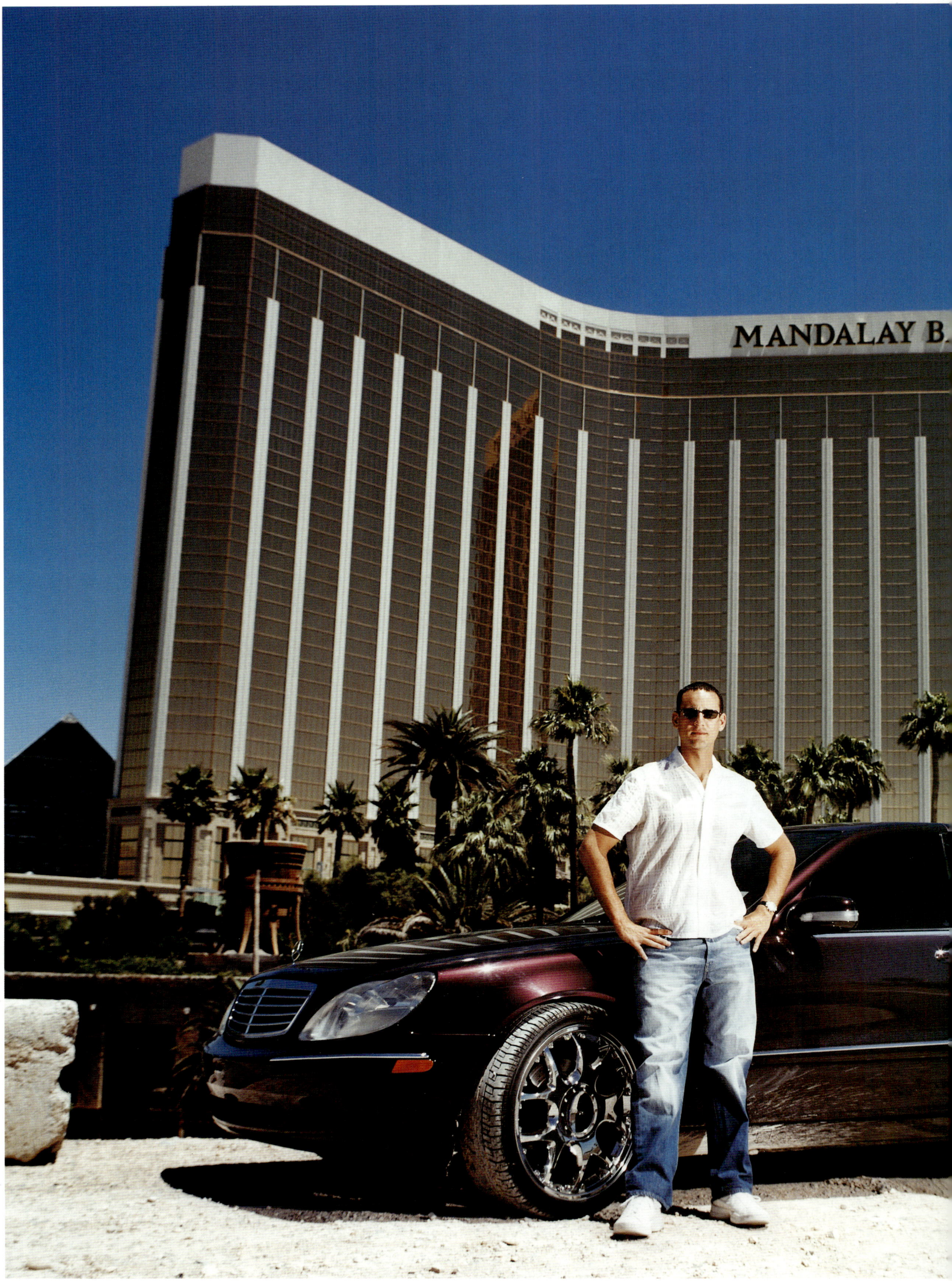
MANDALAY B

# LOST WAGES USA

**WHAT DO PEOPLE WHO WORK IN LAS VEGAS DRIVE? PHOTOGRAPHY AND INTERVIEWS KRISTIAN RANKER**

Drawn rather than born there, of Las Vegas's 1.1 million inhabitants, over half have migrated there in the past decade. Many work in the hotels and themed resorts, which host 34 million visitors a year, boasting the capacity to house a transient population as great as the city's permanent one. We asked a selection of people who work in casinos, from the owner down to the doorman, the high-roller to the chef to tell us what they like about their cars.

**NAME: BILLY RICHARDSON
AGE: 27
OCCUPATION: HOTEL CONTROLLER & CLUB OWNER
BORN: LAS VEGAS
CAR: MERCEDES 500 S-CLASS**

My role is to entertain and make people happy and make sure they're having a good time. I'm kind of like an actor in a way, I'm just playing a part. The Mercedes is a 500 S-class. My mum had one. I kinda like something very easy and simple. I think this is a cruising car. It's a real mellow car. It's my ladies car.
I had another business which I sold and the first thing I bought was a Mercedes. I'd always wanted one, so I got one. It cost me $100,000. I made money on it. I've had that for two years now.
I always had a truck growing up. I went to work with my dad when I wasn't at school [Billy's family own a stake in the 15 casino Mandalay Resort Group].
We came to the hotels to eat. It was exciting. But we grew up like normal kids. A normal childhood, a mum, a dad, a house. I kind of missed having a truck to haul stuff around and put stuff in the back, so I got one about a month ago, a black Cadillac Escalade. It cost $50,000 - I got a deal. They're normally $55-60k.
I like to drive my truck during the day. I use the Mercedes at night for running around town.

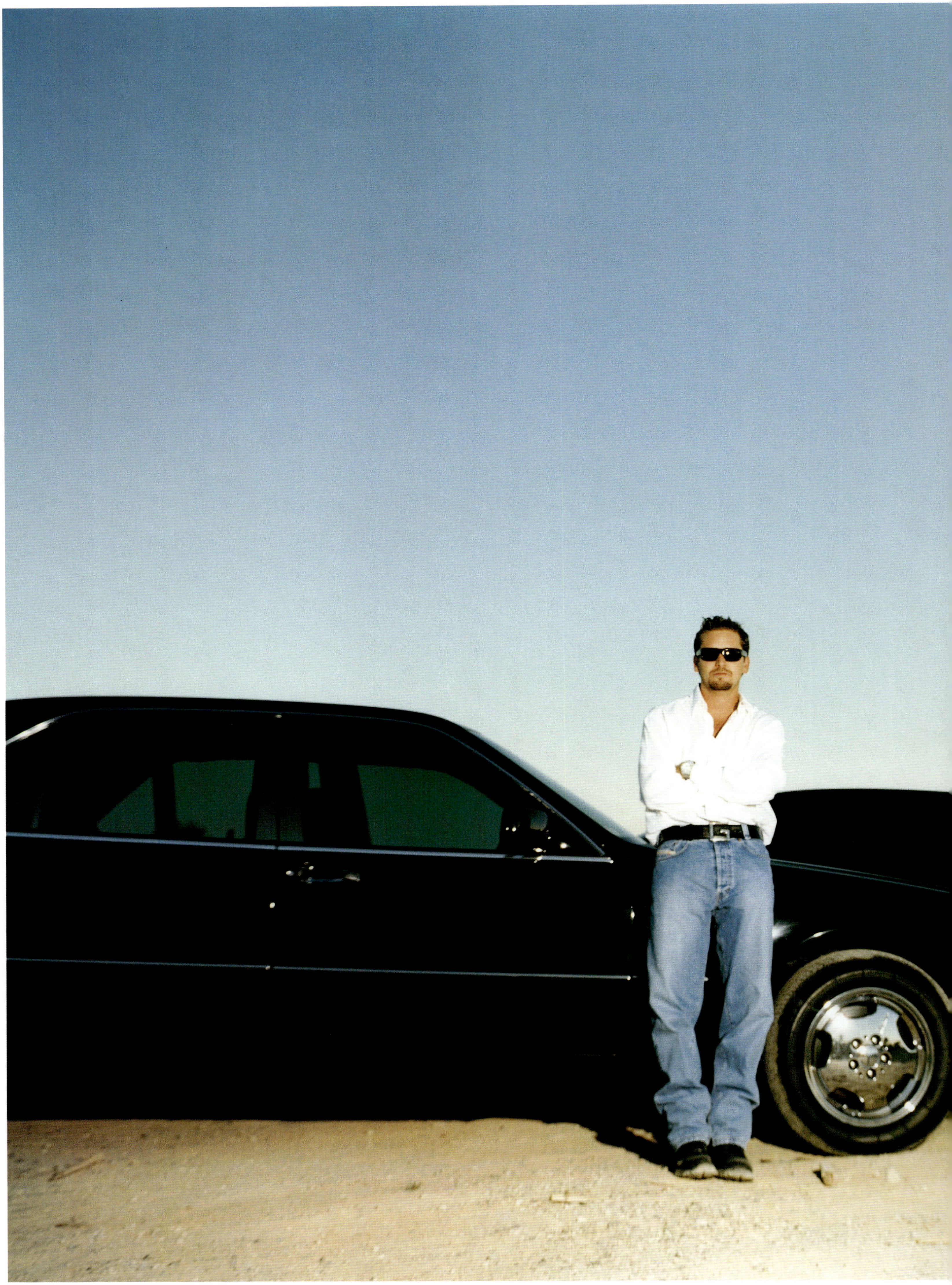

**NAME: NATHAN BAXTER**
**AGE: 25**
**OCCUPATION: GAMBLER**
**BORN: AUGUSTA, GEORGIA**
**CAR: TWO MERCEDES**

I started out working for my dad, who's probably the biggest sports gambler in the world. Pro-football is our best sport. We do basketball, tennis, golf, no horses, no hockey. I'm probably one of the three biggest sports gamblers in the world. We live in Las Vegas because it is still the betting capital of the world. The biggest bet I've ever made was about $25k on a fight which I lost. But my dad has bet over a million dollars on some fights. The thing I love most is sports betters in this town are like rockstars. Every person in Las Vegas knows who they are. If you have a good year, you've got a lot of cash on you and you can go and buy whatever lunch you want, and if you have a shitty year you'll be eating McDonald's. I was a truck man growing up, but mine has always been a Mercedes-Benz family. My mum and dad both have a 600 Merc, and I actually have two. In Las Vegas they seem to be the popular car of successful people and I've never been one for a convertible. I just love them. They're as fast as I need to go. The V12 is like a race horse, it's almost got too much power. Both cars have 18" rims on them and Pirelli tyres. They do tend to get worn if you have too many cocktails on your way home from the hotel at night.

All six cars in our family our black. People seem to recognise you in the town with the same cars. It's really hot so black is not always the best colour, but we've always bought black cars, I don't know, maybe it adds to the mystique of the gambler. It's great to drive at night when the sun goes down and that's when you can really enjoy a black car out there. When I was younger we'd have 10 or 15 cars up front. The big thing in high school used to be to drive up and down the strip and see what kind of trouble we could get into. But now I'm over that, it's not the kind of entertainment I'm looking for.

I think the car fits in real well here. It's not too flashy and its not too unflashy, you know? I love all kinds of other cars and hopefully one day I'll buy a Bentley or something. But my parents are from the south and they've never been into being real flashy and all.

**NAME: ROBERT WARNER**
**AGE: 32**
**OCCUPATION: DESIGN AND PR CONSULTANT**
**BORN: LAS VEGAS**
**CAR: CORVETTE**

I like going to beautiful homes and organising parties, being the one who makes everything beautiful. Growing up I was always into fast cars. And I was crazy about jumping motorcycles, bicycles, jumping bicycles off the house into the pool. Before I was able to drive I had a Volkswagen buggy and we used to take her out in the desert or into the valley where the place was crazily vacant, where you were almost like a free bird out in the middle of nowhere and you never had to worry about getting hurt.

Owning a Corvette has been a big growing up thing. As a kid I always dreamed of owning the best American sports car ever created, and the Corvette has the tempo and character that every man dreams of. I personally feel that you get the respect. One of the things I enjoy driving this car is being able to drive down the road and pulling alongside a lady in a Jag and having her remember that I'm the man with the Corvette.

**NAME: JAMES GUNDY**
**AGE: 29**
**OCCUPATION: DESIGNER**
**BORN: PHOENIX**
**CAR: PORSCHE BOXSTER**

Cars change so often, there's always a new car. As a kid, I was worried the new ones I'd buy when I was older wouldn't be so good.
I love Porsches because they're simple and efficient. There's no cup holders for your drink, and no ashtray. It's a car. Everything is calibrated by hand. I don't really analyse myself that much, but it kind of has a rough, hard sophistication to it.
That's me. That's the car.
Does it go with the city? It works about as well as a pyramid standing next to a castle, or the Eiffel Tower standing across from New York. Everything goes well with Vegas. It doesn't matter what you have. It all works well here.
That's what makes it so great.

**NAME: STEVE GROMER**
**AGE: 31**
**OCCUPATION: HOTEL MANAGER**
**BORN: SAN FRANCISCO**
**CAR: FORD MUSTANG**

I love fast cars and convertibles. Some roads you can find here are phenomenal, you can drive as fast as you desire.

I paid $25,000 for my Mustang. I got a good deal, it normally costs $29,000, but, of course, I know somebody well at Ford!
No matter how much money you have this is a great car - a fine balance between expensive and inexpensive, a fine balance between fast and, er, not too fast.

**NAME: BUDDY GRECO**
**AGE: 35**
**OCCUPATION: HOTEL DOORMAN**
**BORN: NEW YORK**
**CAR: RANGE ROVER 4.6**

With tips, I earn about $80,000 a year. But there are a lot of people out there who are just mean, and don't care what you do for them. I have a Lotus Esprit and a 1996 Range Rover 4.6L, the top of the range. It had 32,000 miles on the clock when I bought it. I paid $42,000 - the dealer gave me a deal.
People don't know how to drive in Vegas. You have to really watch yourself. I see a lot of people with small cars, but this car will save my life, so it's worth it to me.

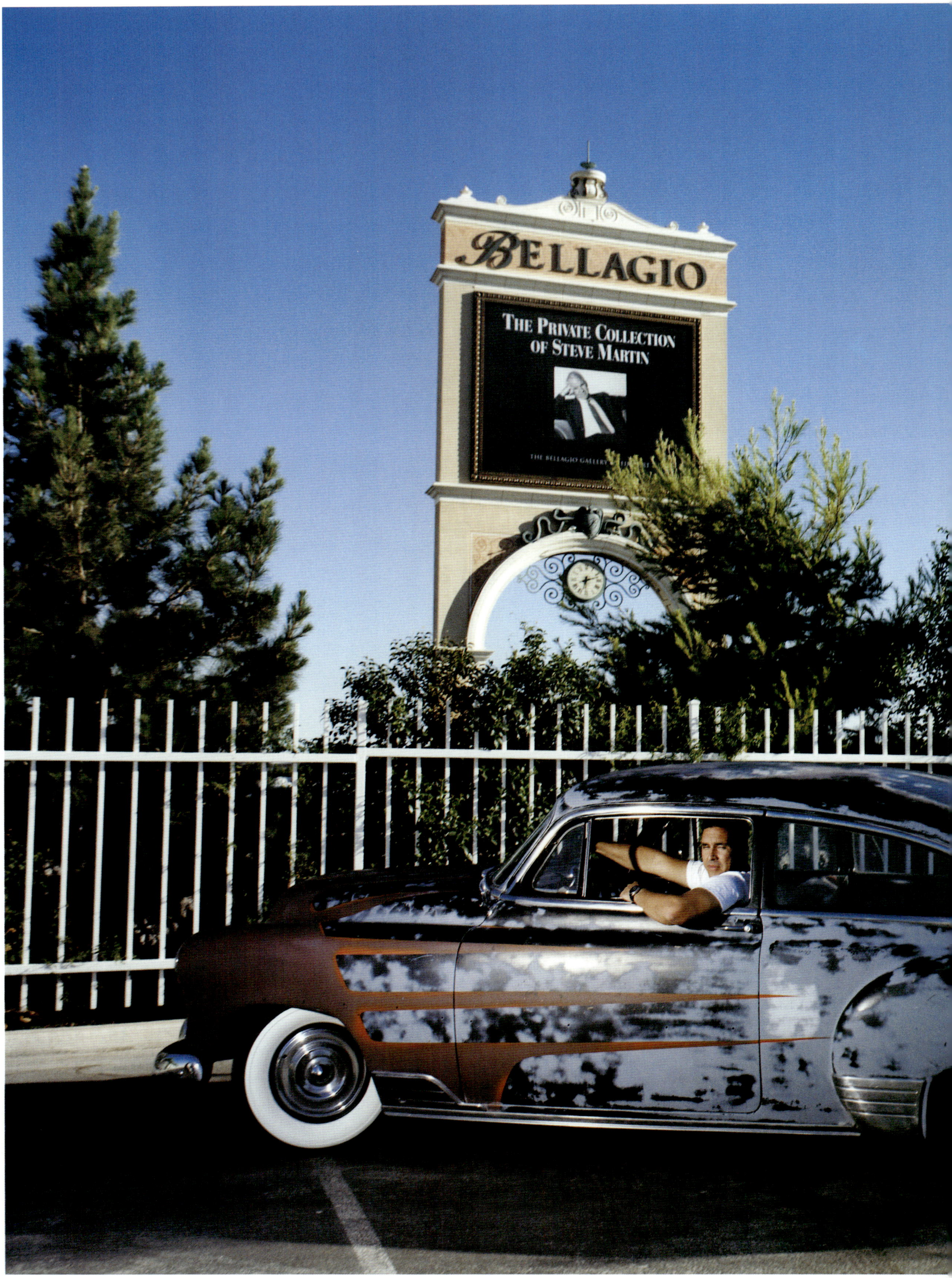
BELLAGIO
THE PRIVATE COLLECTION
OF STEVE MARTIN

**NAME: CHRIS MCGEE**
**AGE: 35**
**OCCUPATION: ENGINEER**
**BORN: SOUTHERN CALIFORNIA**
**CAR: '51 CHEVY**

My father was a big collector so I think that's where I picked up my addiction to automobiles. I didn't know whether I was going to stay in Las Vegas after school, but work ended up making it a perfect home. I tried to create a 1950s type image on this '51 Chevy with '50s Chrysler hub caps, back lights, twin exhausts. I added a car cooler on it, made in the '50s, called a Thermidor, an odd device. You don't see them too much in the warmer places because they don't work too well.

I also own a '22 Willis Knife; a '54 Cadillac X2; a '57 Cadillac; a '60 Cadillac; a '61 Cadillac; a '56 Oldsmobile hardtop; a '58 MGA roadster; a '31 Model A Ford sport coupe; a '31 Chevy truck; a '39 Chevy panel; a '56 Buick; a '64 Lincoln Carmel; and a '46 Pontiac.

I usually buy ones that are restorable, that way I can put my own signature on them. Certain ones I buy because they're not in bad shape to fix up so if I want to sell them on, I can. I've recently turned loose a '47 Cadillac Fleetwood, a couple of T-Birds, and two '62 Thunderbirds. I had fun with them, but too many cars and not enough time. I get help from some friends here. What I didn't learn from my father I turn to them for.

The car I'm getting most pleasure out of driving right now is the '60 Cadillac. It's almost like getting on your favourite sofa and going for a drive around town. The thing I enjoy about driving is the reactions I get. People always make comments, turn their heads, give thumbs up, and want to know what it is. Something you don't see a lot of anymore. That's my satisfaction.

The '50s style cars always get misunderstood. People who spend a lot on their cars don't understand it. It's the roots of hot-rodding that people did when you couldn't afford a lot. You just got something running and had fun with it. What I like to do on cars beyond just a '50s hot-rod, is add a lot of the speed equipment that people couldn't buy normally, it was rare then, and rarer now. For the car enthusiasts, when they look under the hood they know some of the neater tricks that have been done. The cars are an integral part of my life. It's an avenue for expression, just like musicians with guitars or drums. My output is through the automobiles.

I drive the cars daily, they were built to be driven. Newer cars even lend some ideas to what to do with older cars. Chrysler has made a strong move to bring in some new interesting concept cars with an antique or classic look. I've seen some stuff in the future, I just wish that it'd come up sooner.

When I arrived in Las Vegas I didn't know many automotive people but over the years the town has developed into a more enjoyable place and a lot of people have come from California or Montana. I have a car club here called the Road Masters with an outlet for people who like '50s style. There's quite a few car clubs out here now. The '60s cars, they fit in really well in Las Vegas. It gives you the feeling of when people were first establishing the Strip. Particularly the '64 Lincoln Carmel. It's got a gangster motif. I get a lot of comments when I drive around town in that.

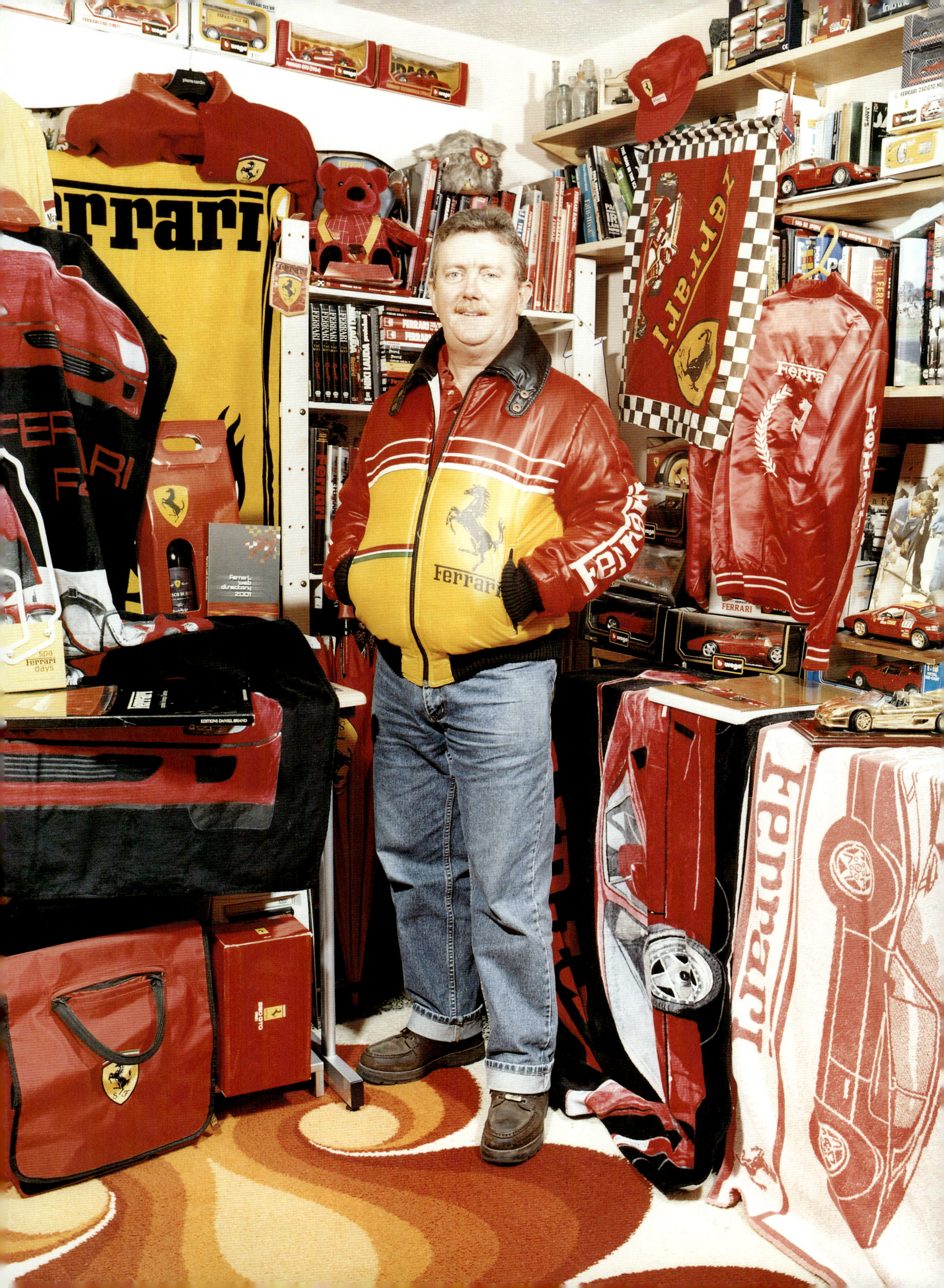
Ferrari
Ferrari web directory 2001
spa Ferrari days

# THEY CALL HIM ENZIO

**TEXT GUY BIRD**
**PHOTOGRAPHY DANIEL STIER**

They call him Enzio at work - after the founder of the most famous racing car brand in the world, Enzo Ferrari - but he's not Italian. Ralph Palmer is married with children yet boasts that he keeps a mistress in the garage - an adapted Ferrari Mondial 8. Walking down a quiet residential street in Oxfordshire, England, a prancing black horse atop a yellow shield carefully painted onto a red wooden-slatted garage door gives the first clue to a preoccupation with Ferrari. Inside the modest house, the motoring theme continues with carefully framed car pictures sharing wall space with prints of Victorian women in their finery and family portraits. Push ajar the small door under the stairs, however, and a whole other world opens up.

Flags are draped over bookshelves crammed with every conceivable publication on Ferrari - sometimes the same book features in several different languages - while beach towels, jackets, hats, shirts, bags, bottles of wine, toy cars, calendars and photographs all vie for the remaining space. For a moment, as Ralph pauses amongst his collection, sporting a mint condition late '70s Ferrari jacket, it is as if his faded blue jeans are the only thing keeping him from merging fully into the revered jumble of memorabilia.

Ralph's obsession began with an epiphany back in '82, and his eyes glaze over as he recalls the dreamy event: "I remember seeing this low sleek car parked in my road one night after work. I walked round it a couple of times, and read on its side 'Dino GT4'. I thought, what the hell's that? I knocked on the guy's door and he told me it was a Ferrari. It was the first car that really got hold of me." The car belonged to the neighbour's boss, and was only borrowed for the weekend, but after discovering it was for sale, Ralph took up the offer of a test drive. A 130mph spin down the local A41 road sealed the deal. "The sound and the way it went - that was it - I was sold. I got rid of my BMW and my motorbike and borrowed £10,000. To give you an idea, the repayments on my house were £88 per month back then, and the repayments for the car were £400. That's how desperate I was to get hold of the thing."

Since then, Ralph has spent most of his spare time and money on the growing obsession. It's not been without sacrifice for all concerned. When he left his wife and two kids behind to go on a European road trip to the Monte Carlo Grand Prix with 16 other Ferrari fans, his family went without new carpets for another two years. Ralph explains: "Sometimes I think back on the money I've spent on Ferrari - I could be sitting in a house with two or three acres, easy. But then I wouldn't have had such a good time. You're only on this planet once, life's not a rehearsal. So many people say they wish they'd done this or wish they'd done that, and the next thing they know they're 70 years old or dead and they haven't done half of the things they wanted to. I've done some things."

Ralph says his wife doesn't mind his fanaticism, as long as the family don't go hungry, although she did draw the line when Ralph suggested calling his first son Enzo Dino Ferrari Palmer. A Ferrari bedspread doesn't cover the marital bed either, though both boys have single Ferrari duvets,

**THEY WOULD NEVER GUESS IN A MILLION YEARS THAT I CLIMB OUT OF THAT TRUCK AND GET INTO A FERRARI**

and a commemorative portrait of the real Enzo on his 90th birthday takes pride of place in the couple's bedroom. Ralph has owned six of the Italian cars in total, but his most intensive period of collecting memorabilia occurred during leaner times when he didn't have a Ferrari at all. "When the repayments became too much and the car had to go it was like a bereavement. I was in a deep depression. I used to buy up all the books I could to feed my hunger for knowledge on Ferrari. That was my boom/bust period. When I had a Ferrari it was boom and when it was bust, I collected. I think there were times, when I didn't have a Ferrari, I would have almost sold my soul to get another one. The churchgoers will love that one, won't they?"

When times got better for Ralph, he moved to a bigger house and started the room dedicated to his passion. Despite all the money he's spent on Ferrari over the years, he claims that most of the individual bits have come pretty cheap or been gifts. The place to get the best stuff is the home of Ferrari in Maranello, Italy. He refers to the factory there as Mecca. "It's got a whole street of shops dedicated to Ferrari memorabilia - you get stuff there you can't get anywhere else." His favourite piece is a photo he took in '83 of the then Ferrari racing driver Rene Arnoux, enlarged and mounted. "I climbed the fence to the pit area - I actually ripped my shorts getting over it - and they were just there. So I just managed to snap the shot before security asked me to leave." But he claims the pursuit of his obsession has never led him into real illegality. His day job - driving a Volvo truck and 40ft trailer for a military distribution network - helps pay for his habit. Ralph says the truck is almost as much fun as his Ferrari: "Both the Ferrari and my truck have power, which I love, but in different ways. The truck has huge power and torque to drag the trailer, but hit 56mph and that's it, whereas in a Ferrari you can reach 160mph. When you see a truck on the road, most people think: 'Bloody hell, I'm stuck behind a lorry.' When I overtake in my Ferrari, a lot more say: 'Flash bastard.' They would never guess in a million years that I climb out of that truck and get into a Ferrari. It's a totally different social scale. I find people don't let me out in either car though."

Is there a bigger Ferrari fan than Ralph? "There are fans in different ways. I consider myself a true enthusiast. Some people follow Manchester United because they are winning, I follow Ferrari through the good times and the bad. My dream was to own a Ferrari when Ferrari won the Formula One World Championship - it took from '82 to the year 2000. It's a love affair. When you go out to see your girlfriend or your wife, you've always got to learn more. It's the same with Ferrari - you never stop learning."

His favourite Ferrari of all time is the 250 Short-wheel base ('59-'61). "It's got a fantastic rear end - it just looks right from any angle, it looks like it was built for the purpose. It was the last real Ferrari car you could take to the circuit, race and then drive home. One racing car driver did exactly that. He picked the car up from Italy, 'ran it in' on the way to a circuit in England and then raced it. You couldn't do that today." Ralph isn't lost for words explaining the magic of Ferrari. "It's the whole thing. The history, the smell - Ferraris smell great. You know when you thrash an engine, it's got its own distinct smell? I can't describe it. When you've just taken it round a track and its sitting there going tick, tick, tick - maybe a combination of petrol and oil. What I love is the power, the way it goes. I'm not interested in what people think about me. Some people buy Ferraris as trinkets - not to drive, but to say 'I've got a Ferrari'. But I bought my car to drive it. That's what it's meant for. It's a moving piece of art. The only way to enjoy it is by driving it." Though Ralph has owned an Aston Martin, a V12 E-type Jag as well as three Porsches, he keeps coming back to Ferrari. As far as he is concerned, it's easy to understand why.

Ralph Palmer publishes the Ferrari Web Directory 2001
Contact: red4racing.com

# ARE YOU ALRIGHT LOVE? GO ON, QUICK THEN

**TEXT GUY BIRD**
**PHOTOGRAPHY NEIL MASSEY**

Mary Holland knows what to do with a lollipop. She may be considerably less than 5ft tall and 76 years old, but the way she boldly steps out in front of her mostly male "audience" and commands their complete attention with just one confident wave of her traffic-halting wand is something to behold. Her stage is a street in the shadow of London's famous Tower Bridge. Her show, put on every rush hour morning and evening, rain or shine, obeys the clockwork routine of the local school children in her charge.

In politically-correct terminology, Mary is a "school crossing patrol person" - one of about 16,000 in the UK. To most people, however, Mary and her colleagues are affectionately known as "lollipop ladies", on account of the standard issue lollipop-shaped sticks with which they command traffic to stop.

Once in the middle of her four-lane work place, she brandishes the tool of her trade, facing down huge lorries and burly drivers caught in the rush to get wherever they are going. Sporting her floor-hugging fluorescent yellow trench coat, black bowler hat, cycling mask and glasses, she looks like a safety-conscious Ewok - replete with stolen light sabre - in a parallel universe *Star Wars* where the storm troopers drive white vans.

Few question her authority. This is her domain. Just one of a whole host of "road people" who delay drivers, Mary enjoys a respect and authority unparalleled by those that dig up roads and place clamps on vehicles illegally parked upon its surface. In Britain, most drivers will have been helped across the road by one of them as kids. They tend to be friendly faces in a sea of angry, frustrated or bored drivers, characters defined by the context they defy. Who are they? Where do they come from?

The concept of having a lollipop lady to help children get across busy roads near schools first came into being in the early '50s as car volumes began to increase exponentially. Along with police and traffic wardens, lollipop ladies are the only citizens legally allowed to halt traffic and have recently had their powers increased to allow them to usher anyone in need of assistance across the street. Lollipop ladies' wages are low - in Mary's case about £5.60 per hour - and are mainly paid for by local authorities. In the past, sponsorship deals with car companies like Volkswagen helped pay for their coats. Mary was born and raised in Ireland and became a lollipop lady on the south side of Tower Bridge after a career as a bank cashier in the City of London, just across the bridge. She is proud of her role but admits it wasn't one she planned. She was recruited after a persistent local policeman (the police used to employ the lollipop ladies) accosted her repeatedly as she took her dog for walks in the park.

"He kept on asking me to join and gave me all the forms to fill in.

**SHE LOOKS LIKE A SAFETY-CONSCIOUS EWOK - REPLETE WITH STOLEN LIGHT SABRE - IN A PARALLEL UNIVERSE STARS WARS WHERE THE STORM TROOPERS DRIVE WHITE VANS**

Eventually I agreed to take the job on for a little while to help him out until he got somebody else. I've been here 13 years now and not a child has been in trouble… There have been accidents in this area, but not where I work. (*At this point Mary bangs her tall lollipop stick on the pavement for emphasis, making a clicking sound*)

No one (*click*) I can honestly say no one (*click*) will know how many lives I've saved, I'll tell you that. (*Pause, then double click*)

When I put this lollipop stick up for everybody to see, there's no excuse for cars going past, because everybody can see this." (*Click*)

She expands on her high stick technique: "The idea is that the cars at the back will know why the van in front is stopping. You see? It's extremely dangerous here sometimes…"

She was a natural from day one.

"The first day I came here, I went out into the middle of the road and stopped the traffic and that's my training. Nobody showed me what to do. It's true."

While her place of work would appear to be an unpleasant fume-filled environment to most onlookers, Mary enjoys working on the road.

"I love it. I like seeing the children across the road. When I see them across the road, I know that it is safe…" (*Suddenly alerted to some pedestrians crossing cautiously, she interrupts our interview to usher them across*)

"Are you all right, love?… Go on, quick then!"

In her opinion, the pollution where she works has got better since she first started, though she has always worn a mask.

"On my first day out there it was awful with traffic. Both sides of the road were chock-a-block. I was standing out there and I said 'oh my God'. I went into the police station and said 'I've got to get a mask. I can't stand out there, it'll kill me!' So the duty sergeant makes me wait a minute, and then comes back with a World War II gas mask."

After that, she settled on a wrap-a-round cycling mask. She is aware her image may look strange to some people.

"I didn't wear it for anyone, I wore it for myself, but… it has brought a lot pleasure to a lot of people. I've seen people here and they're looking at me and they're having a good laugh. And I know what they're laughing at, because I do look funny, especially when I've got the big long coat on. They laugh away but I don't mind, I'd rather have them laughing than being miserable, you know what I mean?"

Mary's affinity with "her public" - pedestrian and driver - comes from enjoying both roles. She passed her driving test in her '60s, after her husband became ill, and clearly appreciates the freedom it affords. She used to give lifts to pensioner friends out to clubs until recently, when her Ford Fiesta was stolen. "If I could, I would have a little Vauxhall Corsa," she confides.

Her image is ripe for adoption by the green lobby as some sort of anti-car mask-clad symbol of humanity fighting for pedestrian power amidst a polluted capitalist urban chaos. But she doesn't see herself that way. "I like cars, I have no problem with them. I'm happy and content. I can't moan at all."

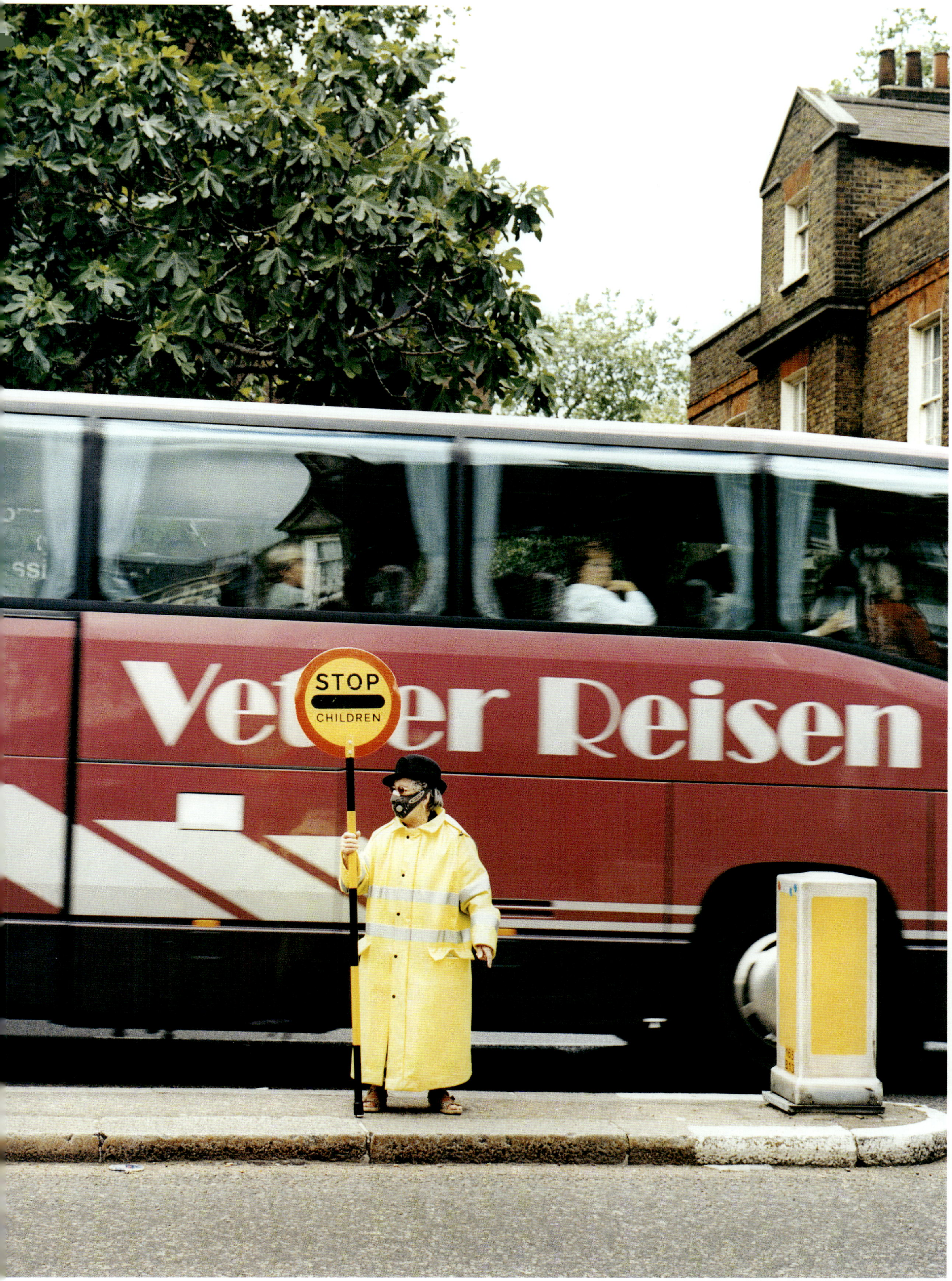
STOP
CHILDREN
Reisen

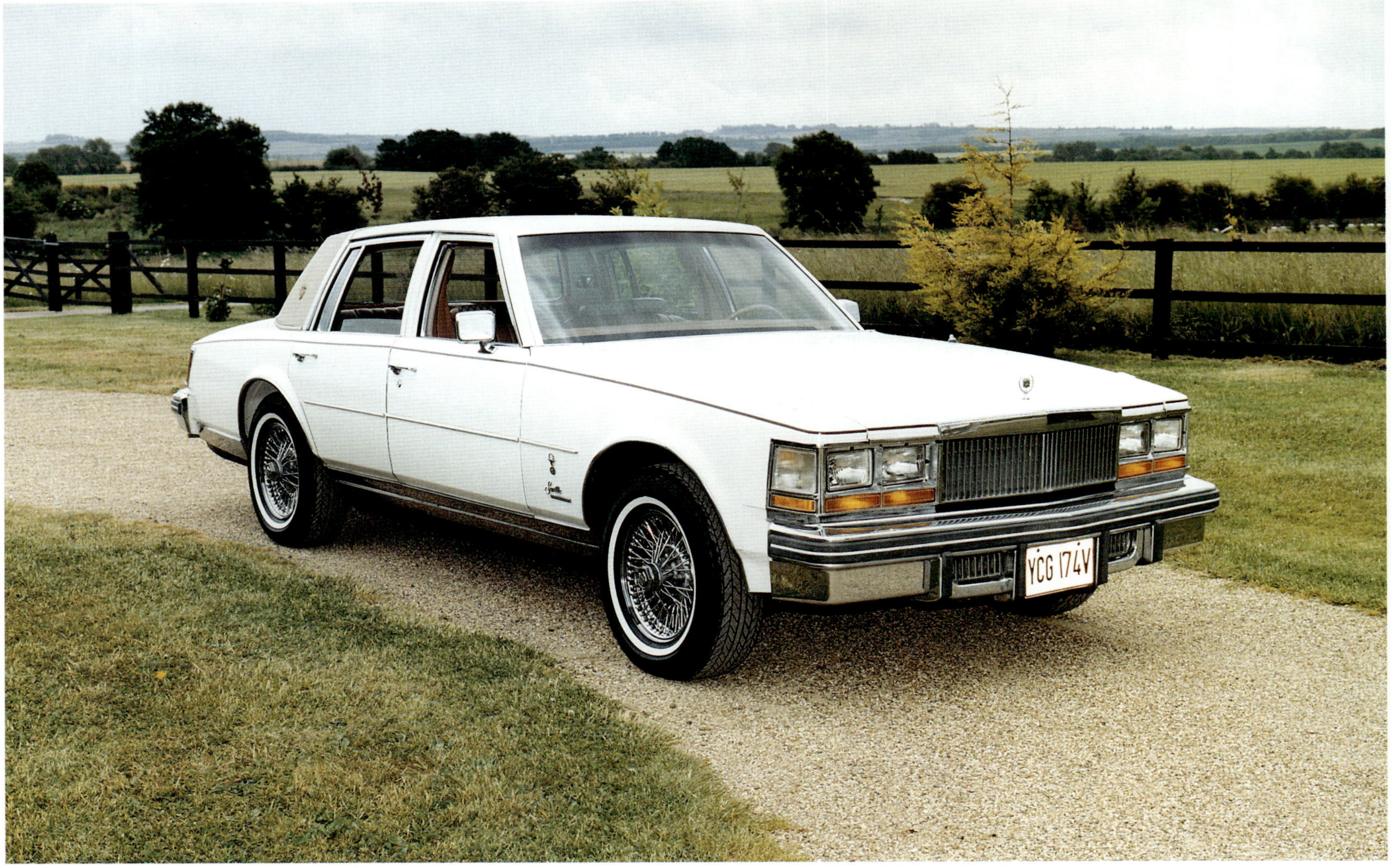
YCG 174V

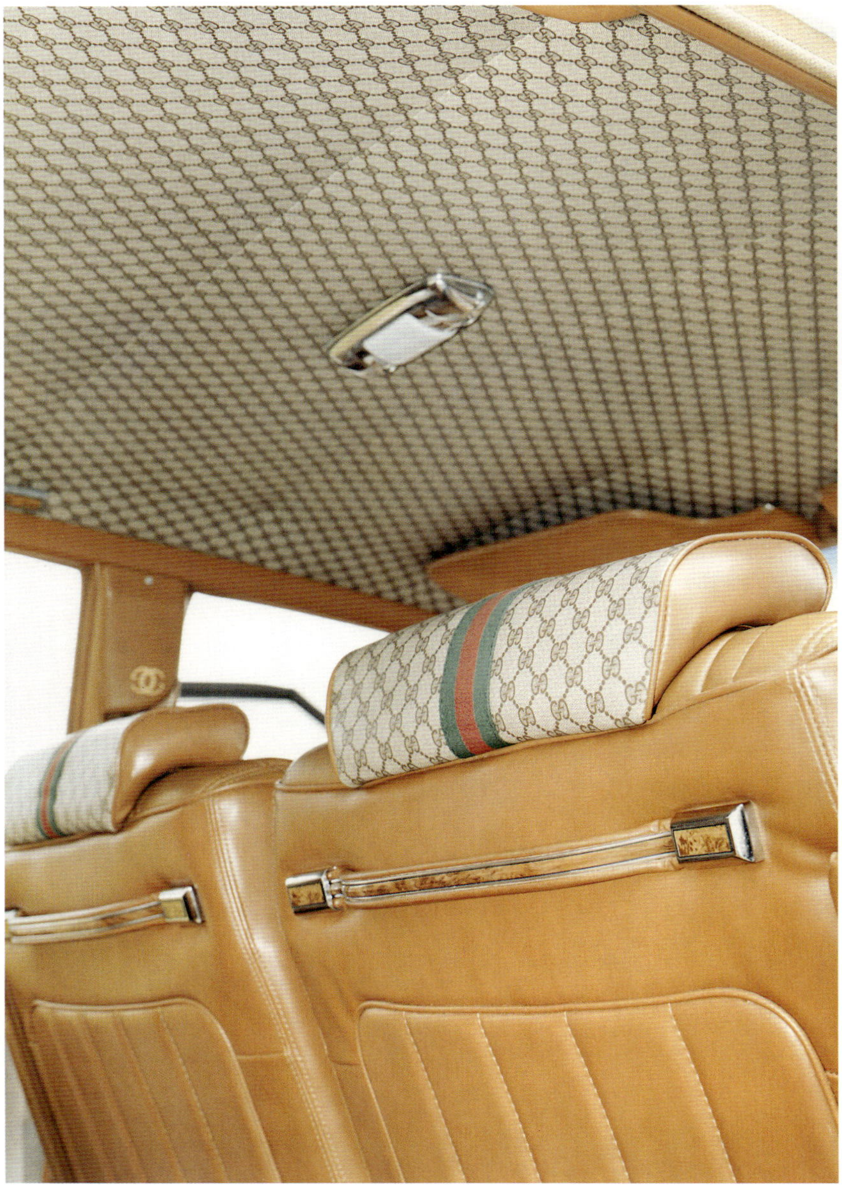

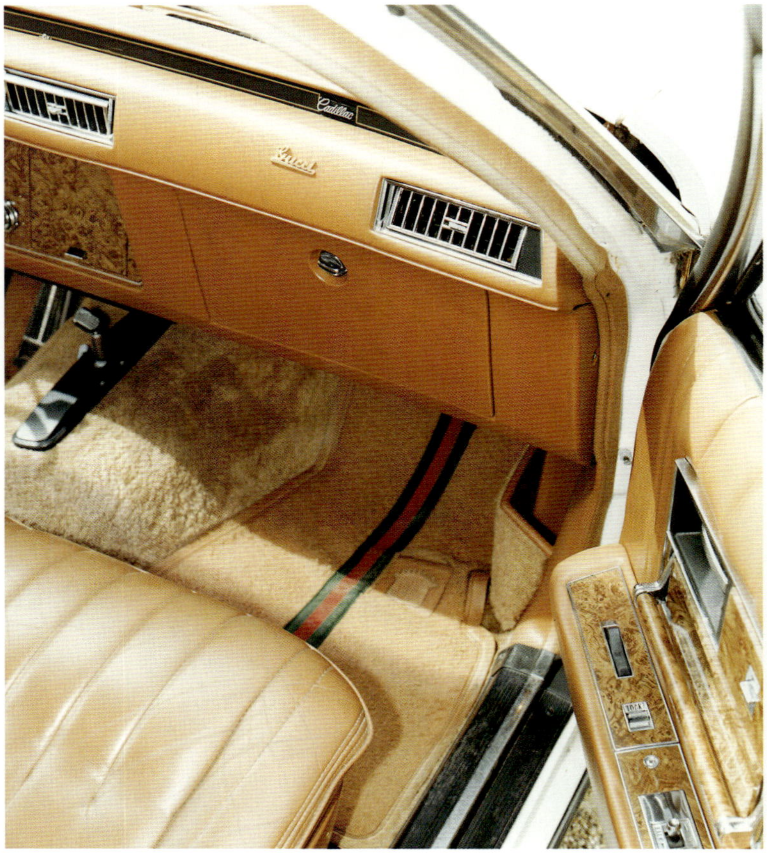

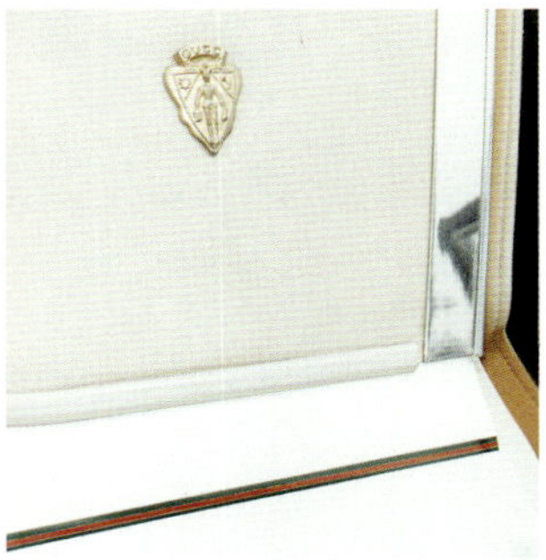

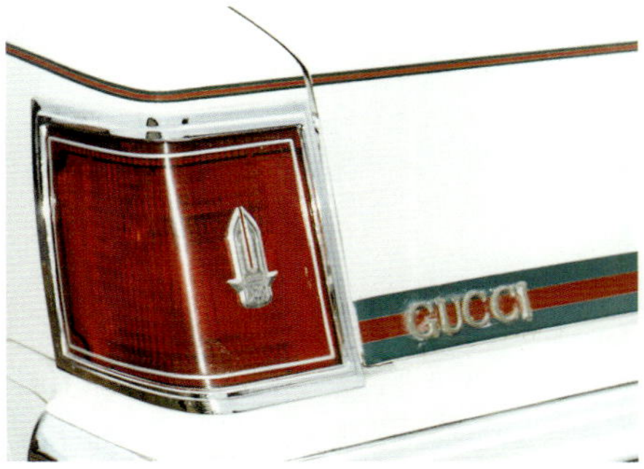
GUCCI

# GUCCI CADDY

**TEXT EMMA E FORREST**
**PHOTOGRAPHY DANIEL STIER**

It's the ultimate in ostentatious fashion accessories, one that would make the average Gucci dog bowl-owning footballer's wife salivate with desire. Built between 1973 and 1979, the Gucci Cadillac Seville even includes its own bespoke set of luggage featuring the signature Gucci snaffle. The Gucci Seville is a car that combines classic Italian design with US technology. This special edition Caddy comes painted in black, burgundy, brown or white, with an interior lovingly lined with white or caramel leather, and Gucci-designed trim wrapped round the head and armrests, upholstery, and dashboard. On the outside, interlocking Gs replace the Cadillac laurel crown on the bonnet and the hubcaps, and the Gucci crest brands the rear pillars. Gucci licensed Braman Cadillac of Miami to produce the cars in 1976, with the first vehicle officially presented to a Mrs Mimi Abel of Coral Gables, Florida, that year. Few facts remain about why this unusual beast was born, but 200 of these designer vehicles were planned and built. The experiment was fairly limited as the exclusive model was not as widely embraced as, say, Pierre Cardin's AMC Javelin with its jazzy, silky black seats and white, purple and red stripes flowing throughout the interior, or the Levi's AMC Gremlin with its copper buttons, jean door pockets and red tabs. "Nobody really wanted to pay the extra money for a few bits of luggage and a souped-up interior", explains one Gucci Seville owner. At the time, the Gucci cars cost $7,000 more than the standard model, and that's about all they are valued at right now. But the subsequent demise of AMC and rise of Gucci vindicate the accessorised rarity retrospectively. If not as yet credited as a classic within car culture, its symbolic status is in the altogether more exclusive category of car couture.

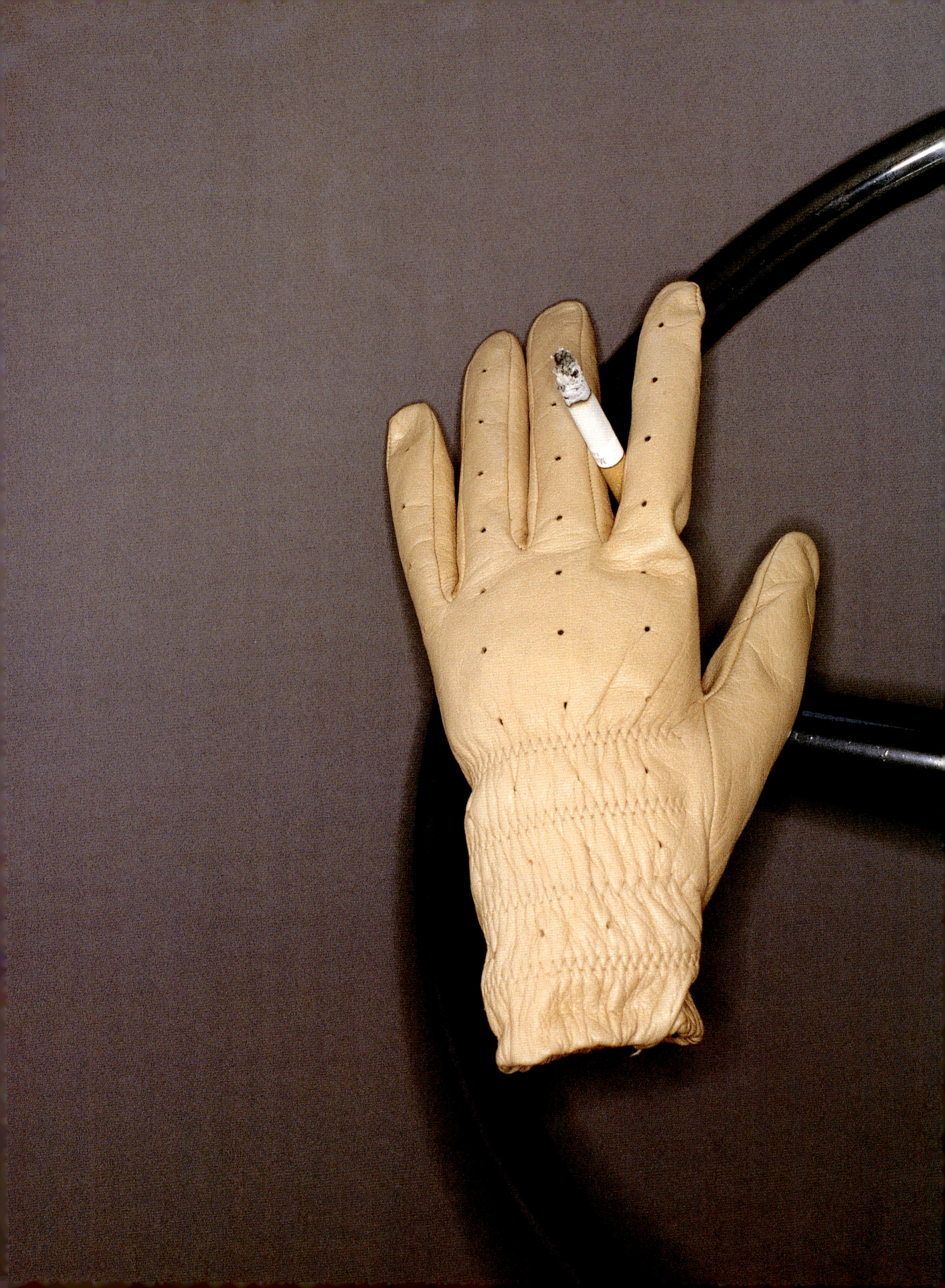

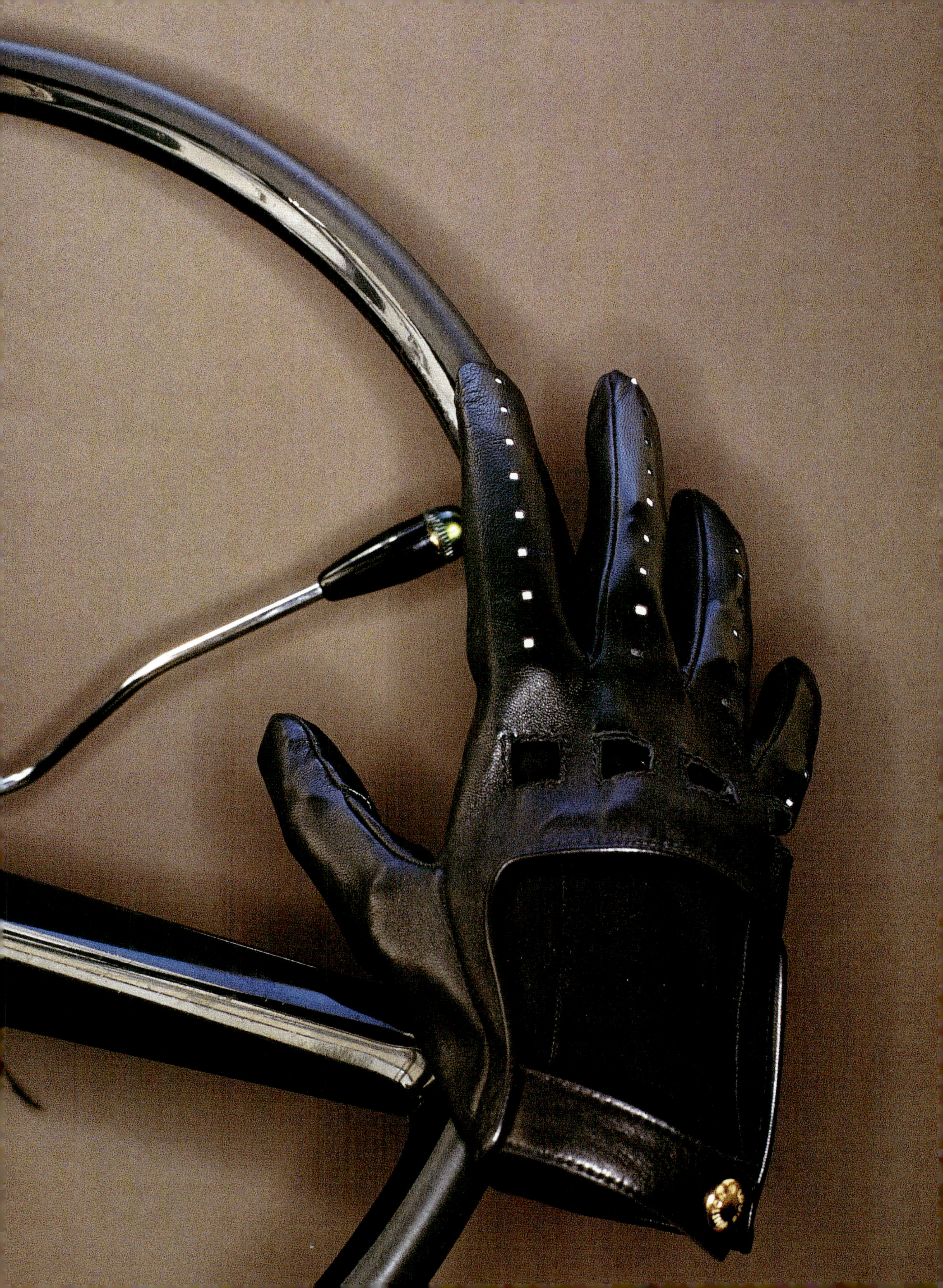

HAUT
92
Rueil
Vaucresson
Châtillon
Malakoff
Montrouge
Bagneux
VILLEJUIF
Lecourbe
Vaugirard
Losserand
Zola

# GLOVE STORY
# PHOTOGRAPHY
# CAMILLE VIVIER

**STYLING**
**MIRANDA ROBSON**

**THANKS TO CLAIRE DUPONT**
**MODEL AGNIEZKA BARANOWSKA**
**CAR: 1966 AUSTIN PRINCESS VANDENPLAS**

**PREVIOUS SPREAD LEFT:**
**CREAM LEATHER PERFORATED**
**DRIVING GLOVES BY HERMES**

**PREVIOUS SPREAD RIGHT:**
**BLACK LEATHER DRIVING GLOVES**
**BY LOUIS VUITTON**

**LEFT:**
**OLIVE GREEN AND CREAM PERFORATED**
**DRIVING GLOVES BY HERMES**

**NEXT SPREAD:**
**TAN LEATHER GLOVES WITH WOOL LINING**
**BY VERSACE**

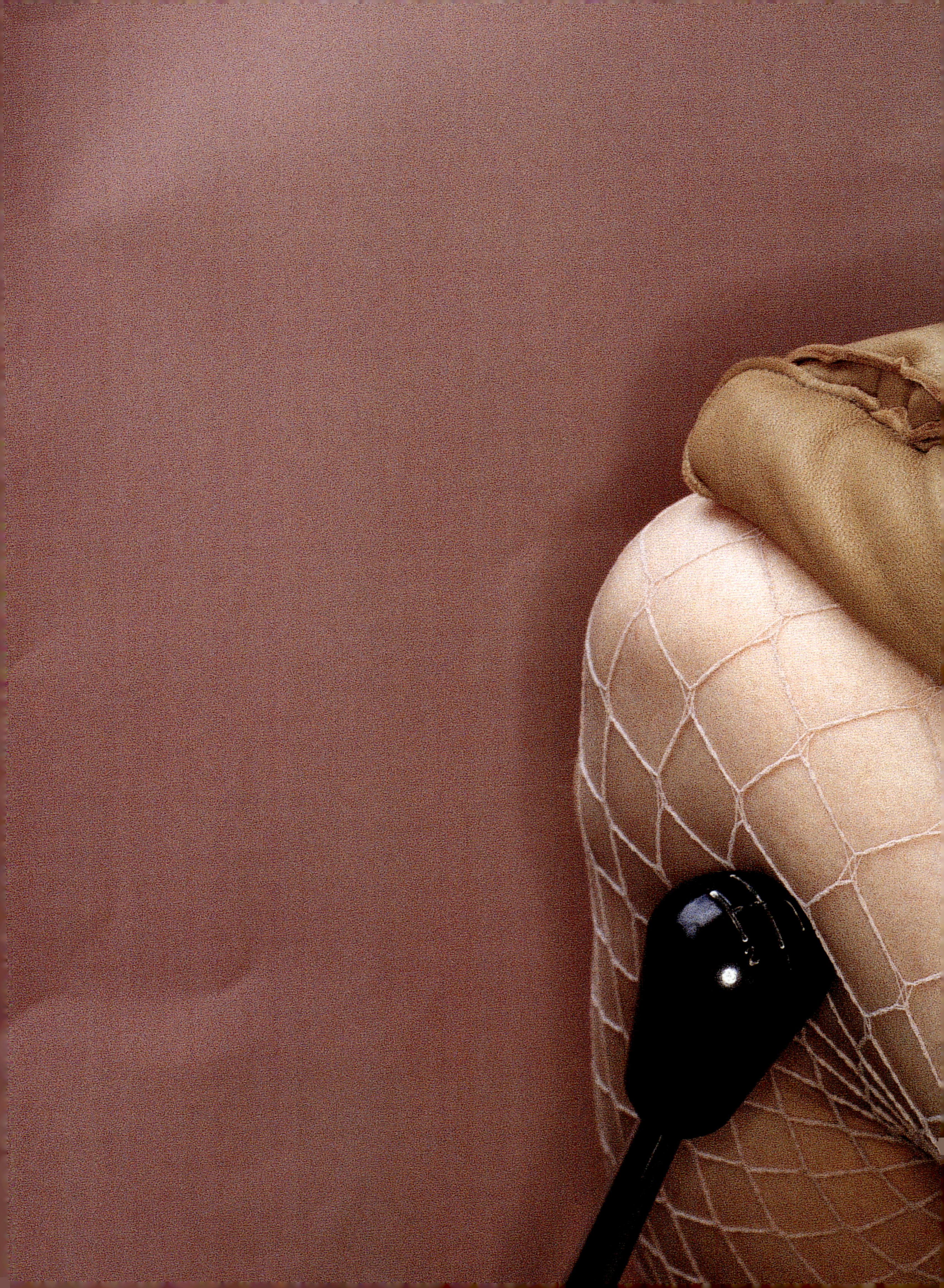

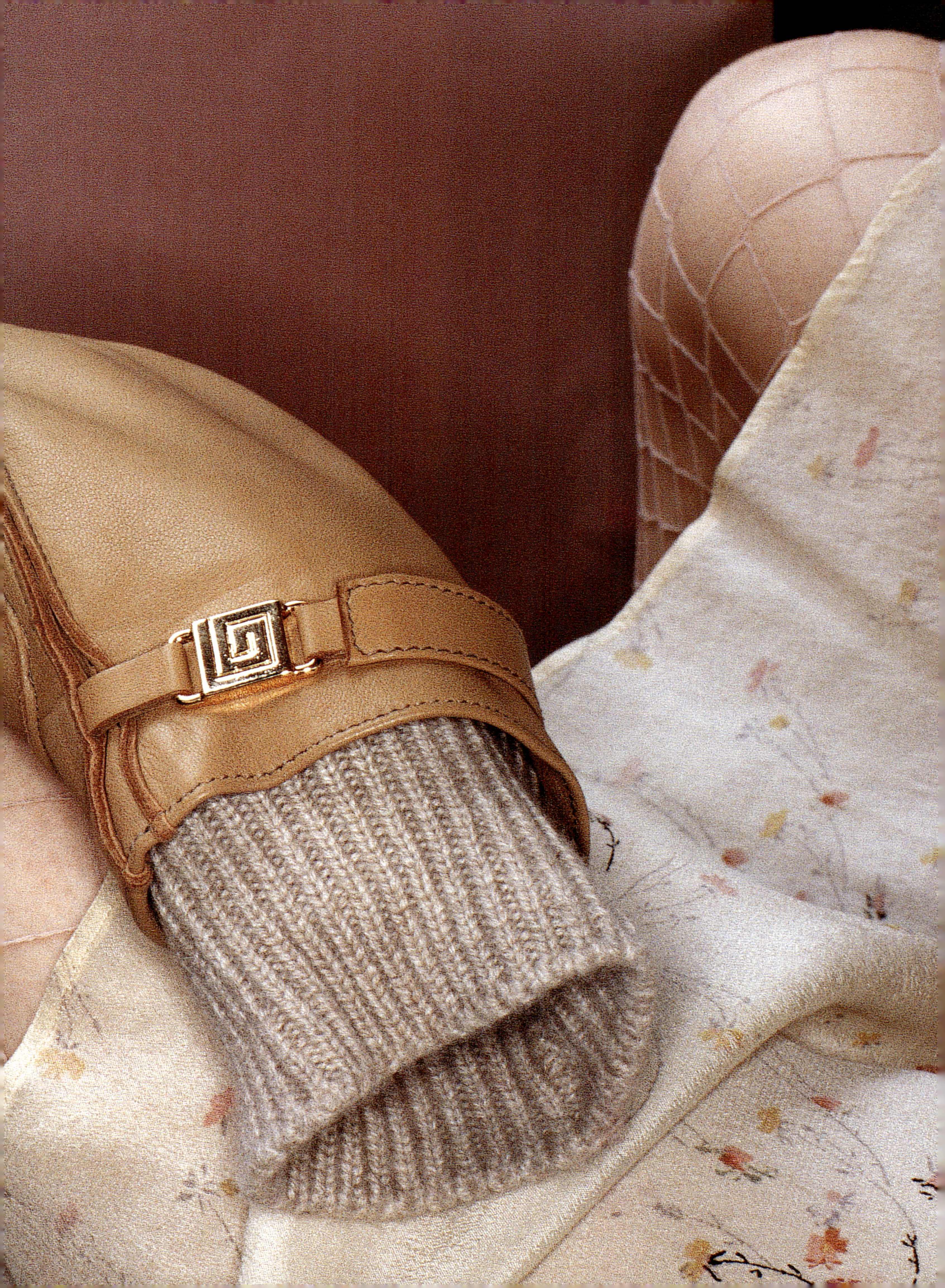

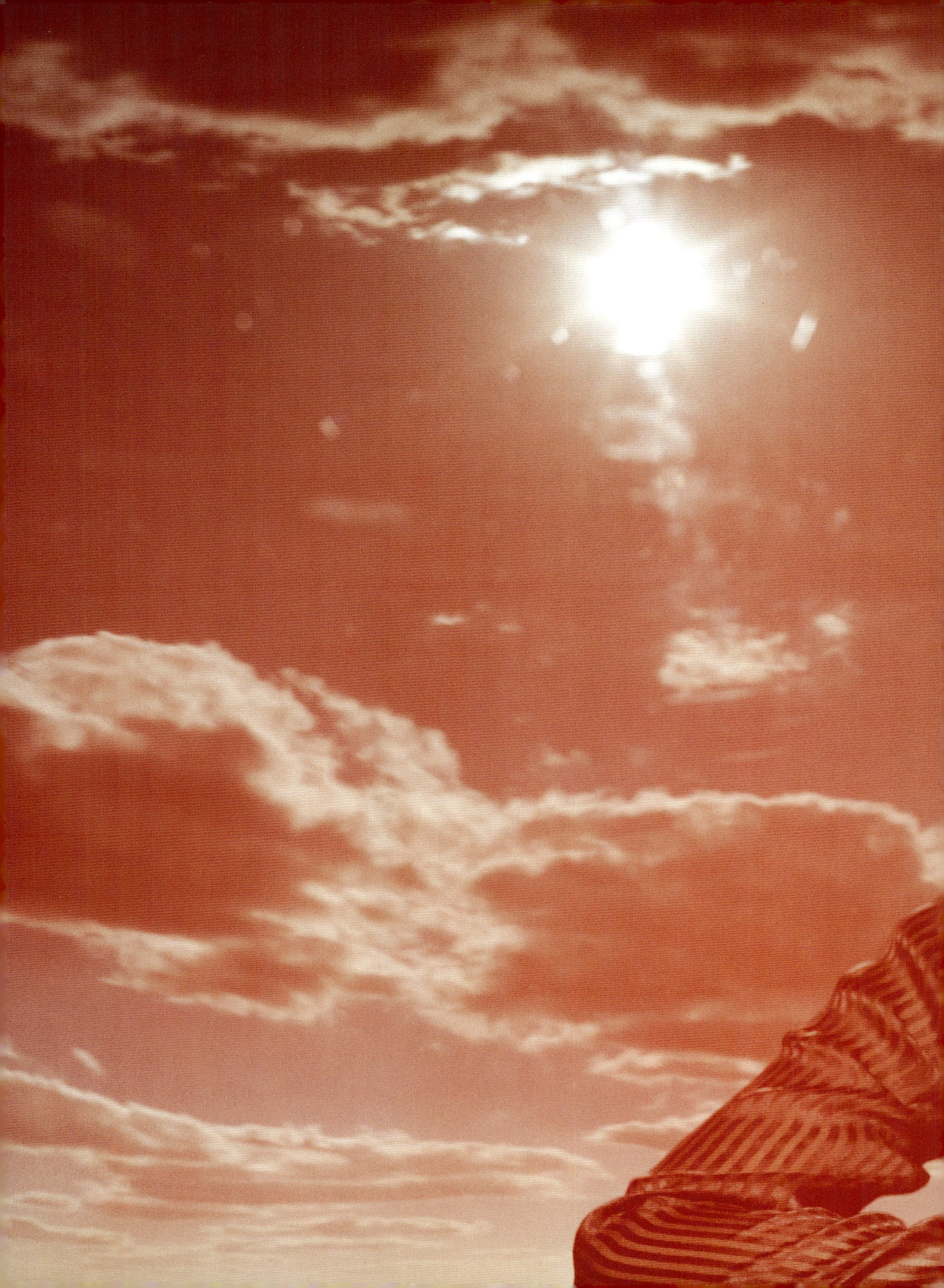

# ON REFLECTION

**PHOTOGRAPHY
JAMES DIMMOCK
STYLING
MIRANDA ROBSON**

BLACK SILK SHIRT BY SPORTMAX
GOLD CHAIN BY H SAMUEL

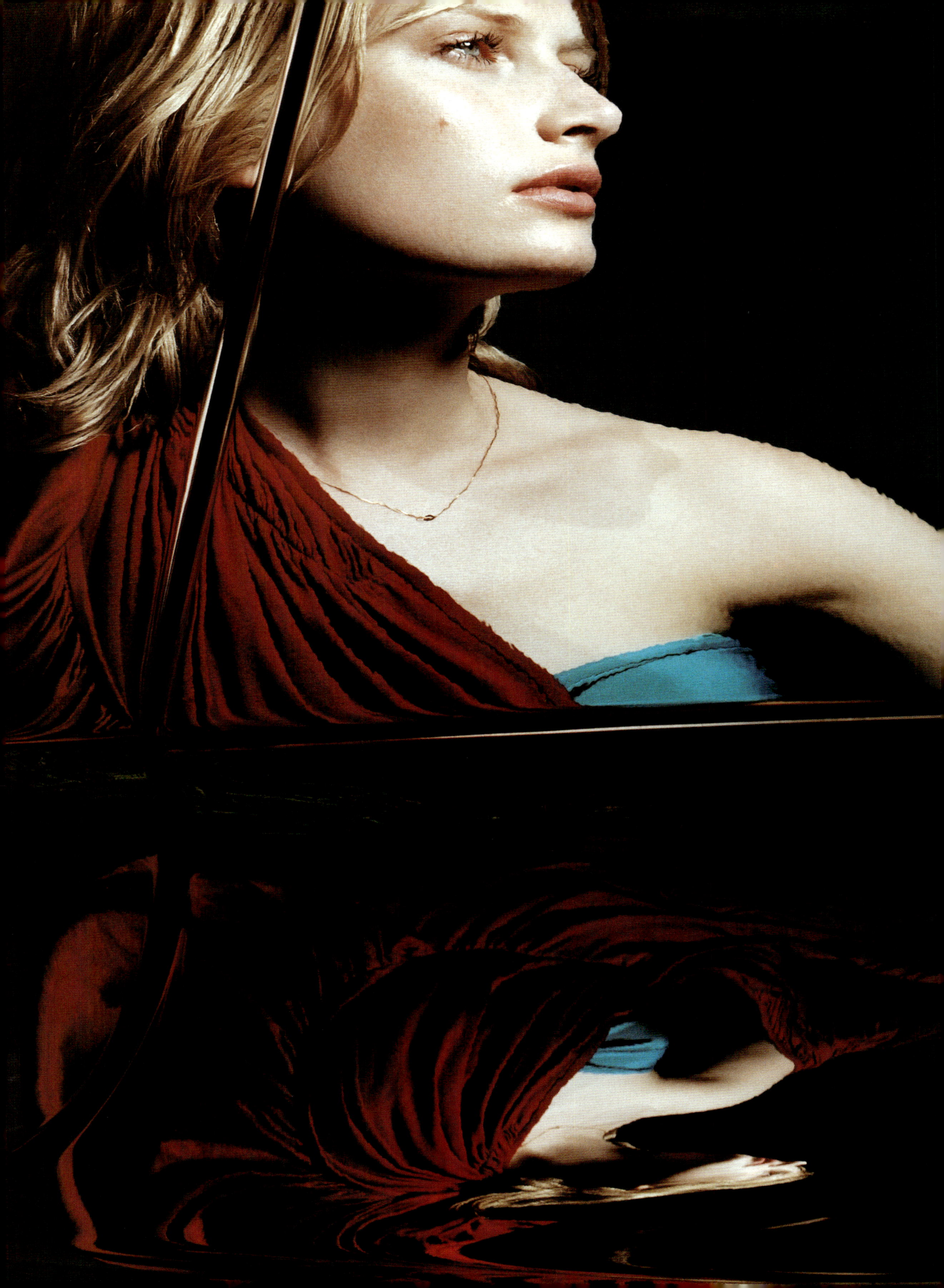

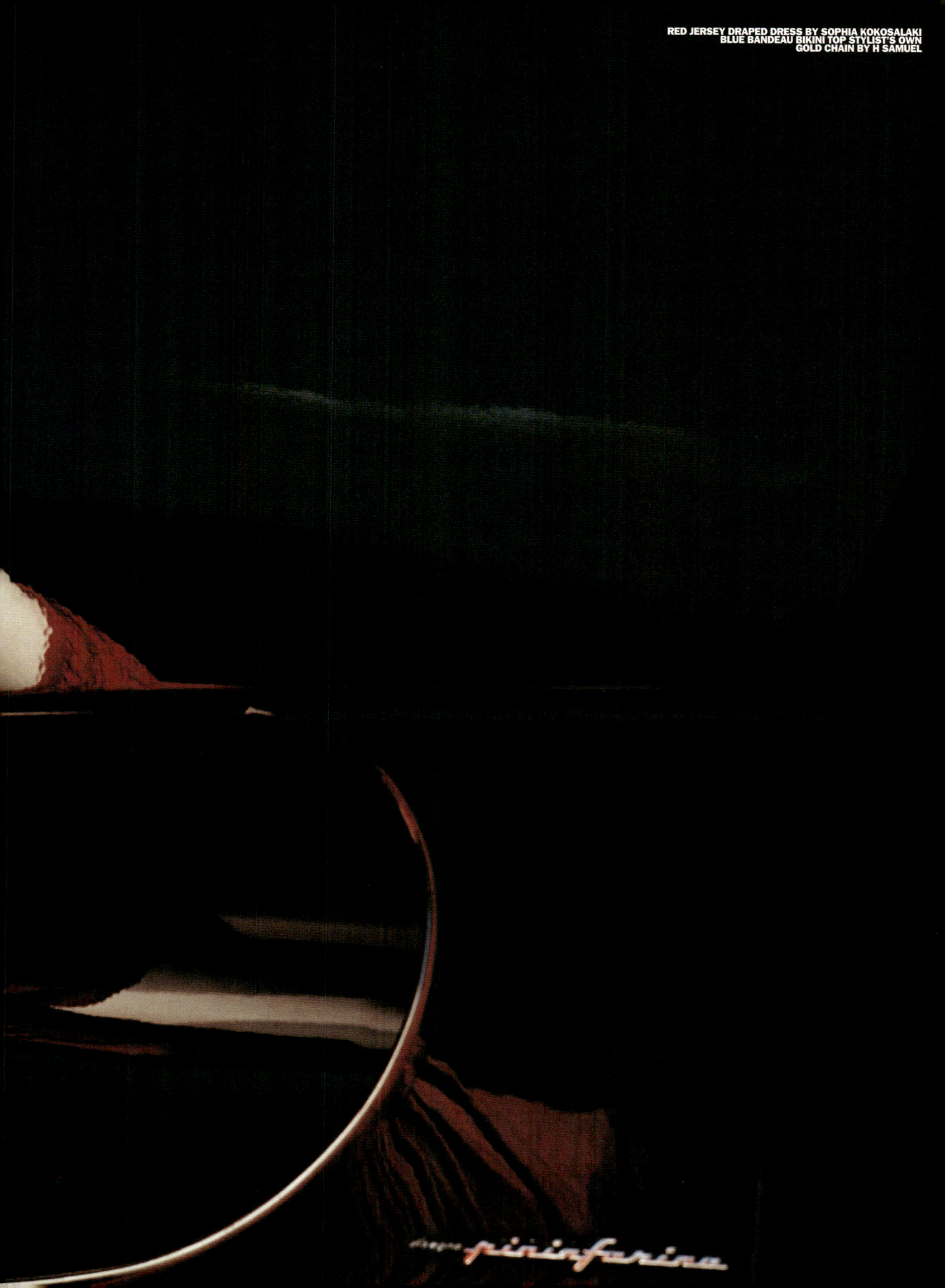

RED JERSEY DRAPED DRESS BY SOPHIA KOKOSALAKI
BLUE BANDEAU BIKINI TOP STYLIST'S OWN
GOLD CHAIN BY H SAMUEL

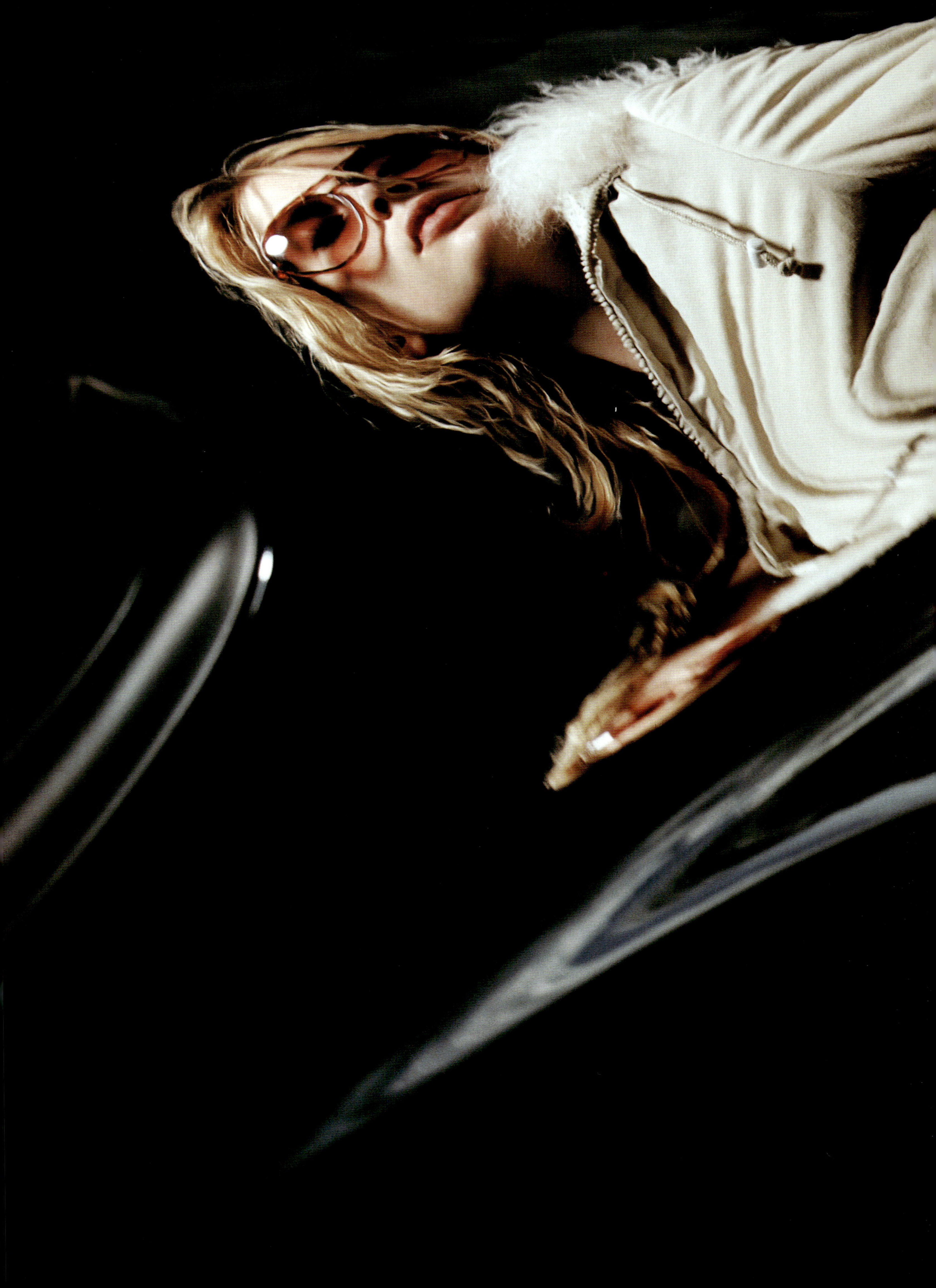

CREAM BOMBER JACKET BY JIGSAW
GOLD SEQUINNED CHIFFON SKIRT BY BLUMARINE
SUNGLASSES STYLIST'S OWN

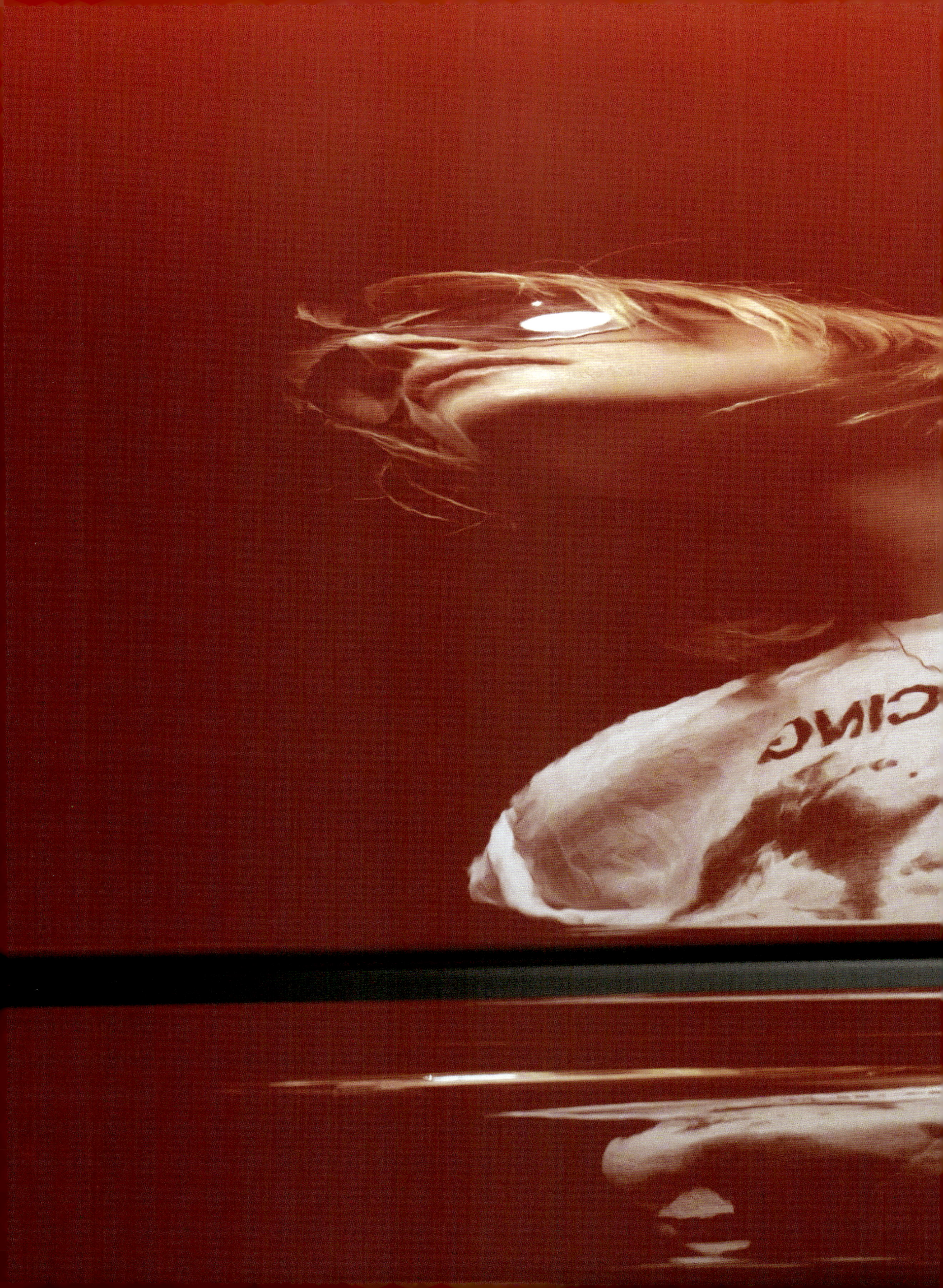

T-SHIRT FROM PORTOBELLO MARKET
DISTRESSED LEATHER SKIRT BY SPORTMAX
ORIGINAL SUNGLASSES BY FERRARI STYLIST'S OWN
GOLD CHAIN BY H SAMUEL

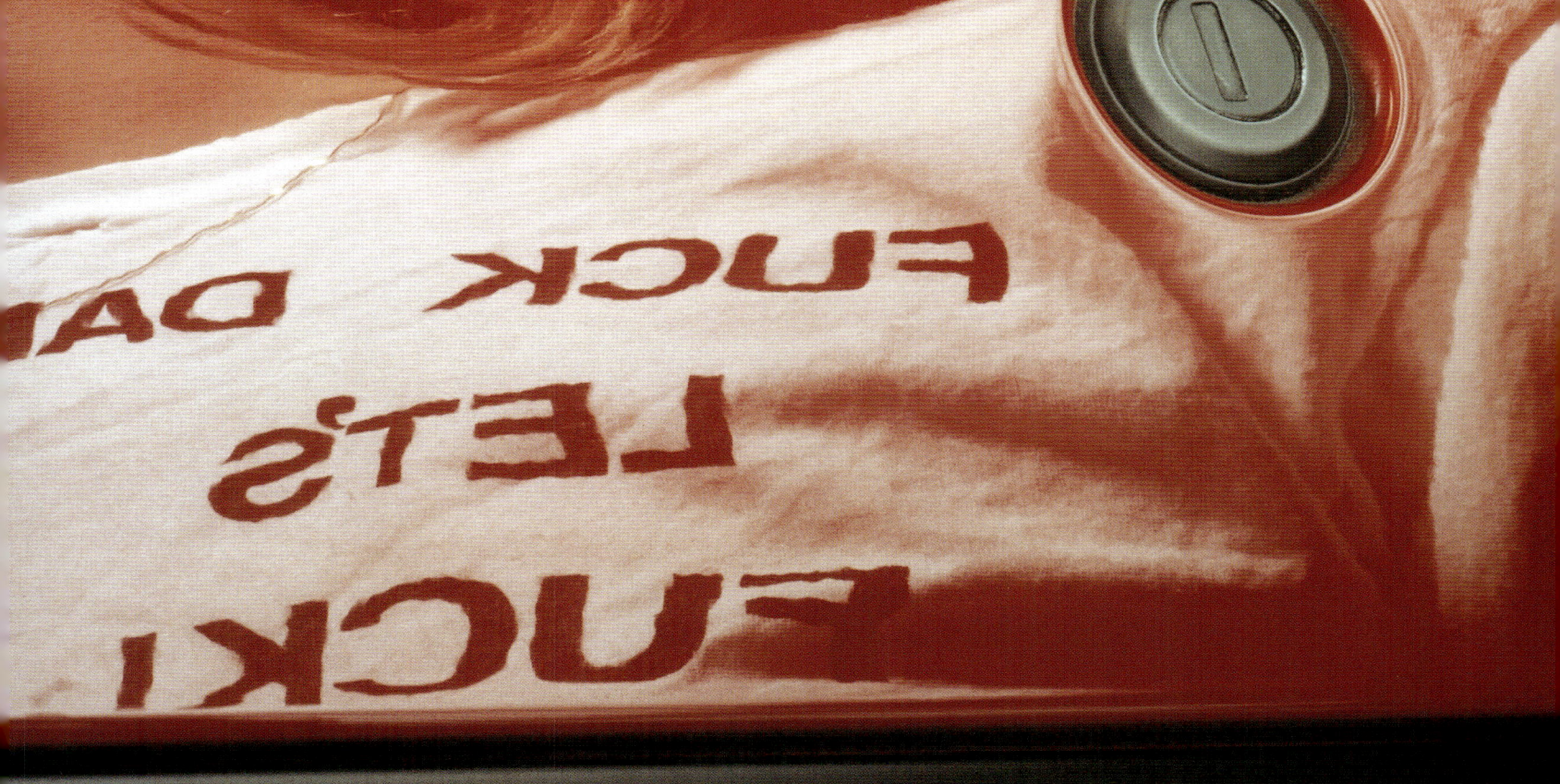

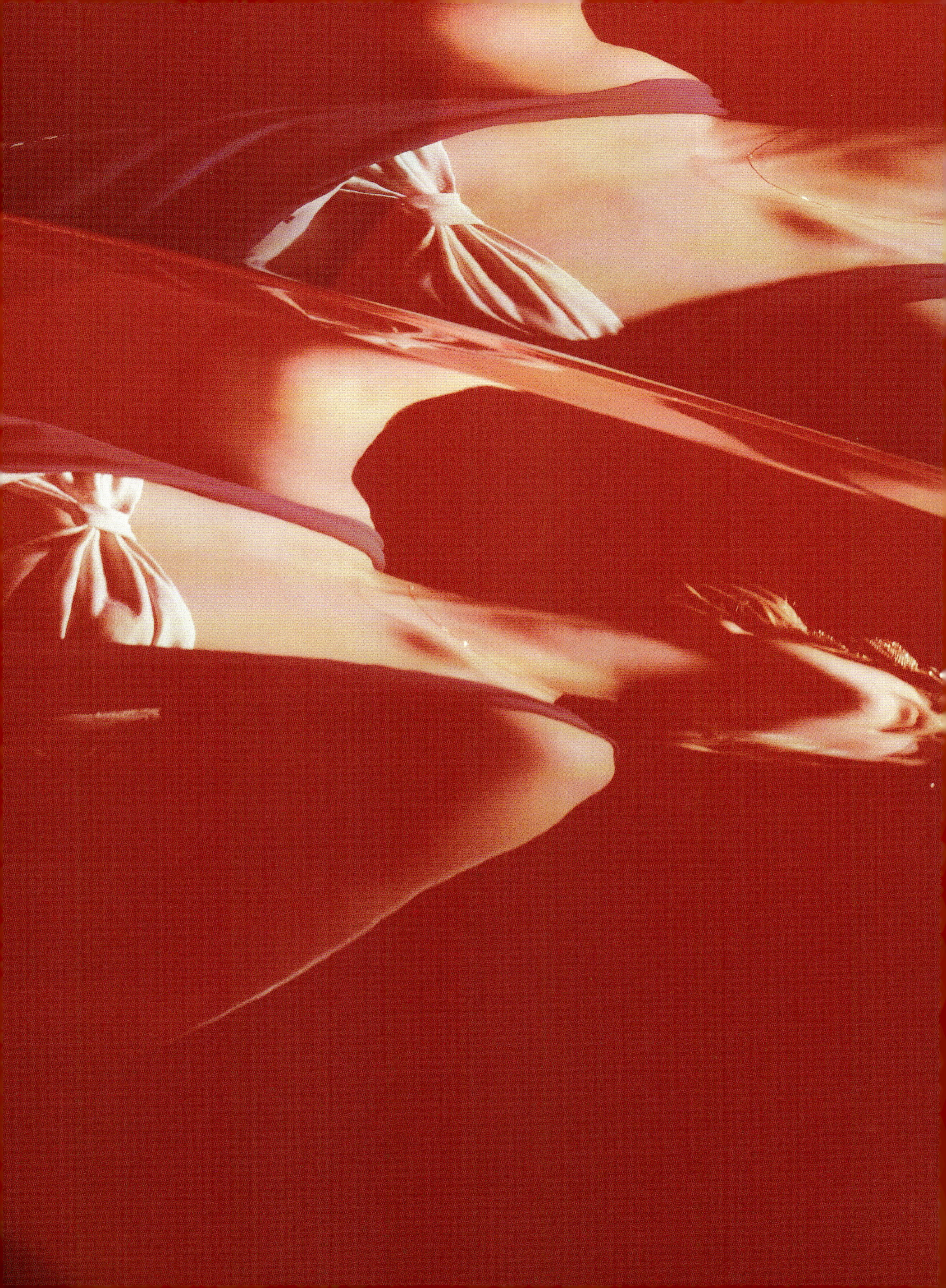

BLUE DRAPED DRESS WITH LADIES FACES PRINT LINING BY EMMA COOK
WHITE BANDEAU BIKINI TOP STYLIST'S OWN
OFFICERS CAP BY MARIA CHEN CUSTOMISED BY LARA BOHINC
GOLD CHAIN BY H SAMUEL

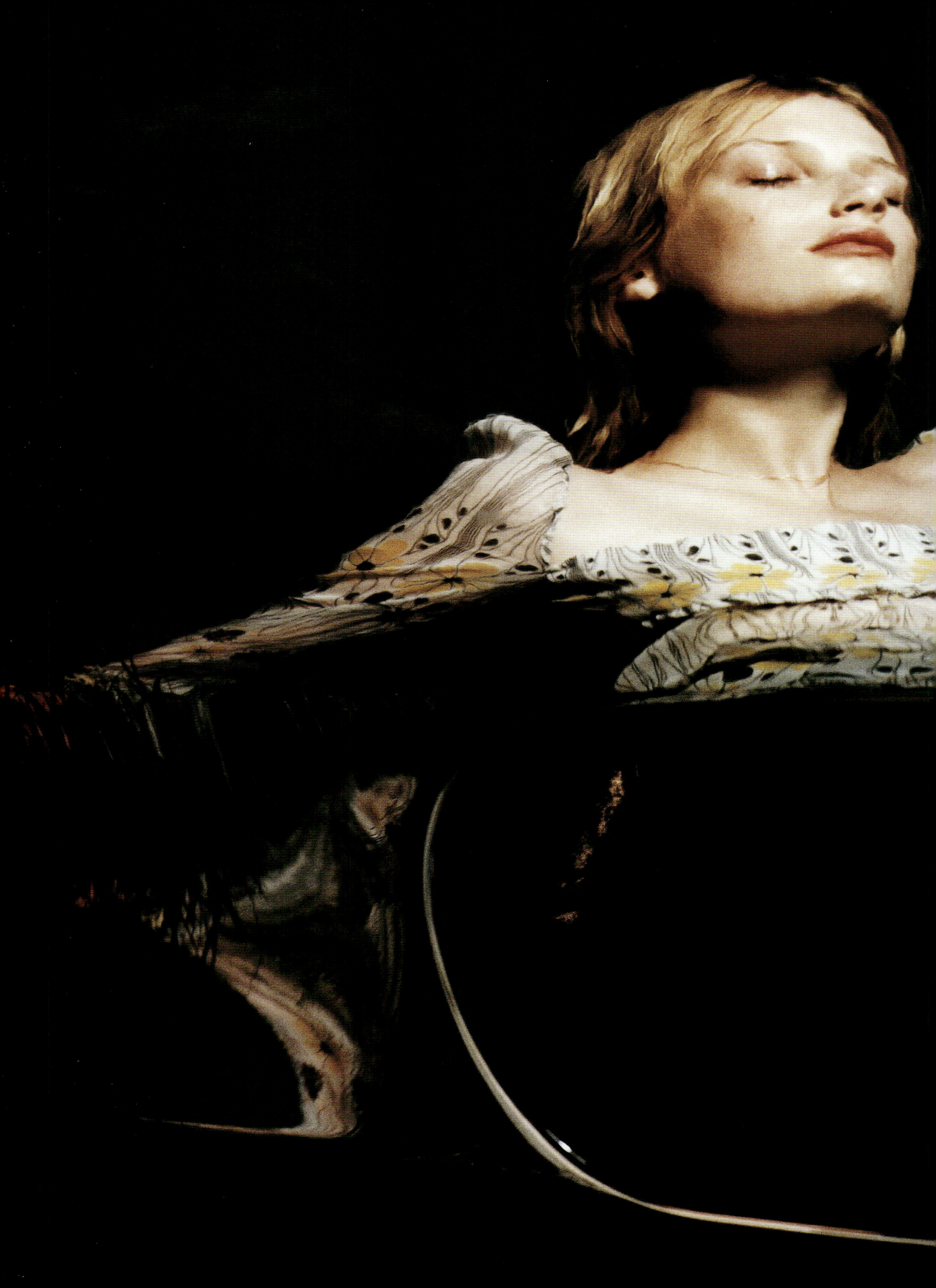

FLOWER PRINT CHIFFON DRESS BY MIU MIU
GOLD CHAIN BY H SAMUEL
VINTAGE DENIM SHORTS BY LEVI'S

HAIR SHINYA NAKAYAMA FOR CUTS
MAKE-UP EMMA LOVELL AT SMILE
MODEL NINA HIEMLICH AT SELECT
CARS: BLACK FERRARI 360 MODENA
RED FERRARI 355 F1
THANKS TO H R OWEN CANARY WHARF

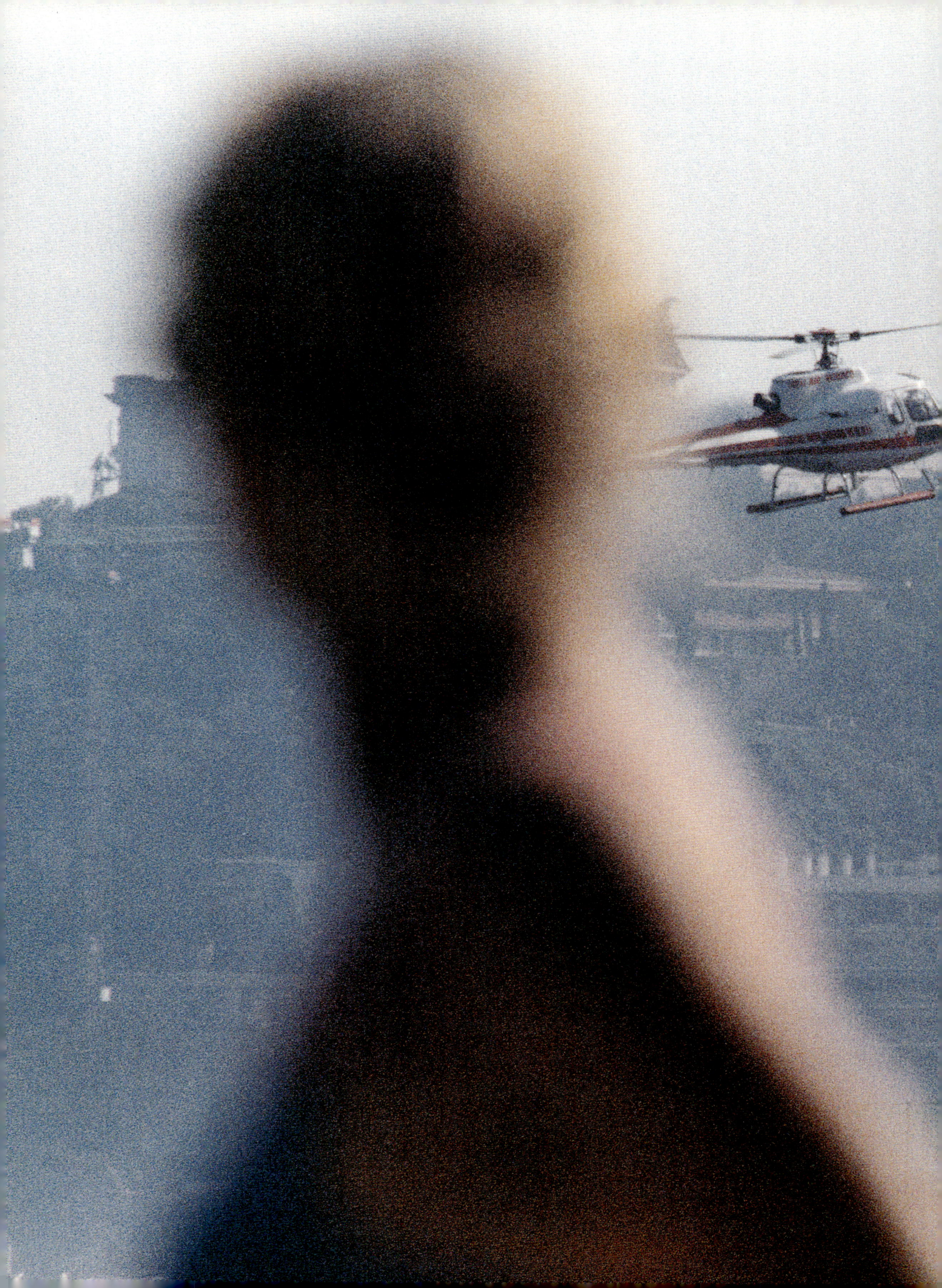

# A DAY AT THE RACES
# PART 1
# MONACO

GRACE KELLY USED TO OPEN THE GRAND PRIX WITH PRINCE RANIER. HIS ANCESTOR LOUIS II HAD SUPPORTED THE INITIATION OF THE ANNUAL EVENT IN THE PRINCIPALITY IN 1929.

IF YOU ATTENDED THIS YEAR, YOU MIGHT HAVE FINALLY SEEN THE POINT OF JOINING THE WAITING LIST FOR A ROOM AT THE HOTEL DE PARIS IN THE EARLY '90S. OF COURSE, YOU CAN JUMP THE QUEUE IF YOU HAVE THE REQUISITE MEANS OR CONNECTIONS. LESS PRESTIGIOUS PLACES TO PARK YOUR LUGGAGE CAN ALSO BE FOUND. $13,000 MIGHT HAVE BEEN ENOUGH FOR AN APARTMENT WITH A TERRACE FOR THE WEEK. CHEAPER STILL, $3,300 SECURES A VIEW FROM LA RACASSE, THE RESTAURANT ONLY INCHES AWAY FROM A HAIRPIN BEND. IF YOUR OWN YACHT WAS STILL IN THE CARIBBEAN BEFORE CROSSING THE ATLANTIC FOR A MEDITERRANEAN SUMMER, YOU COULD HAVE HIRED ONE. $45,000 GETS YOU ON THE WATER, BUT BERTHS ARE IN SHORT SUPPLY.

200,000 ATTENDANTS MANAGED TO CRAM INTO THE 195 HECTARE (0.75 SQUARE MILE) TAX HAVEN, NORMALLY INHABITED BY 30,000 FOR THIS YEAR'S EVENT. THE CRAMPED PITS AND NARROW CIRCUIT MEAN EVEN DRIVERS ARE SQUEEZED FOR SPACE.

AYRTON SENNA MANAGED TO CONFINE A SUPERIORLY POWERED, FRESHLY TYRED NIGEL MANSELL TO SECOND PLACE IN 1992 BY SIMPLY STEERING DOWN THE MIDDLE OF THE TRACK FOR THE LAST SIX LAPS. THIS YEAR, CAPITALISING ON AN UNEXPECTED HEAD START, MICHAEL SCHUMACHÉR TOOK THE TEN POINTS FOR VICTORY AFTER DAVID COULTHARD'S POLE-POSITIONED MCLAREN STALLED. PLAYING CATCH UP, COULTHARD'S CONSOLATION PRIZE WAS THE FASTEST LAP TIME, RACING AROUND THE 3.3KM CIRCUIT IN ONE MINUTE 19 SECONDS.

BUT LAPPING UP CHAMPAGNE IS WHAT THE MONACO GRAND PRIX IS REALLY ABOUT. AS PUFFY MIGHT SAY, "IT'S ALL ABOUT THE BENJAMINS."

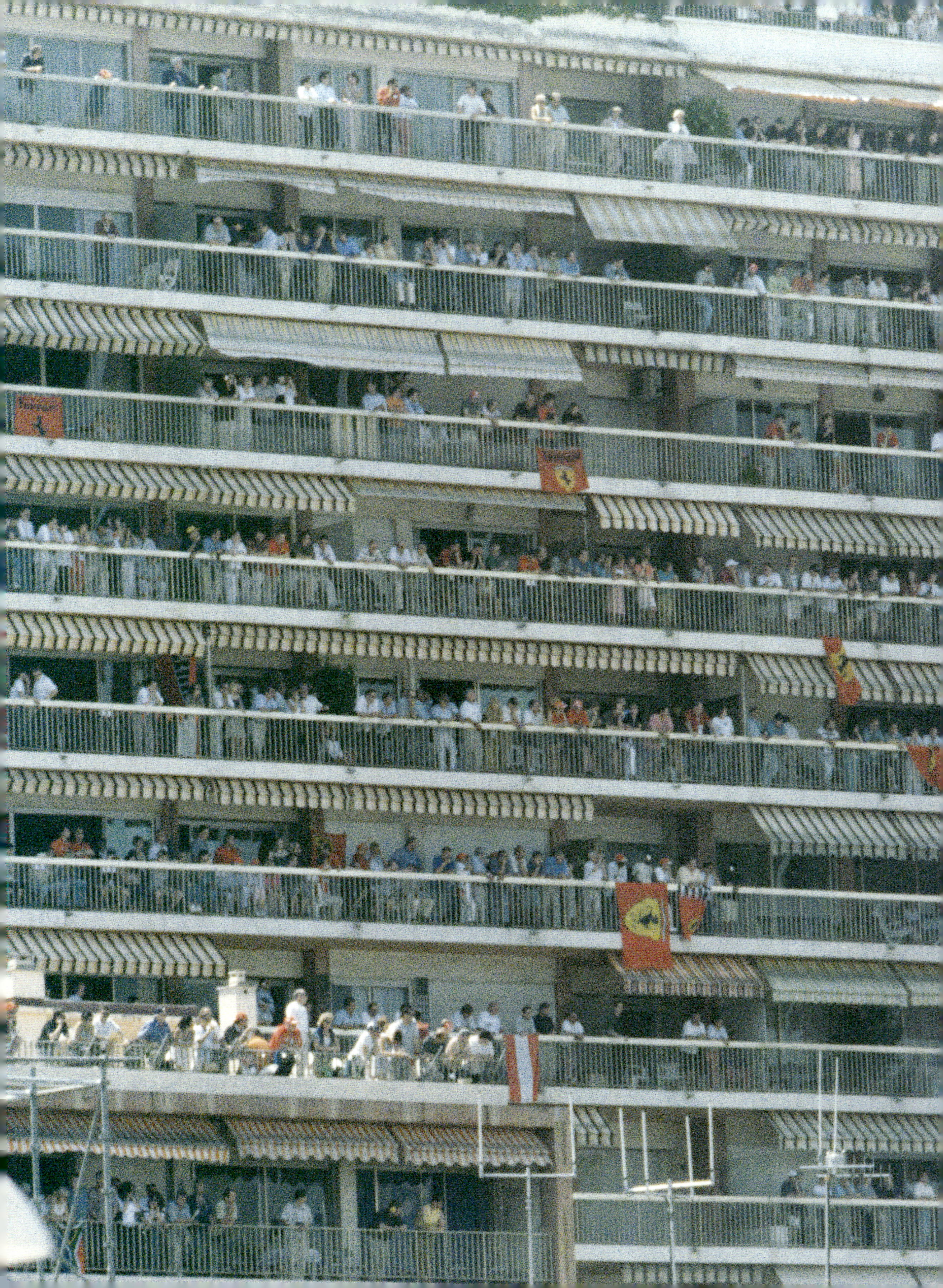

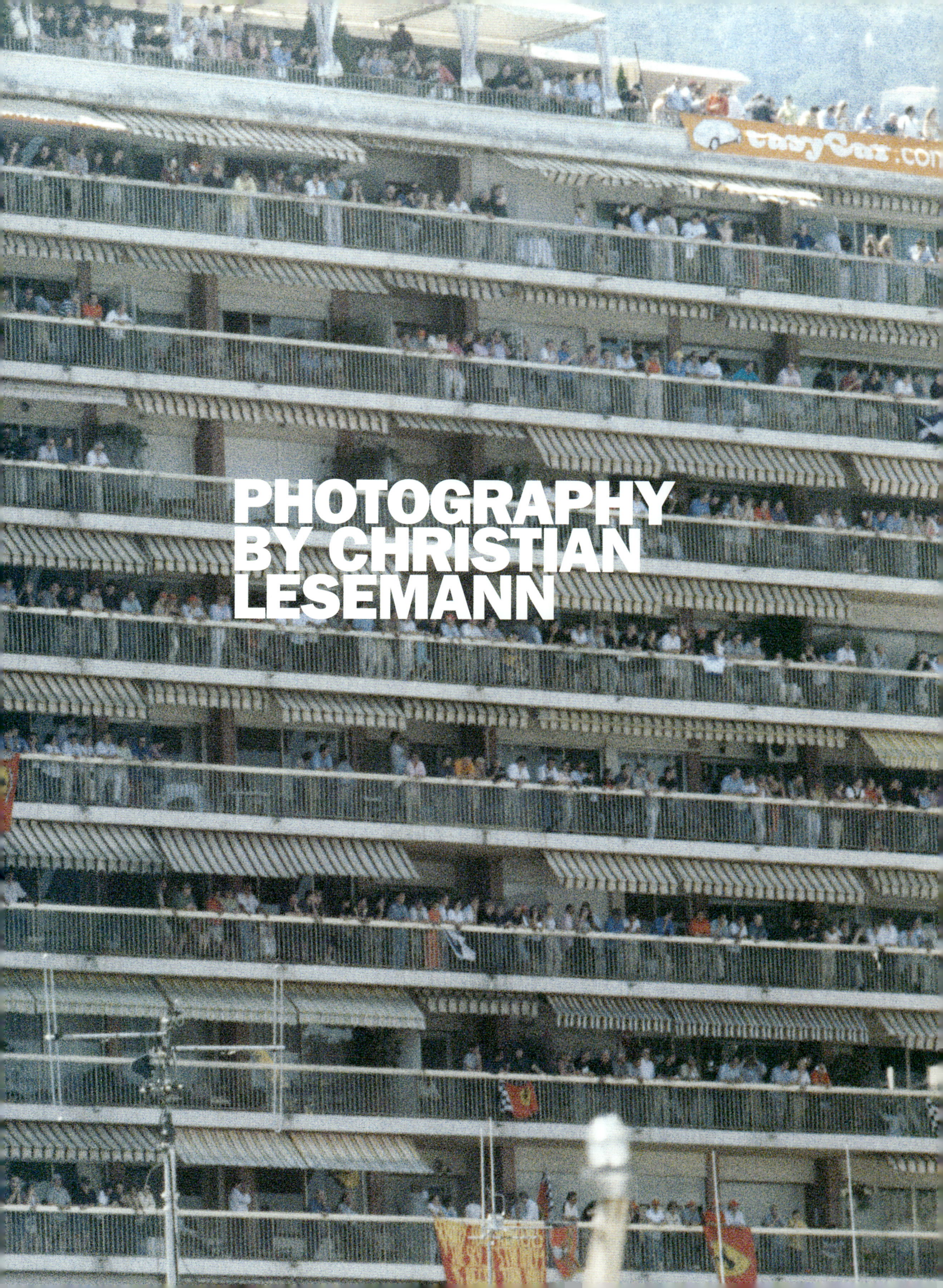

PHOTOGRAPHY
BY CHRISTIAN
LESEMANN

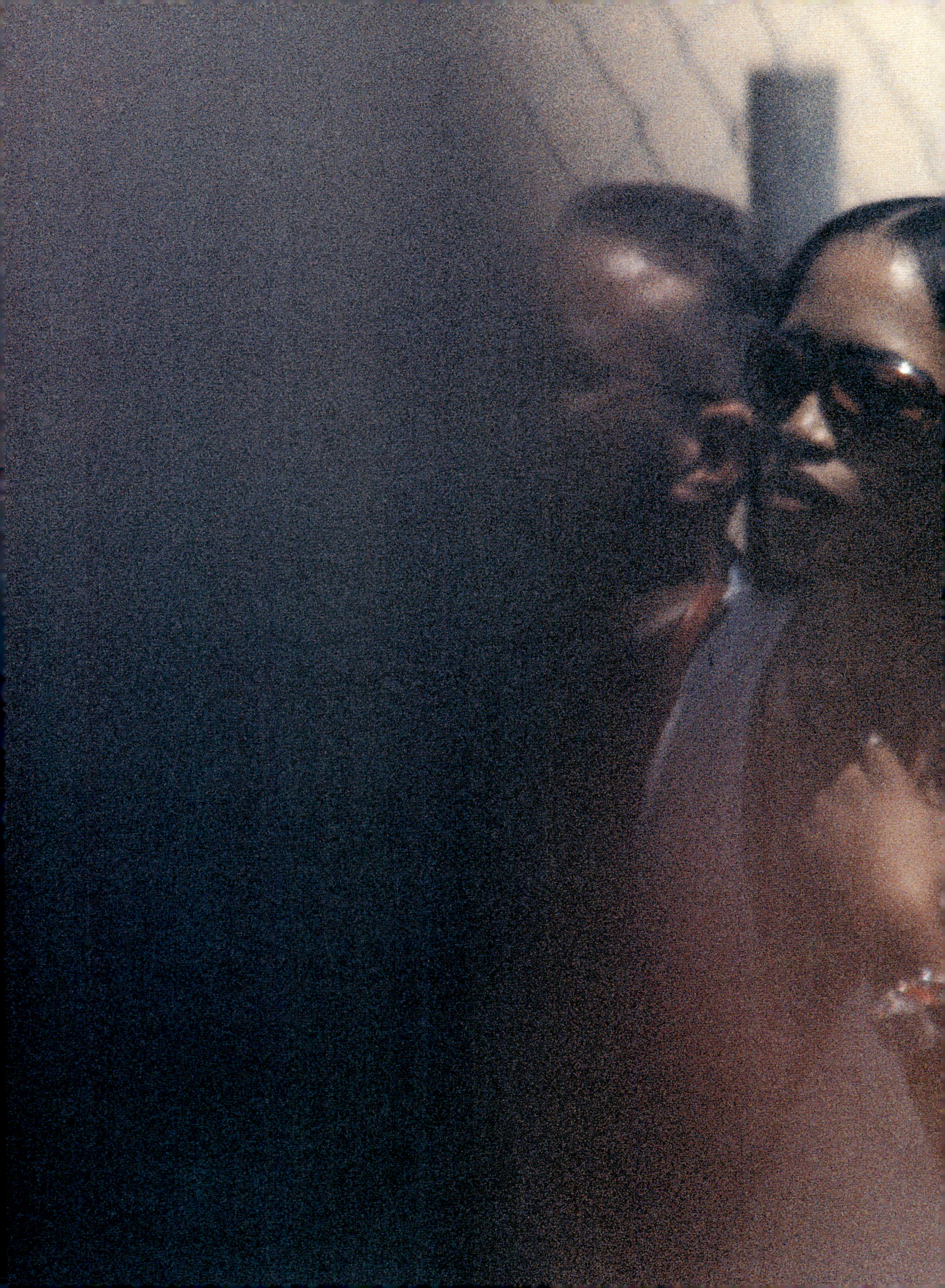

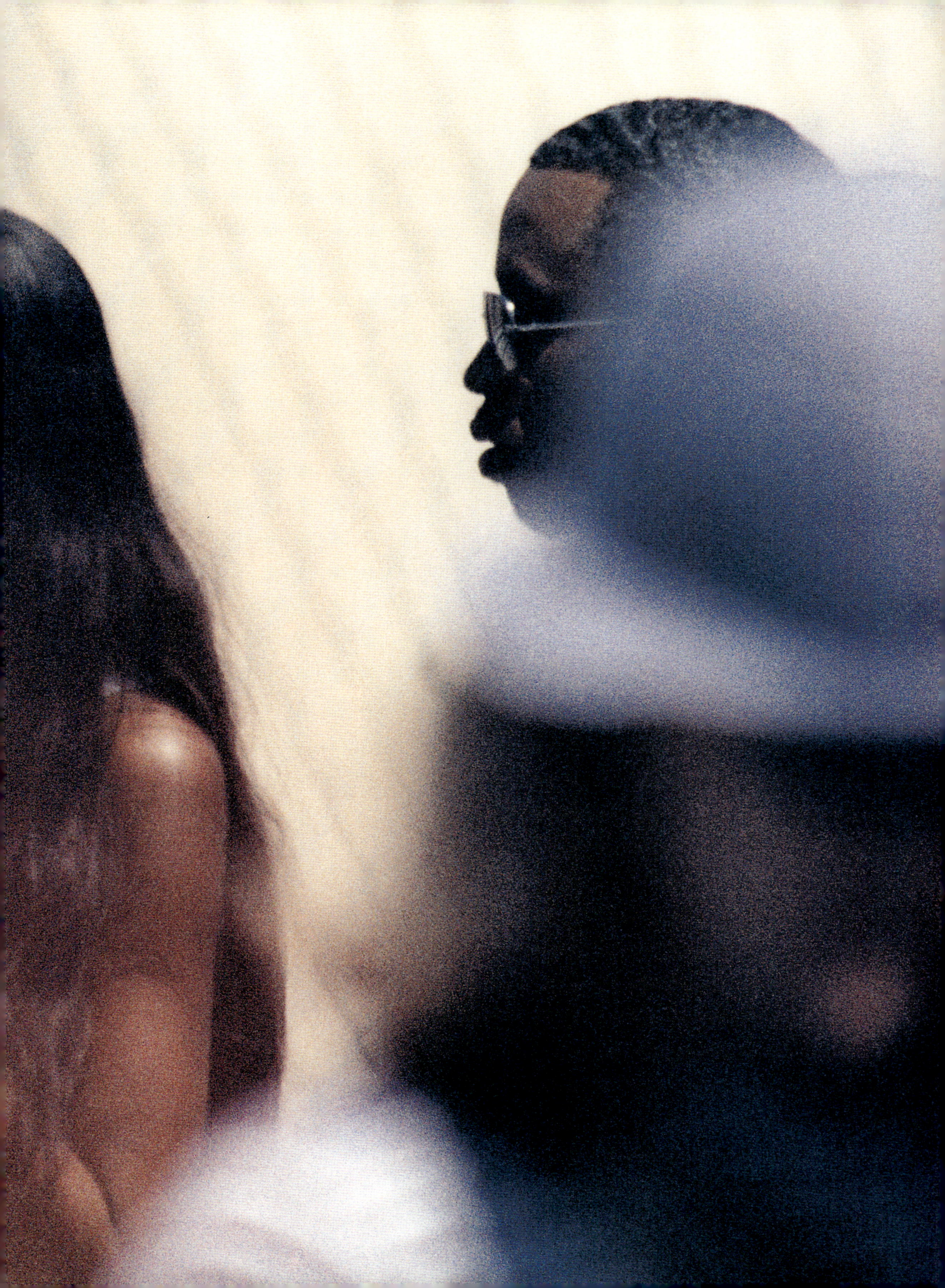

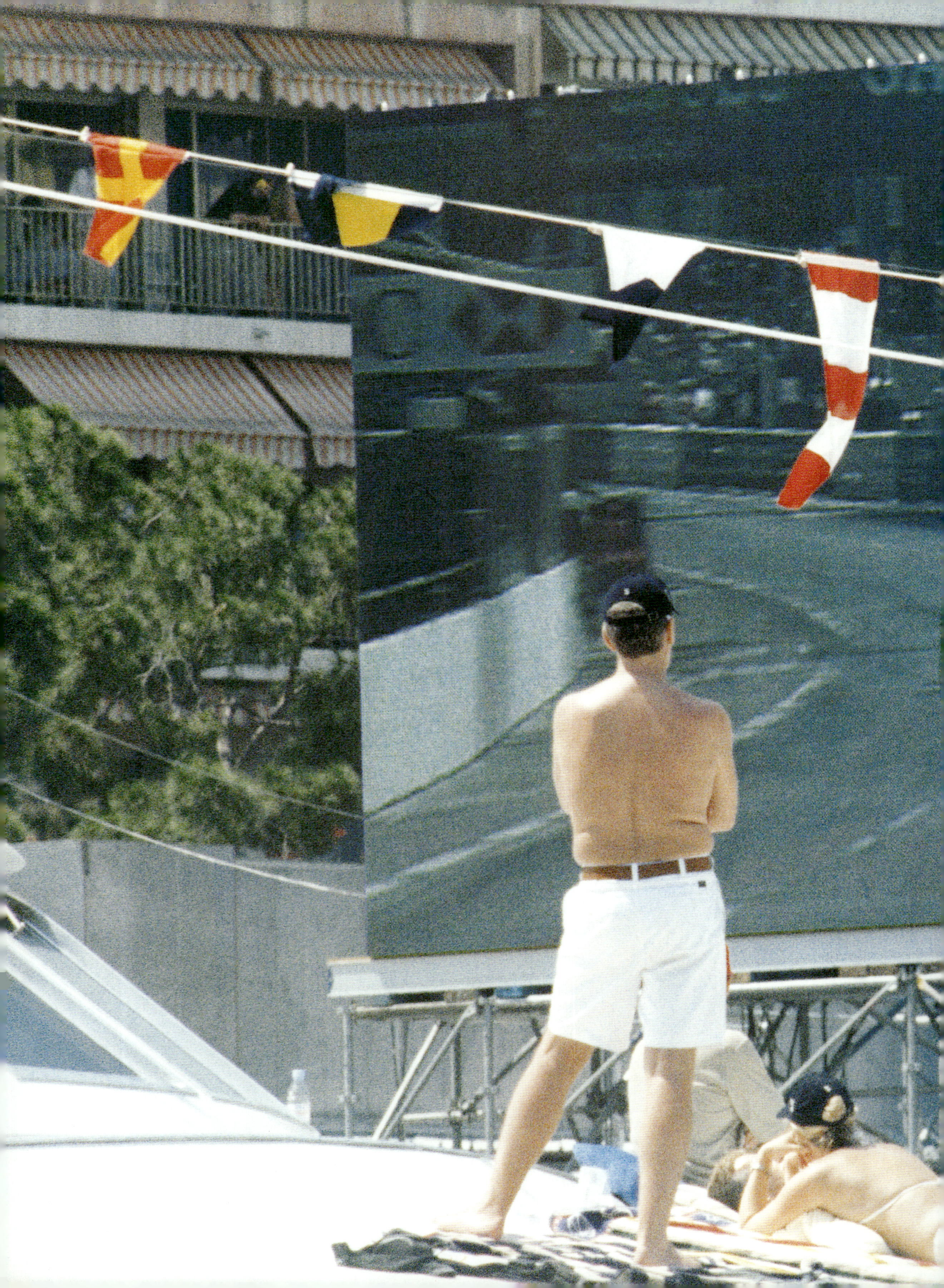

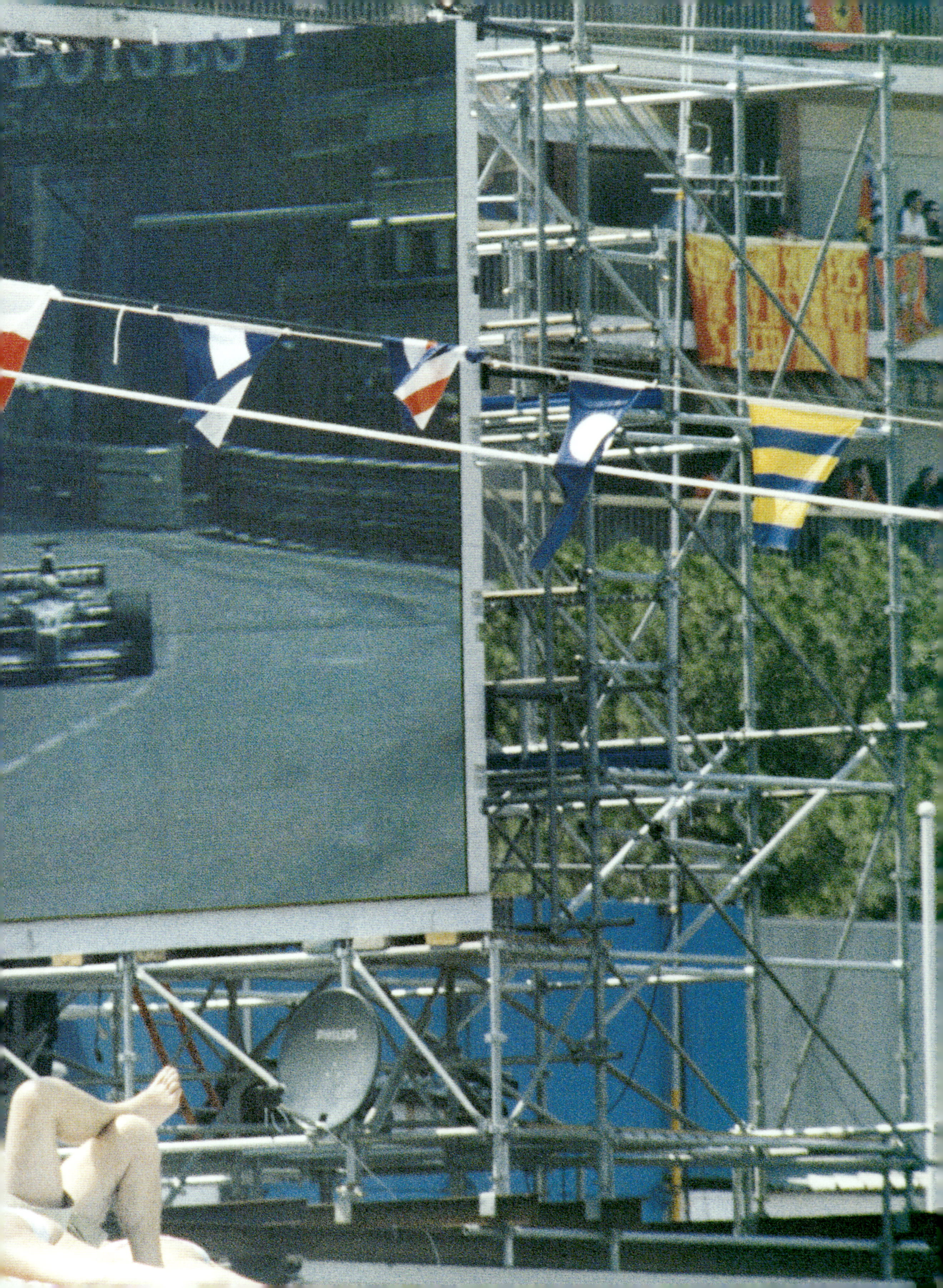

BAD OEYNHAUSEN

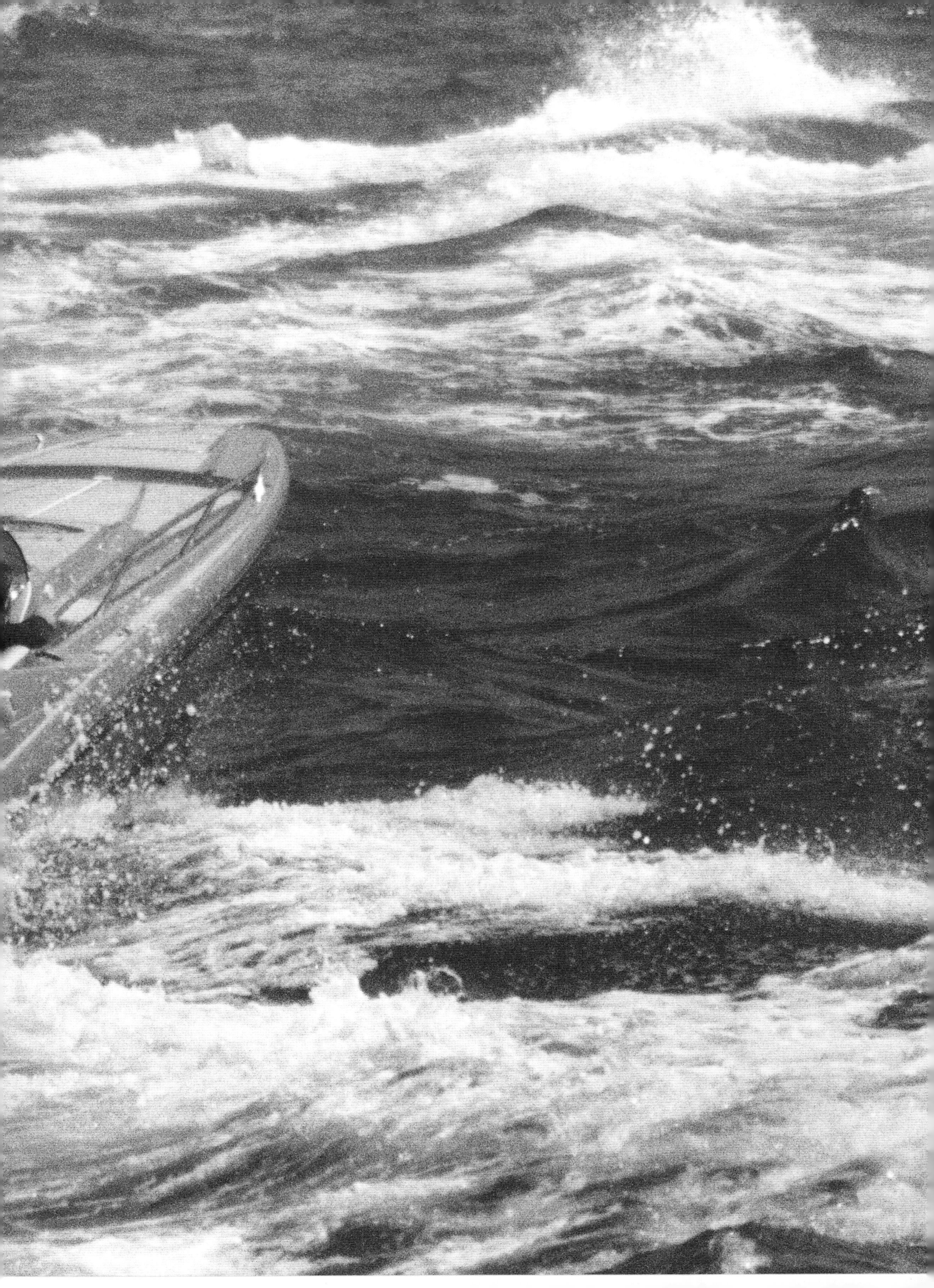

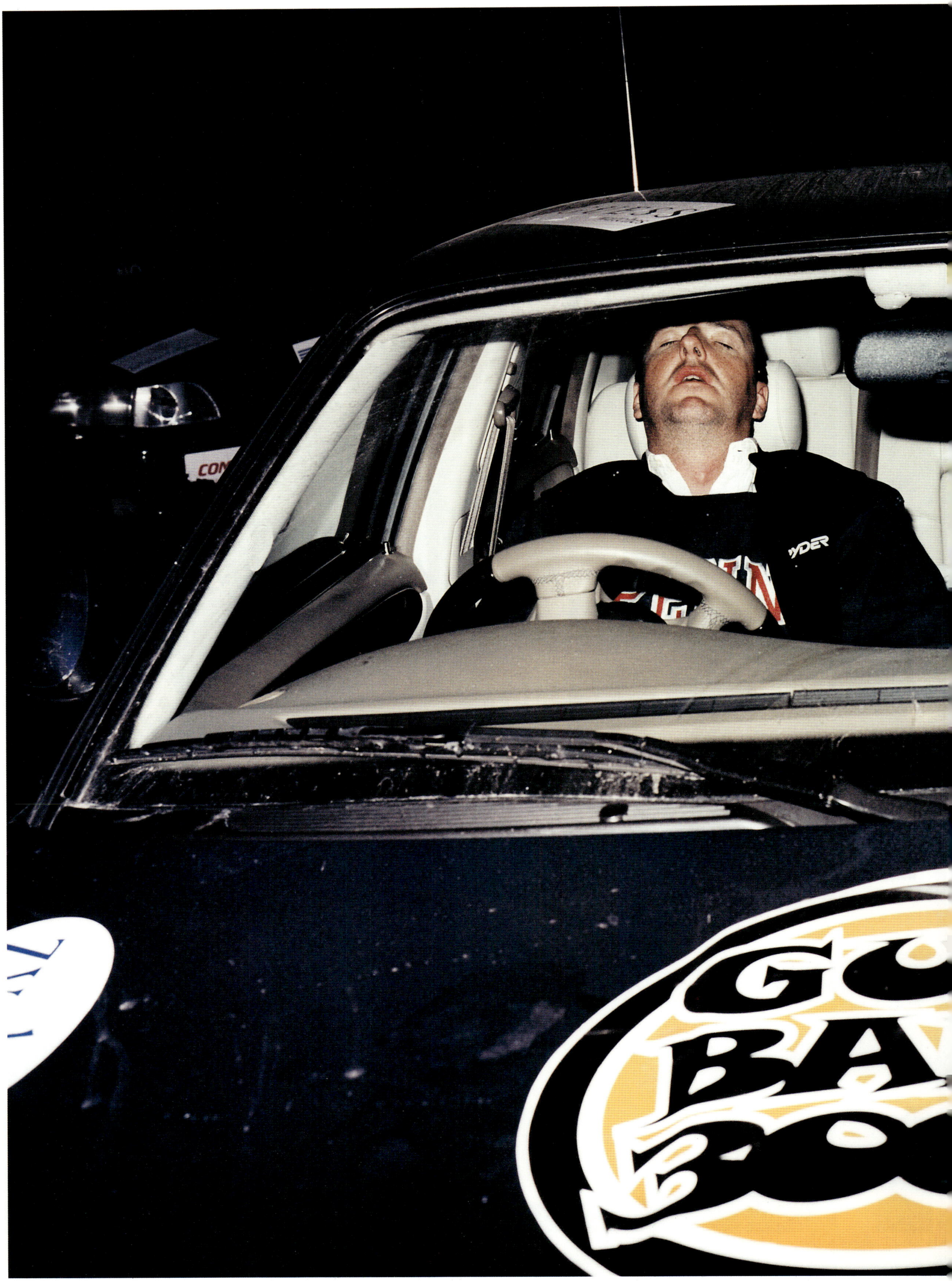

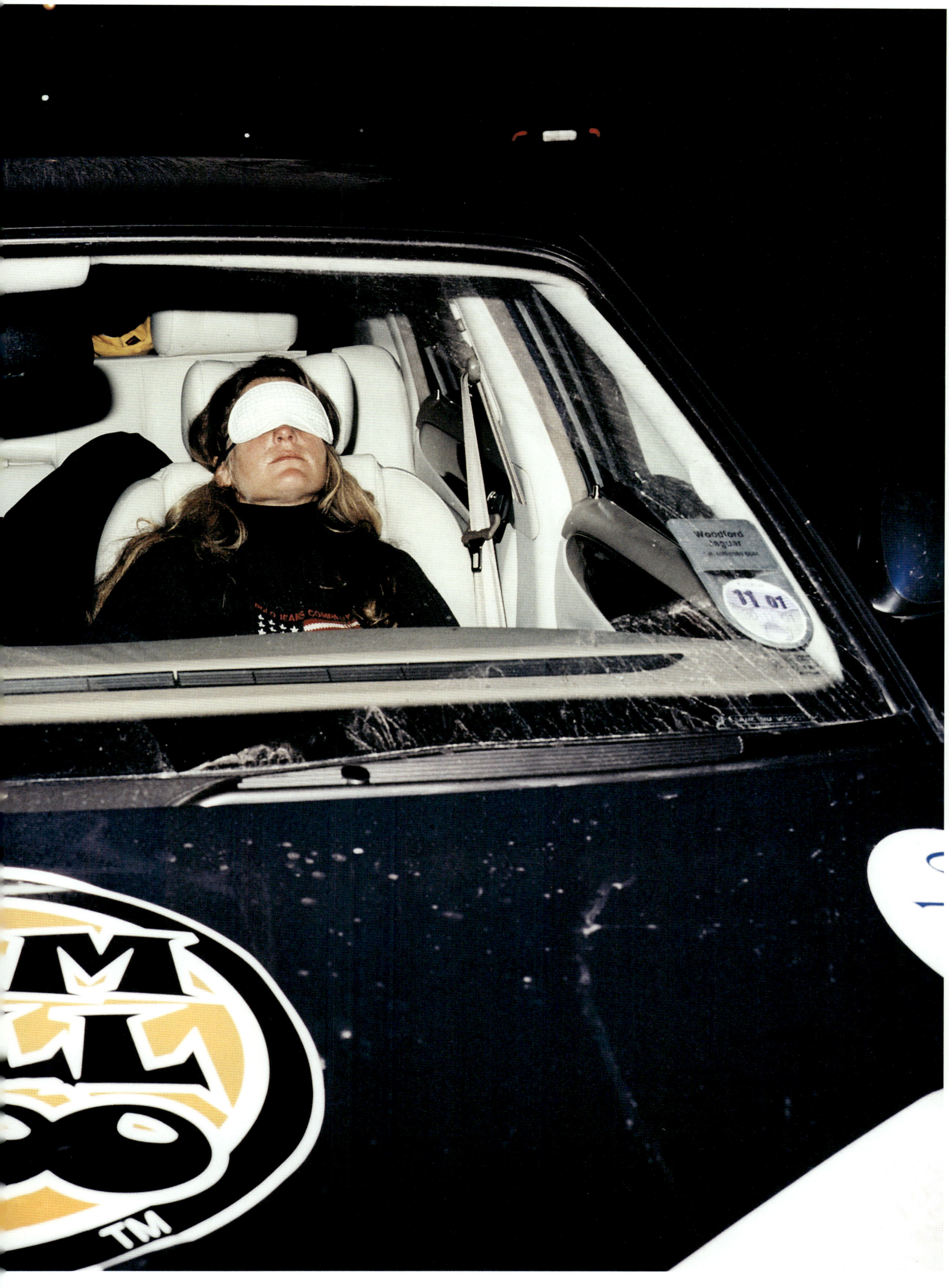
Woodford Jaguar

**IN APRIL 2001, THE GUMBALL RALLY TOOK A HUNDRED LUXURY CARS ON A 3,500 MILE ROAD TRIP FROM LONDON TO ST PETERSBURG AND BACK AGAIN IN JUST FIVE DAYS.**
**TEXT DAN ROSS**
**PHOTOGRAPHY FREDERIKE HELWIG**

### I. THE PLAN

With a name harking back to the illegal street-races that culminated in the infamous transcontinental American dashes of the '70s, the recent British-based incarnation of the Gumball Rally is the brain-child of the extravagantly named Maximillion Cooper. With a name like a Bond villain and a background uniting reputed rock-aristocracy parentage, stints as a racing driver, fashion and then law student, Maximillion is the enigmatic self-appointed champion of a new motor racing chic. Born out of frustration at the business culture that has engulfed Formula One, which he had come to love as a child and hoped to compete in as a teenager, the Rally is Max's stepping stone towards his ultimate ambition of forming his own Formula One team. Four years ago he put together an unsuccessful £12 million bid for the Tyrrell team (now BAR, owned by British American Tobacco). He was 23. He says on reflection that he wasn't ready.

Having failed in his bid for the F1 team, the scenic route back to that finishing line started taking shape in the form of the Gumball. The plan that hatched then, and is being played out now, was to unite the wealth, connections, and cars of his ever-increasing circle - which includes friends liberally spread across media, finance, entertainment, racing and government - to generate a spectacle which in turn would create an iconoclastic aspirational brand. A rally, open to all who can afford it, which encapsulates and reinvigorates the spirit Max felt had been drained from motor sport, and, by implication, society. The spirit which might be summoned by watching one of the *Cannonball Run* movies, or the lesser known (but widely held as superior) '76 film *Gumball*, starring Gary Busey and Raul Julia. In the big screen view of a rally which uses open public roads as its course, the aim is to confound the cops and defeat the elements whilst playing fair, not that a little mischief is out of the question. The idea plays on the childhood cartoon fantasy of *Wacky Races*, and adolescent daydreams of an open road full of opportunities for manly displays of skill at the wheel, conspicuous assertions of status, and sexual conquest. Gumball, in its reincarnation, is pitched as a hedonistic ticket to ride with the jet set and play "all licenced fool" to convention. It is couched in terms of sportsmanship, rebellion and team spirit, but this is disingenuous. Its appeal is more visceral, complex and, certainly, less pure.

At the outset, a collection of wealthy friends and acquaintances having fun for a few days driving around western Europe, picking up speeding tickets, Gumball was a very loud event that mostly made noise within a small but well placed international social circle. The cast was assembling - 50 cars took part, and many would become enchanted with the Rally, returning the following year.

In 2000, the second Gumball made large blips appear on the radar screens of the international media, achieving some of the defining moments in the mythical story. To call it mythical isn't to deny that much of it happened. It's to say that whatever did happen instantly obtained the transglorification of fact into fiction that all great stories achieve, becoming timeless in the way that tales of "unforgettable nights out" grow the minute the hangover has been beaten into submission the following morning.

Thanks to over a thousand articles, broadcasts and web-reports, not to mention the live spectacle of the cars on the street, the trademarked

### ON THE DREAM GUMBALL YOU GET TO BE FAMOUS

Gumball 3000 brand is now known worldwide. With three European events completed including this year's road trip to Russia, and a fourth, final Rally scheduled to take place in the United States in 2002, the Rally is soon to be released as a game on PlayStation 2, with massive sales predicted. According to the current plan, Spike Jonze, director of *Being John Malkovich*, will turn the last Rally into a feature film, an updated immortalisation of the Gumball experience. Max's Rally will then swap the street for the racetrack, where for obvious reasons many say it belongs.

### II. MYTH BUILDING - THE PREQUEL

So, as far as we know, what did happen last year? The Rally started in London, where the Gumballers (as participants are known) received their first instructions. To maintain suspense, prevent cheating and, most pragmatically, to elude unwanted attention from the police, the exact route is kept secret until the last moment, progress being made between checkpoints. Checkpoint one was Stanstead airport, where three Russian cargo planes were waiting to fly the cars and their occupants to southern Spain. A quick dash through the country led to a party at the Bilbao Guggenheim, Frank Gehry's modern cathedral of art and bendy metal. It is available to hire, apparently.

Speeding tickets were issued as never before. In Germany, Europe's highest ever fines were awarded to two racers, £18,000 and £10,000 respectively. Celebrity racer Chris Eubank was stopped speeding in France, but escaped more lightly, signing his autograph for the police in lieu of a cheque. But then, unlike the others, he wasn't doing 180mph. He was driving a slow pickup truck, part of a collection of eccentric Gumball cars including classics, curios and supercars that would, in the subsequent Russian rally, be whittled down to a more pragmatic selection of sports cars.

Heads of banks took part alongside industrial magnates; a beautiful It girl drove topless; rock and dance stars jammed on improvised instruments as champagne flowed freely from the generously uncorked, seemingly bottomless reservoir of the Count who owns Veuve Clicquot. The jazz age was here once again. The beautiful and the damned careered through Europe and the flamboyant, almost-famous and, for a few days at least, the fastest-living from the worlds of art and commerce came together to celebrate all the possibilities that money and its tactical deployment could supply.

That's the story. At least, that's how I heard it. The first time. As myth, rumour, press release, and finally as the pitch, Max's honed way of instilling the Gumball dream.

### III. MYTH BUILDING MADE EASY

Gumball generates three types of coverage in abundance. The first I'll term "the participants' version", the category into which the tale that follows inescapably falls.

Characterised by an implicit willingness to buy into the Gumball dream (fast cars, exotic locations, danger and its James Bond-promised rewards of glamour and fawning beauty), it is tempered with a sobering dose of reality. The stark contrast between the dream and the reality becomes apparent early in the Gumball experience. On the dream Gumball you effectively get to be famous. You draw attention wherever you go, and are exempt from unpalatable rules (such as exist are consensual between those involved, with external authority reduced like air pressure at 30,000ft). You live like a star, and sprinkle stardust from your exhaust. In the dream, opportunity comes with very little opportunity cost. But through actualisation, the dream distils inevitably into something more like real life. What is left is the kernel of the dream, its pip. By attempting to grasp that which had seemed ungraspable, the participant feels privy to the secret that dreams rarely come true. And that in itself is the heart of the dream

*Right:* Maximillion Cooper, organiser of the Gumball Rally

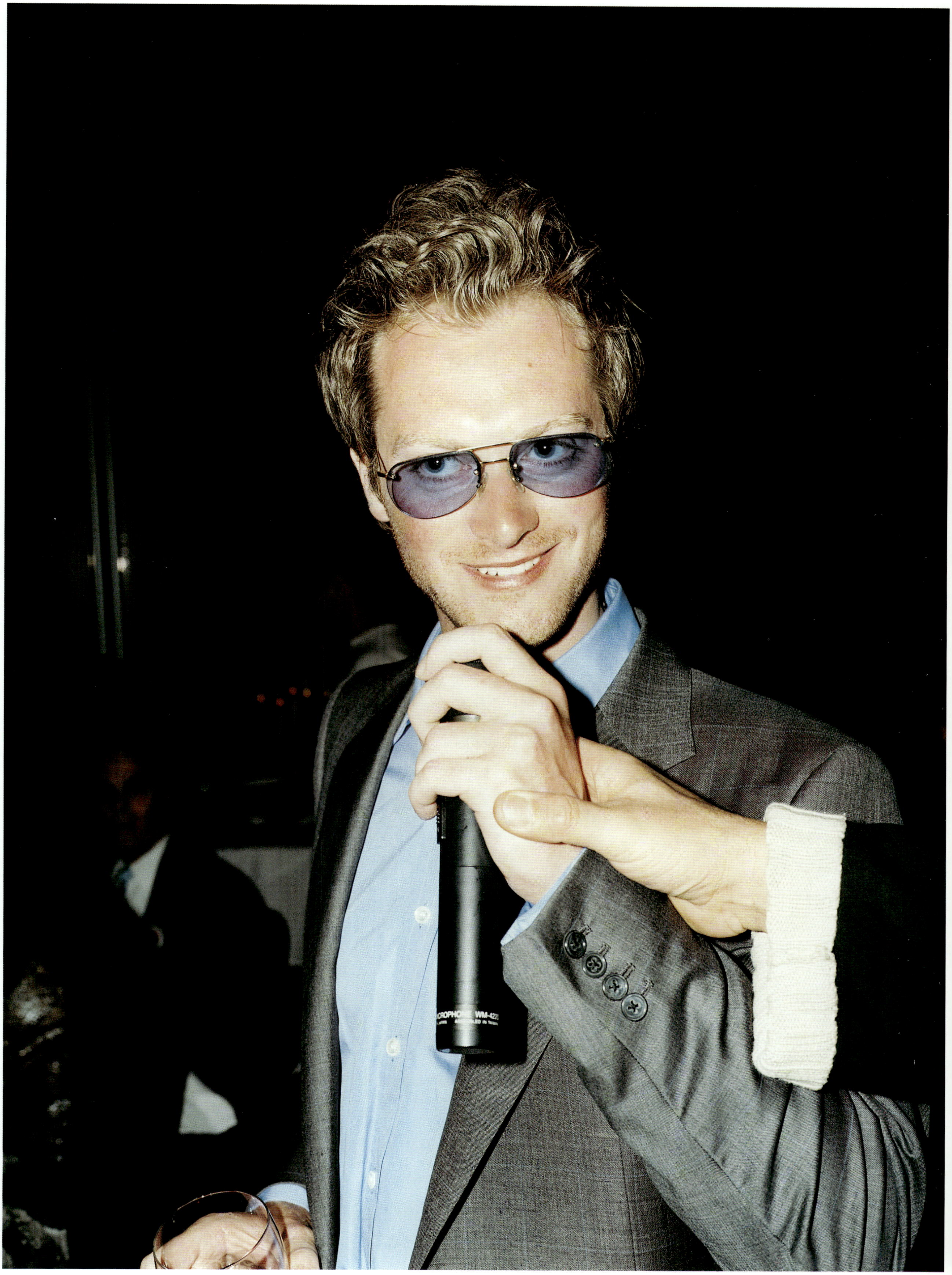

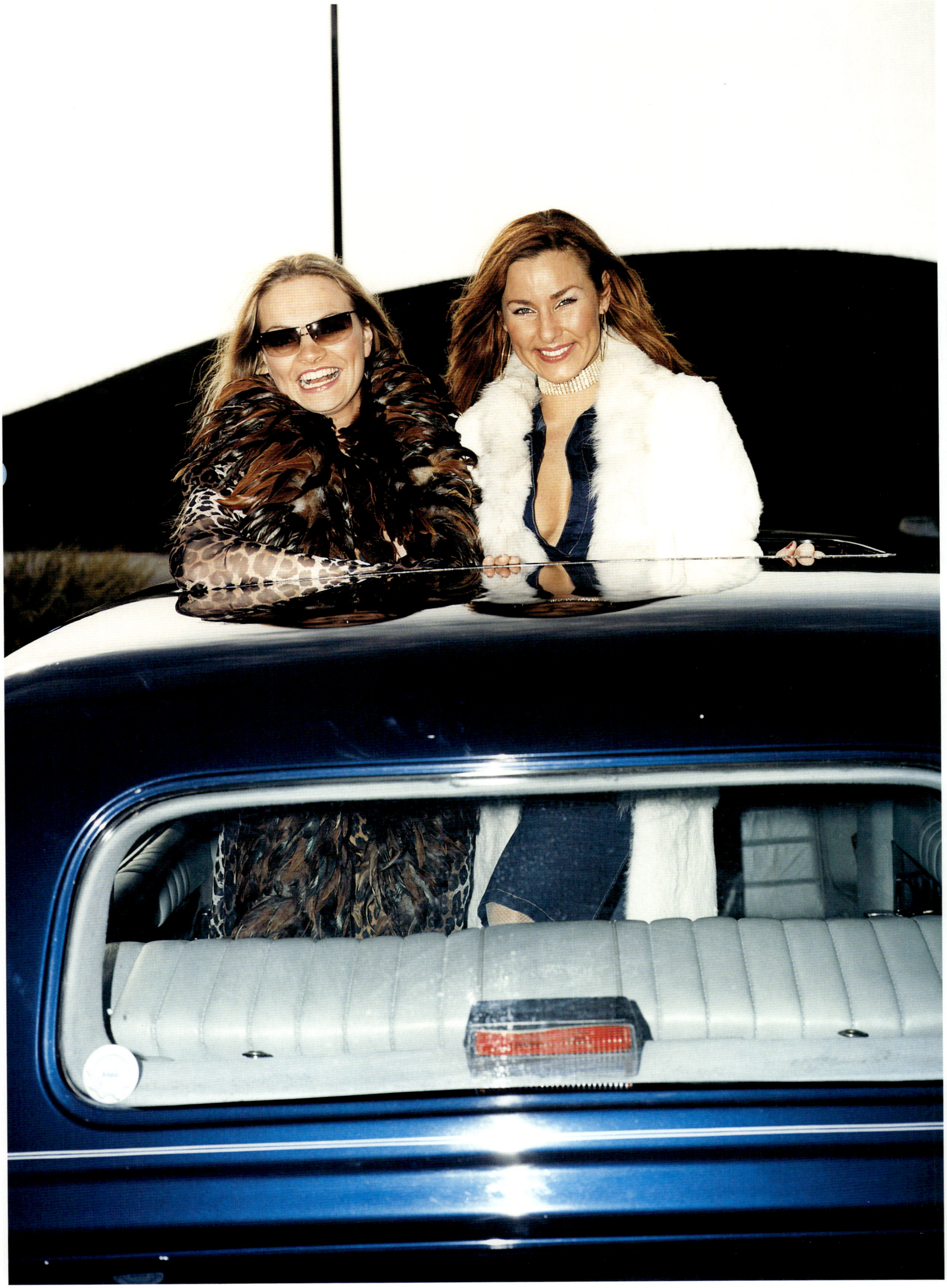

- an indelible insight that is gained through an exceptional, exclusive experience.

The participants' version appears with certain traits given varying emphases like journalistic enthusiasm ("wouldn't it be great if the dream came true"), and nonchalance ("I never really thought it would come true"). It carries an obligation to bring some form of objectivity (the odd remark about rich people running riot through poor countries), without making explicit moral judgement. It calls for an "angle", that trail of detail or filter of perspective that animates the report with the personality of the medium. The reader or viewer thereby gets to buy into the dream then watch it fall apart, and finally have it stuck together again in a way that leaves them the richer for their expenditure of attention. Whatever they say, their participation is an endorsement, and their coverage makes it live beyond the five or six days of its duration. Like all Gumballers, the participant buys into the dream in some way and then gets to live it. For better or for worse.

The second form is perhaps best termed "the outsiders' version", for it seeks to define itself by being wholly apart from the Gumball. As such it ignores the "why" to concentrate on the what, the where, the when. It takes the form of a news report, but is a condemnation of the event above all, a moral reassertion of "normalcy" over the "lunacy" of the race which calls itself a rally.

This variant sometimes overlaps with a third, "the aspirants' version", which, distinct from the participants', doesn't concern itself with the actualisation, and distinct from the outsiders' isn't a condemnation, isn't bothered with the facts. It finds the dream, or, perhaps more accurately, the press release, as containing the start, middle and end of the story. It will typically list names of celebrities associated with the Gumball and judge it accordingly. Whether they are past participants (Beverly Hills 90210 star Jason Priestley, model Jodie Kidd, socialite Tara Palmer-Tompkinson, band the Fun Loving Criminals), mooted current racers (Goldie, Damon Hill, the Happy Mondays, Vic Reeves) or those who attend the numerous parties (Madonna, Nicholas Cage, All Saints) before, during or after the event, the names blind the author and dazzle the reader.

The third version and the second together take care of the masses. The first covers the rest. Gumball is built as a story that you are destined to hear, one way or the other.

### IV. PARTICIPATING

I met Max at the end of 2000 through a mutual acquaintance, and heard the pitch with my jaw open - the audacity of the idea, the contacts, resources and gall to carry it off, the business plan and its ambition. If not entirely trusting him, I liked Max. Tall, blond and slim, styled in off-duty racing attire and speaking with a clipped, upper-case accent, his icily cool surface cracks charismatically to revealed his amusement at the world and what it is letting him do. Having entered, as the start approached our main concern became which car to take part in. Would it be slick and techno, like the Japanese team in *Cannonball Run*? Loud and fast, new or old? Another Gumball myth, which again isn't to say that it is only a myth (although, as it turns out, in this case it is), is that in the first year someone had written off their new Lamborghini in a crash and went straight to the nearest dealership to buy another. If you look at the Gumball as a party, your car is your outfit. The ability to rip a precious item of clothing and replace it without a second thought marks out the person who can afford to party with true abandon. On the Gumball, the journalist plays the part of Cinderella.

Appropriately, the Rally starts and ends with a ball. The climax of the trip was to be a black-tie James Bond-themed party, the archetypal teenage "Sloane" event writ large and vindicated on our hotel destination in St Petersburg, the Rocco Forte owned Astoria. But on the road too it conforms to the format of a ball. Cars dance with each other, often pairing off to race, a custom which had produced the celebrated five-figure fines in Germany the previous year. Dress sense being displayed

**DRESS SENSE BEING DISPLAYED BY WHAT CAR YOU DRIVE, THE UNWRITTEN CODE IS STRICT**

by what car you drive, the unwritten code is strict, but allows, generously, for style to compensate for lack of speed. So, whilst most Gumballers opt to bring their Porsches, Ferraris, Maseratis, classic roadsters, or stealth bombers such as the Audi S6, a few make do with what jeeps or saloons they can persuade Hertz or a manufacturer to lend them. Initially attempting to camouflage a limousine, we decide (like most others) to forego the military theme which Max had given this year's Gumball, largely due to practical concerns. A descendent of Otto von Bismarck had hired a limousine to chauffeur him the length of the journey, and to have the same car would cause embarrassment. (The ubiquitous red Ferrari driver was obviously oblivious to this dilemma.)

In the end, we opted to create a mock "secret test car", out of a new, needless to say borrowed, Lexus LS430 which we painstakingly and very carefully covered in semi-permanent black vinyl, with a couple of cardboard-achieved appendages in strategic places to complete the effect. It felt suitably Blue Peter, and we drew approving murmurs from all quarters at the starting line. We'd made it into the ball.

### V. GATECRASHING

Of course, Gumball is a gatecrashers' ball. For every Prussian who leaves his imperialist ancestry behind for a few days fun, there is an entrant to whom the Rally is a badly needed chance to show off their newfound wealth and its prized signifier, the flash sports car. And the field is wide enough to pit an art dealer next to an estate agent, an American TV star next to a Danish princess. Everyone pays the same £3,000 per car entry fee. This unlikely group then shares an intimate, trying experience together, melding them briefly into a tentative social whole.

A week before the trip, a cocktail party allows Gumballers to meet. The event is mundane - an odd assortment, full of men who look ordinary without their cars, hardly any women and, conspicuously, no stars. The next warm-up event, the night before the start, is more fun, and delivers the requisite A-list count which forms the basis of the hype-building pre-launch Gumball press release. The next day, the start of the Rally is a media and mechanical circus. The car from the film version of *Judge Dredd* lines up as if it is taking part (it isn't). Most celebrities that are supposedly taking part according to the official line don't. Damon Hill is there to promote his private driving club, the logo of which is plastered on most of the cars along with those of other sponsors, but he doesn't make it out of England. I hear some of the touted "names" couldn't face the journey; others maybe sensed they were being lured into a media ambush.

Red Bull and Fubu have entered cars, the latter filled with perennially energetic Danish girls, the former energised by calculatingly vast supplies of the drink. We escape covering our car with sponsors' logos as the sticker-application procedure has backed up, and in the queue chaos reigns. We receive our official launch briefing from Max and the head of Gumball security, ex-SAS man Bill Skully, in the underground car park, the gist of which is "Be careful", and are told to assemble down the road at the centre of the roundabout at Hyde Park Corner. Although much about the Gumball is impossible to verify or deny, I hear that Max has no permission to launch the Rally from the high profile spot. Watching the carnival unfold, with 100 cars, and a fast-forming crowd of onlookers, press, attention-seekers and a sparse and overwhelmed police presence, this should be obvious, but, inside the Gumball bubble, isn't. Awaiting the start, an impatient Kim Schmitz covers our matt black shell with smattered mud and grass as his tyres churn up a *Back To The Future*-style strip of lawn at Westminster Green. Kim, or Kimble, as he's better known, is one of the Gumball's great characters. Obnoxious, hugely tall and weighing in at 19 stone, he is a world-famous computer hacker turned internet millionaire. He takes the Rally very seriously - jets will fly him spare parts, and his car is accompanied by a support vehicle. He is here to speed.

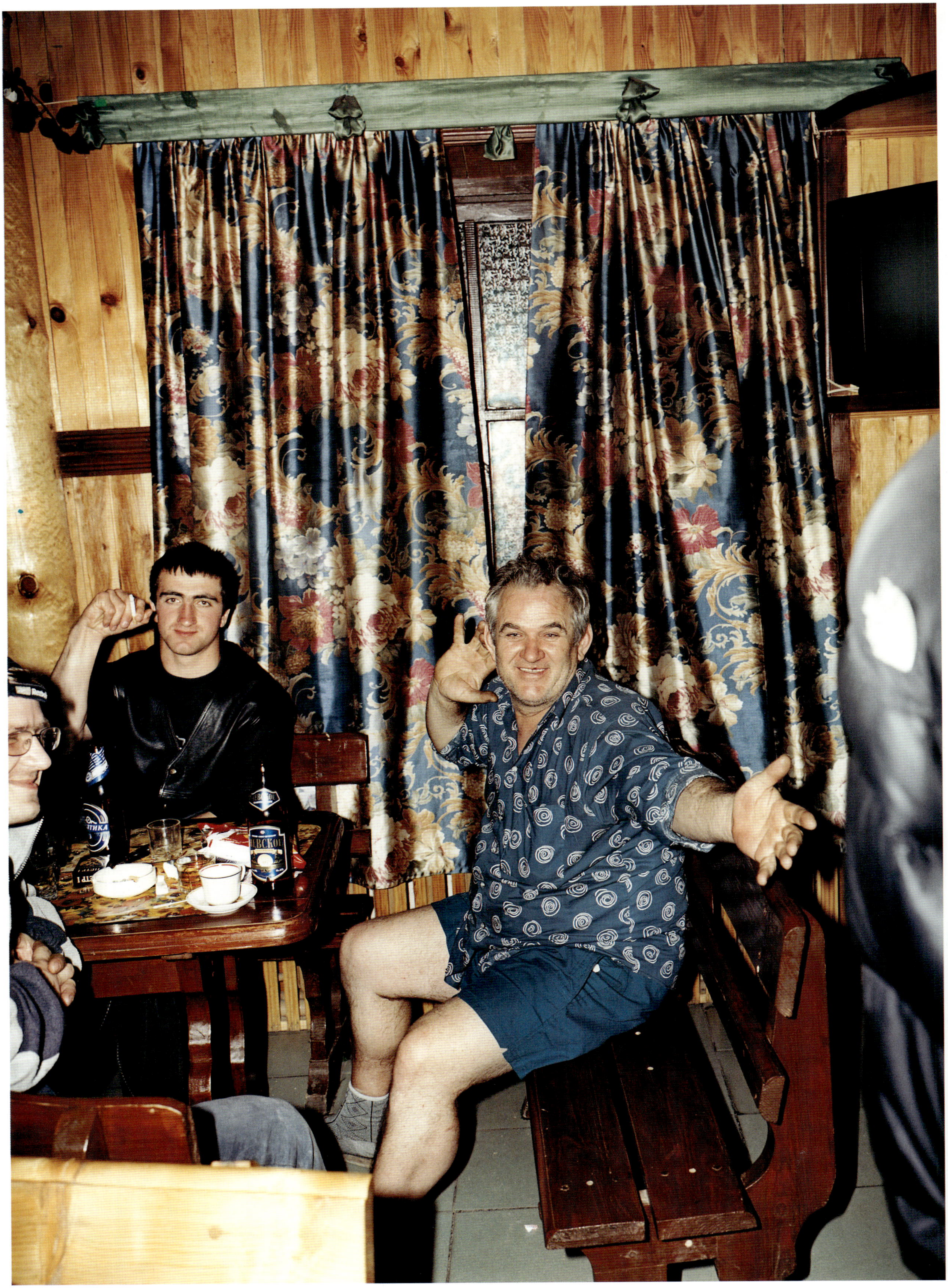

We achieve the camouflage effect after all, and marvel at Max's first brazen signature stroke, which we would find repeated 14 hours later at the first checkpoint, Berlin.

From Hyde Park corner, our car's GPS system leads us to London's worst traffic jam, and we make half-hearted attempts to circumvent it before rejoining the stuttering procession. Our mood is still buoyant when we board the Eurostar (channel tunnel train), having enjoyed the amused and curious glances our car had attracted on the way to Folkestone, looking back at the commuters, kids and shoppers of South London with a sense of nostalgia that we were leaving all that behind. The guards gamble a fiver on whether our disguised car is a Lexus or Mercedes. An L on the steering wheel finally gives us away, making one of them a little richer.

Arriving at the Aldon Hotel, next to the Brandenberg Gate, at 6am, we have already fallen to the back of the Rally. Landing on Europe's clear roads, the others left us standing. The GPS is slowly regaining our confidence and after inadvertently breaking the CD-player we settle in to the periodical purr of the sultry navigator voice, adjusting itself to the local dialect with an inviting "next right for Ha-noufffer". Led effortlessly into Berlin, we pick up a straggler, the Rally's oldest entrants, a couple in their 70s driving a Morgan Aero 8, the car the driver helped design. Outside the hotel the police are moving the last cars left on the street, and on a trestle table is an empty pot of coffee and a tired Rally security staffer. The older couple are so relieved to reach the hotel that they are visibly wounded by the news that it isn't our stop for the night. They both look as if they could collapse. Max has warned me that the first day's drive lasts 24 hours, but for most it is to be a not altogether pleasant surprise.

Instead of a room, we all get directions. Checkpoint two is in eastern Poland. The desk manager tells us that he first heard about the Rally at midnight, when the organisers' car arrived. Its occupants, they said, had told them a few cars were passing through, and could they set out some coffee. Asking for a cup, we are told curtly that there is no more, and that we must leave.

### VI. OUT OF RANGE
From Berlin, we are on our own. We lose sight of other Gumball cars, and the GPS falls silent. It's still, and the city is asleep. Except for a lone prostitute, the streets are empty of pedestrians. Sailing down tree-lined roads into a beaming morning, the mood in the car is peaceful. We're tired and the adrenalin flush of leaving London has spilled itself on the traffic, the motorway, the empty city, leaving us floating on the hallucinogenic mist that sleeplessness delivers.

The four of us in the car, including my girlfriend Vivien, Guy, an editor from the magazine, and Fredricke, our photographer, pull into a noiseless village, where we notice pockmarked houses, the bullet holes vestiges of a brutally violent past. At dawn, in these strange surroundings, placid calm and instant tension are thinly separated. It's as if the sleeping inhabitants could wake at any minute, as if they pose some threat. We'd been told at the hotel that the planned crossing was heavily delayed, hence our attempted diversion, and we are conspicuously lost. Though alert enough to drive safely, and doing nothing illegal, we panic on seeing a police van. Once we overcome our paranoia, we admit to them this simple truth and they offer to lead us to the border we're looking for. Once again cruising down country roads, we drift over the speed limit reassured by the tentative pleasure of following a police car. The van is from border control, suggesting an easy crossing. This is not to be. At the border, two things happen which twist the fragile mood. The first is that my girlfriend is taken away into a concrete building with no windows. The second is that we meet Brett.

### VII. BORDER
Vivien is Canadian, and whilst Max has taken care of visas for Russia, paid for a smooth passage through Latvia, hired a helicopter escort to St Petersburg, and seemingly

**OBNOXIOUS, HUGELY TALL AND WEIGHING IN AT 19 STONE, HE IS A WORLD-FAMOUS COMPUTER HACKER TURNED INTERNET MILLIONAIRE. HE TAKES THE RALLY VERY SERIOUSLY**

employs a fair proportion of the ex-SAS, he hasn't discovered that Canadians need a visa to enter eastern Europe. Why they do but Americans, for example, don't is a mystery. A gentle, sympathetic guard with a moustache tells us "there's no problem, you can go - but she must go back". We explain that we'd rather not leave her alone with no form of transportation in eastern Germany, that we don't wish to stay in Poland longer than is necessary to drive across it, but our argument is as incomprehensible to him as his is to us. Vivien is taken away to be interviewed for a visa.

Parked in between countries are two other cars. One carries Alex, a gallery owner from London, and Polly, a features editor on assignment from a style magazine, in search of a sexy celebrity story which will never materialise. They are our friends, and are driving a black-matted, though decidedly less secret, sister-car to our Lexus, in the form of a Ford pickup truck. Having failed to escape the stickering line-up, it is covered in garish, prominently positioned Gumball stickers, and the logos of a dozen sponsors. It is a moving advertisement not only for the Rally but for its potential bounty of rich, vulnerable, western inhabitants who are where they should not be.

The other car is a Jaguar saloon occupied by a horizontal, sleeping man and an English woman whose haughty self-conceit is unchallenged by the discordant surroundings. Their absent passenger is Brett, an Australian in his 20s who has a problem which has put him in a similar predicament to my detained partner - his passport is full, and the guards can't issue him a visa because it won't fit.

Five hours later, through a series of events that only make sense when you're struggling to stay awake at a Polish military installation with an Australian playboy, Vivien and I are alone in the pickup, hopelessly mis-navigating what appears to us to be a closed-loop of abysmally surfaced, unsignposted road inside Poland.

### VIII. IMAGINE THAT YOU ARE STRUGGLING TO STAY AWAKE AT A POLISH MILITARY INSTALLATION
When Vivien is taken away, we are relatively unconcerned at first, our friendly guard dispelling any darker thoughts. Boredom and creeping exhaustion fill the time for a while, until minutes start to pass uncomfortably. Fredricke calms me with her unflappable disposition. Alex laughs that this is his first holiday for two years. Polly is anxious to get to St Petersburg where she thinks her story will be. After waiting an hour and a half, I tell the others to go on without me. I think that Vivien will be issued a visa, it's just a matter of waiting a little longer, and we swap cars so I am left with the pickup, the others now all in the Lexus. We arrange to meet at the next checkpoint, a castle in the Polish town of Malbork.

Another hour passes and, now alone, the dark thoughts return and won't go away. I find myself pushing up against the detention area's metal railings, trying to control my involuntarily surfacing anger and fear as I enquire what's become of her. Brett comes out briefly to tell me he has seen Vivien and that she is okay. But he goes inside again, and the thoughts return. Men with guns, an attractive girl, only a thin veil of discipline, a foreign language and a remote landscape. These separate thoughts make connections that conspire to nag, playing on and feeding my utter sense of powerlessness.

The guard reassures me that she is okay, which I only really believe when Vivien emerges shortly after. Interviewed alone, and asked why she had no visa, she had then been moved to another room where she'd met Brett, her visa application eventually denied. But she is animated rather than dismayed, and tells me tales about the Australian with whom I'd only exchanged a few genial, pragmatic sentences. I phone the others - I have all their belongings along with their car, and it doesn't look like I'll be able to give them to them, at least not in Poland. They

us. Vivien is held alone and we can't see her. This makes the young guard more anxious. After an hour, the answer we get is that she can't go on. A General is phoned. Allegedly, Max paid something in the region of $40,000 to ensure an easy ride into Latvia, money which was obviously taken with no intention of doing anything in return. But the General gives permission for a visa to be issued.

Some paperwork and officially claimed dollars later, we are finally in the car and able to leave. The young guard sighs heavily and emotionally. What caused his relief, what we have to be grateful for, beyond the visa, he doesn't tell me. We offer him some money, not a bribe but a tip, which he declines. He tells us to go quickly and we do.

## XII. RUSSIA

Some hours later, we are at a border bar just inside Russia, drinking soup of unidentifiable content bought for a dollar. We have, with 40 other cars, made it intact in a convoy through Latvia. At the table next to me, Gumballers are challenging locals to arm-wrestles. A beautiful Russian girl is dressed in the '80s look so popular in London - here it is still on the original cycle of fashionability. Shane, a middle-aged art dealer dressed in what seems to be the same elegant suit for most of the Rally, is challenging the local barflies to a drinking contest. Thankfully he is not driving. There seems to be a natural affinity between the Gumballers and the local mix of young mercenary-looking men and worldly-wise women.

Everyone has accumulated a fresh set of Gumball stories, which, matching the Top Trump cards Max licenced from the previous Rally, are traded in a market where brushes with danger replace brake horse power as the unit of currency. Many remain personal, or shared within small groups, whilst the better ones, the ones that ring truer, or simply the ones that are better told, enter the common pool. Our own story, one chiefly of detention at borders, intersects with that of Karta, heir to an American potato chip fortune whose road-focused joie de vivre is unflinching. Karta and his co-driver lost their Caterham to a pot-hole in Latvia, having backtracked to search for a Canadian airforce helmet that had flown off onto the road. At the time they didn't know, but the aforementioned helmet, built and bought for its space-age strength, had lodged under our front left tyre, sending us skidding for 20 metres until it popped off, never to be seen again.

In the dark Latvian woods, their crippled car made them a sitting duck for the supposedly lurking bandits. The hyperactive Fubu girls, in their promotional truck, had come to the rescue, but as Karta saw the blacked-out, imposing vehicle race towards him, he took out his knife and ran into the foliage. The way he tells it, the car screeched to a halt and four Danish girls burst out to the pumping R&B of Destiny's Child's "I'm a survivor", and performed a sort of Bat Dance around his wounded car, scooping him up to safety. The story is not only told well, but it also rings true.

After the bar, I attempt to drive to

St Petersburg, but enter a long debate with Vivien about what we'll listen to on our borrowed CD player, which is now wired into the tape deck. Both tired to irritability, the conversation saps my last reserves of energy. Failing to secure Jay Dee's *Welcome To Detroit* another play, I sink into the reclinable rear seat, switch on the seat heater, adjust the massage

**MINUTES LATER, HE IS IN TEARS, ON HIS KNEES IN FRONT OF AN EMBARRASSED AND FORGIVING ALTHOUGH NOT DISCERNIBLY EMPATHIC MAX**

setting to match the 130bpm of her Vladislav Delay CD, and disappear into a comatose sleep.

Six hours later I wake up in St Petersburg, and hear about Fredericke and Vivien's *Thelma And Louise* adventure, outrunning a Russian police car. (Would you stop? we had been warned that these could be car jackers in disguise, a convenient excuse should your conscience demand one). The opulent hotel has rooms waiting for us, but Gumball security tell us we don't have time to stop. I share a somber coffee with the security team, who would like to catch up for a stern word with Max, said to have hop-scotched the route in a helicopter. Outside the hotel, Brett is there, as are Alex and Polly. The party, planned as the highlight of the trip, suffered from one problem - practically no one was there.

Five minutes after arriving in a surprisingly sunny, temperate St Petersburg, I'm behind the wheel following a full Gumball convoy of perhaps 80 cars onto the road towards Finland, where we'll catch an overnight ferry to Sweden. Gumball takes over the streets of St Petersburg for a formidable display of arrogance, speed and corrupted authority. Driving through the city, we race behind a police car paid to lead us to the border. A few Gumballers scream through the urban streets at over 150mph. The bottle red-head Ferrari driver shouts "I'm living in the fastlane mother-fuckas!" as if the bemused locals should bow down. As if they care. But on the wide, near-deserted motorway out of the city, I confess to enjoying keeping pace for once with the rest of the Rally. Nearing the border, I see Brett overtake me driving a car he'd been hitching a lift in earlier. He is going 100mph over a bridge, on the wrong side of the road, at a brow, around a bend. He misses an oncoming car by a few feet, and pumps his arm in the air. Minutes later I tell a border guard, "No, I'm not carrying any weapons", and we're given permission to leave Russia. Leaving Russia is a relief. Once inside Finland, we're back in a country where the police can't be hired to escort those breaking the law, where a reasonable proportion of people speak English, and where, should we choose to, we can survive without any assistance or direction from the Gumball.

## XIII. GUMBALL BY NIGHT

We have two nights in the company of the Gumball. The first, on the ferry from Helsinki to Stockholm, is relaxed and fairly homely. We are the last but one car to make the ferry before it departs. Others are less lucky. This pervades the mood like the stiff upper-lip propaganda reel memory of comrades lost in war - an inevitable, regrettable fact best not dwelt on. The ship has an impressive internal atrium, hundreds of bedrooms, and a boulevard of restaurants, bars and shops, at the end of which is a casino which Max has hired for the evening. Max sits in a prominent booth, which seems positioned both to conspicuously survey the crowd and retain some distance from it. There is a logic at work here. When I pass, I hear him receive one of many eventual angry reproaches, the subject matter of which varies from the poorly planned route and the amount of money paid to drive non-stop for 2,000 miles to the morality of the whole scheme. In the background, a video-screen plays footage from cars racing at terrific speed, which raises cheers from the audience.

Having rested, and navigated an easy day's drive down to Copenhagen, the next night all are buoyant. MTV's cocksure correspondent tapes a segment from the lobby of the minimalist Hilton. Stories and champagne flow. Shane, who it isn't unfair to describe, at least on my experience of him, as an alcoholic, repeatedly heckles the organiser's dinner speech, which goes down well nonetheless. Minutes later, he is in tears, on his knees in front of an embarrassed and forgiving although not discernibly empathic Max. Shane later tells me he ran into trouble trying to leave Russia, as he had stopped in St Petersberg for some sleep, and his visa, like all of ours only valid for a day, had expired.

118

Presumably drunk, he had hit the border official, and was eventually beaten into submission by several guards. Wild-eyed, he shows me the bruises.

Gumballers offer their views on the Rally. To Kimble, the massive 28-year-old German internet millionaire, "It is about one word only - speed!" Another familiar face, always animated, enthuses about the local prostitutes. He favourably compares the woman he has just had sex with to the girls the concierge in Lithuania procured, saying she was like "a little version of Pamela Anderson". He laments not having had the chance to sample what Russia has to offer; had he arrived earlier, he would have been impressed by the choice that had apparently been available. Gumballers are strong personalities. Each brings their own perspective, their own stylistic traits. Karta, who looks like a modern day muskateer, enjoys it straight-faced as an adventure. He is Max's model Gumballer. Television's Ruby Wax, and the MTV *Jackass* cast of stunt pranksters, approach it as another episode in professional lives spent satirising or goofing around, trying not to be fazed by the madness that their jobs keep them thinly separated from. Others come to escape the pressure of their businesses, or the boredom of wealth without purpose. To them, adventure is a more loaded term, their experiences part of an endless process of self-assertion - they go fast to try to outrun themselves.

This night a party materialises as planned, as scores of fashionable locals, cast for their looks, populate the hotel's ballroom. We join the counter-culture in the lobby. Someone takes us to see their mangled car. On it, with a marker pen, has been written "You are the weakest link". Another Gumballer takes us to see their car, parked with dozens of other expensive, road-dirtied cars. Drunk, he spins donuts on the concrete floor. Late at night, in the lobby, a maudlin playboy snorts cocaine from his fist, *Jackass'* Steve-o walks down a soaring centrepiece staircase on his hands, and we all order more champagne. Others go into Copenhagen in search of more fun.

*Below*: the Intersection "secret test car"

The next day we set off late to be caught, on the long drive back from Copenhagen to London, in a rush-hour traffic jam in Holland. Reality threatens to engulf us again, and the cathartic principle of the Rally registers. A welcome break from normalcy, an excuse to traverse huge distances, create short cuts where the law says there aren't any, the opportunity to make new friends and experience new places. To borrow a line from Stanley Kubrick's *Full Metal Jacket* that equally captures the duality of the Gumball, it is about wanting to see "interesting and stimulating people of an ancient culture", and overtake them. Leaving it is a return to morality and mortality, to law and order, to limited resources and little time to spend freely. A return to real life, for some at least.

In a final flourish, our GPS system, back online, leads us onto a small country lane, then twists us through an industrial estate. Man and machine collude to carve a route through the service area of a restaurant, then back onto the motorway, out of the traffic, an open road ahead.

### XIV. HOW THE STORY ENDS

It's customary to end the story with a fact relating to the final party, in Beaulieu, England, which we didn't make it back in time for. The party where Kimble's spare car, driven

**ON GUMBALL YOU GET TO OVERTAKE CARS NOT ONLY SLOWER, CHEAPER AND UGLIER THAN YOUR OWN, BUT YOU ARE GOING FAR FURTHER THAN THEY EVER WILL**

by someone who forgot to change sides of road from Europe, crashed head-on with an unsuspecting local. Thankfully, nobody was seriously hurt. What will happen if someone dies on the Gumball, or, worse, because of it? The other way to end the story is with a moral judgement. Will I break with the Gumball, having tasted its thrills, or assert my membership of its fraternity on behalf of myself and the reader, and pledge to be there next year? Actually, such thoughts played heavily on my mind as I wrote about, and relived, the experience.

Gumball is a microcosm of the modern, spectacle-driven, money-spun, grey, brutal and brilliant world. It is a summation of the highs and lows of life, accelerated for those who want to escape an age that some feel is speeding out of control.

As Holden Caulfield says in Salingers' *Catcher In The Rye*, "Take most people, they're crazy about cars. I'd rather have a goddamn horse. A horse is at least human, for God's sake." On the eastern Europe leg of the Gumball you get to drive your car through countries where some people still ride horses. You get to drive your car through towns where it could buy a whole street. You get to overtake cars not only slower, cheaper and uglier than your own,

but you are going far further than they ever will, in their cars or by any other means. Your car is a symbol of your freedom, your tangible currency, and your relative celebrity. In the dream, your high doesn't trade off another's low. It's a magic, rubber burning bubble. Keep moving fast enough and maybe it won't burst. Gumball is in a way about control. Controlling the media, controlling the laws that constitute the modern, regulated, policed and PR'd system, feeding it and teasing it at the same time. At times we rightly feel like pawns in a game Max is playing, put on a leash long enough to hang ourselves with. Gumball is like a rollercoaster at a dodgy fairground - it offers thrills without real danger, except when the machinery of the ride itself falls apart. Its purchase on the legacy of great road trips famous and unsung perhaps as shallow as buying a VIP pass, it nonetheless taps the same desire to escape the mercy of daily reality, to break free of the crowd - a universal desire. And sometimes we do all feel truly, joyfully free. Max is right in one way. The true reward of participating in the Rally really is to enjoy a shared present tense, to be welded to it, and, however pathetic or maladjusted some characters are, we are joined to each other by the challenge of navigating from one minute to the next.

A friend advised me not to dignify it by writing about it. Why did I? Because it is a compelling story. Constructed for me and thousands of others to relay. For millions of people to watch on TV, read about or hear in myth, perpetuated and accentuated by Chinese whisper. It's a story that is in itself a myth, in which ugly fact is subsumed in a greater narrative. It's already becoming hard for me to separate the experience from myth in my mind as its peaks spike in my memory, all the more giddy for the troughs they tower over. I had fun on the Gumball, but then I have a get-out clause. I'm a journalist. If I didn't, such an admission would be less comfortable to make.

As for the myth, it is burning itself out, and the next Gumball, the last, will exhaust the energy it has snowballed around it over the past three years. If all goes to plan, it will burn off into media smoke, into which it can vanish to re-emerge as a mass-market brand. As I write at the end of July, this year's Rally has just been screened as a *Jackass* special on MTV. 22 million people tune in, making it the most popular TV show in the country that month. Next year they'll have the chance to see it again, as Max attempts another act of bravado - selling his update of the Gumball dream back to America, where, for obvious reasons many say it belongs.

# A DAY AT THE RACES PART 2 LE MANS

VISIT LE MANS AND YOUR HOME WILL MOST LIKELY BE A TENT, AND YOUR FELLOW SPECTATOR AN ENGLISHMAN, AS OVER 80,000 ATTEND THE ANNUAL FRENCH EVENT.

PITCHED IN THE FIELDS NEXT TO CLASSIC SPORTS CARS AND THEIR MODERN EQUIVALENTS, YOU WILL BE ABLE TO HEAR THE WHINE OF THE RACE - YOU MAY NOT BE AS CONCERNED TO WATCH IT. TUNE INTO THE RADIO AND KEEP TRACK OF THE ACTION. THIS YEAR'S RAIN MEANT BEING IN THE OPEN FOR LONG PERIODS WAS ONLY FOR THE DIE-HARD. BUT FIND A GOOD VANTAGE POINT, ESPECIALLY AT A KINK IN THE MULSANNE STRAIGHT, AND WATCH THE BENTLEY TEAM TRY TO RESTAMP THEIR AUTHORITY ON THE EVENT THAT THEIR RACING ANCESTORS, FAMED AS MILLIONAIRE PLAYBOYS, WON FIVE TIMES BETWEEN 1924 AND 1930.

THIS YEAR BENTLEY CAME AN IMPRESSIVE THIRD IN A CAR WHOSE STYLISTIC VICTORY WAS SEALED BY A NUMBER THAT GLOWS IN THE DARK. AUDI CLAIMED FIRST AND SECOND PLACE WITH THEIR WORKS R8S, AS THEY HAD THE YEAR BEFORE. BORROWING LAST YEAR'S WINNING CARS, PRIVATEER TEAMS FAILED TO LAST THE 24 HOUR, 2700 MILE (4,367 KM) RACE.

COMPETE AND YOU WON'T DO THE DRIVE ALONE - YOU WILL WORK IN SHIFTS. PIERRE LEVEGH PROVED THAT YOU CAN'T GO SOLO IN 1952, ALTHOUGH HIS 23 HOUR ACHIEVEMENT WON HIM A FATEFUL PLACE IN THE MERCEDES TEAM. THREE YEARS LATER HIS CAR LAUNCHED INTO THE CROWD, KILLING 80 SPECTATORS AND THE DRIVER.

DANGER ISN'T CONFINED TO THE TRACK, ALTHOUGH IT IS THE THRILL OF LAPPING AT 200MPH IN THE DARK THAT STILL DRAWS DRIVERS TO TEST THEIR ENDURANCE HERE. ON THE PUBLIC STREETS, SOME OF WHICH ARE INCORPORATED INTO THE TRACK'S EIGHT AND A HALF MILES (13.6KM), ANOTHER SPECTACLE TAKES PLACE. A CROWD GATHERS TO WATCH A MAN STOP EACH PASSING CAR AND MAKE THEM REV THEIR ENGINES AND SPIN OFF, SOMETIMES VEERING TOWARDS THE CHEERING CHILDREN, PARENTS AND DRUNKEN REVELLERS. CATERHAMS, TVRS, E-TYPE JAGS, A MASERATI, A LAMBORGHINI, EVEN A LAND ROVER DEFENDER ENTER INTO THE SPIRIT (WITH VARYING DEGREES OF VOLITION) UNTIL THE POLICE APPEAR.

STEVE MCQUEEN'S 1971 MOVIE, LE MANS, MAY HAVE BANKRUPTED HIM, BUT ITS CULT STATUS LENDS THE CIRCUIT A MYSTIQUE. CAPTURE IT BY WATCHING THE CARS, SETTLED INTO A LONG NIGHT, BURNING OFF FUEL TO ILLUMINATE A CORNER AT 4 AM, HALF WAY TOWARDS THE FINAL, 321ST LAP.

3
SCORP
LUC ALPHAND AVENTURES
MICHELIN
BERU
CESAM
sparco
stand21

**PHOTOGRAPHY BY NEIL MASSEY**

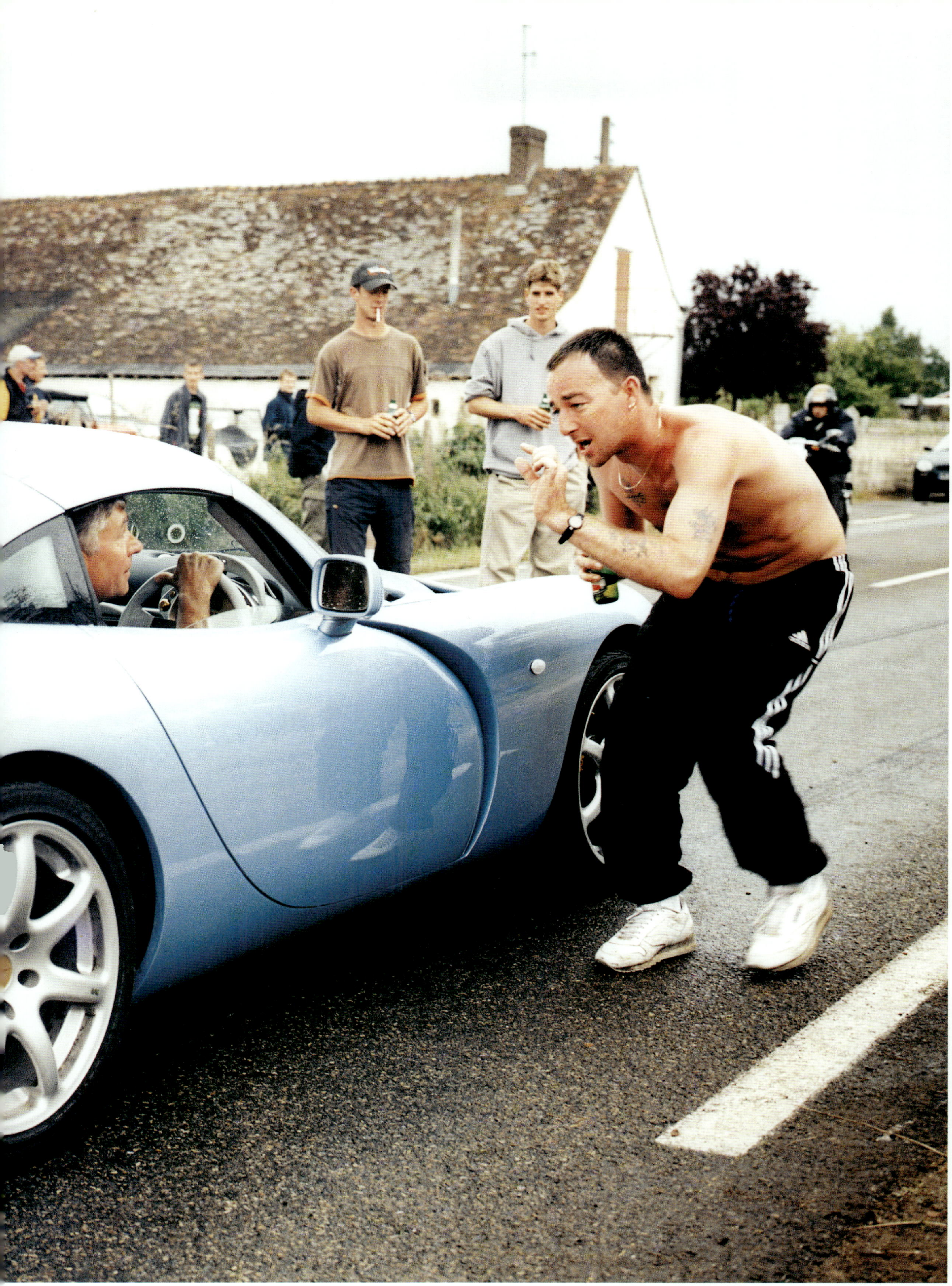

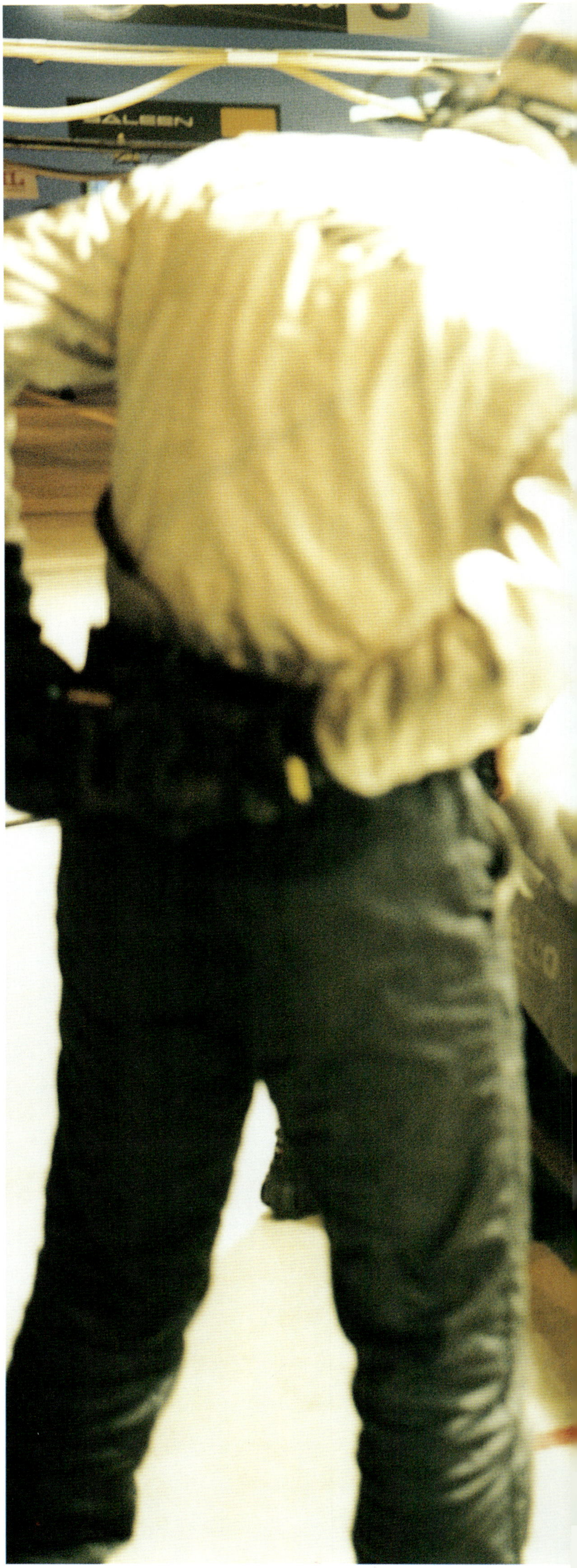

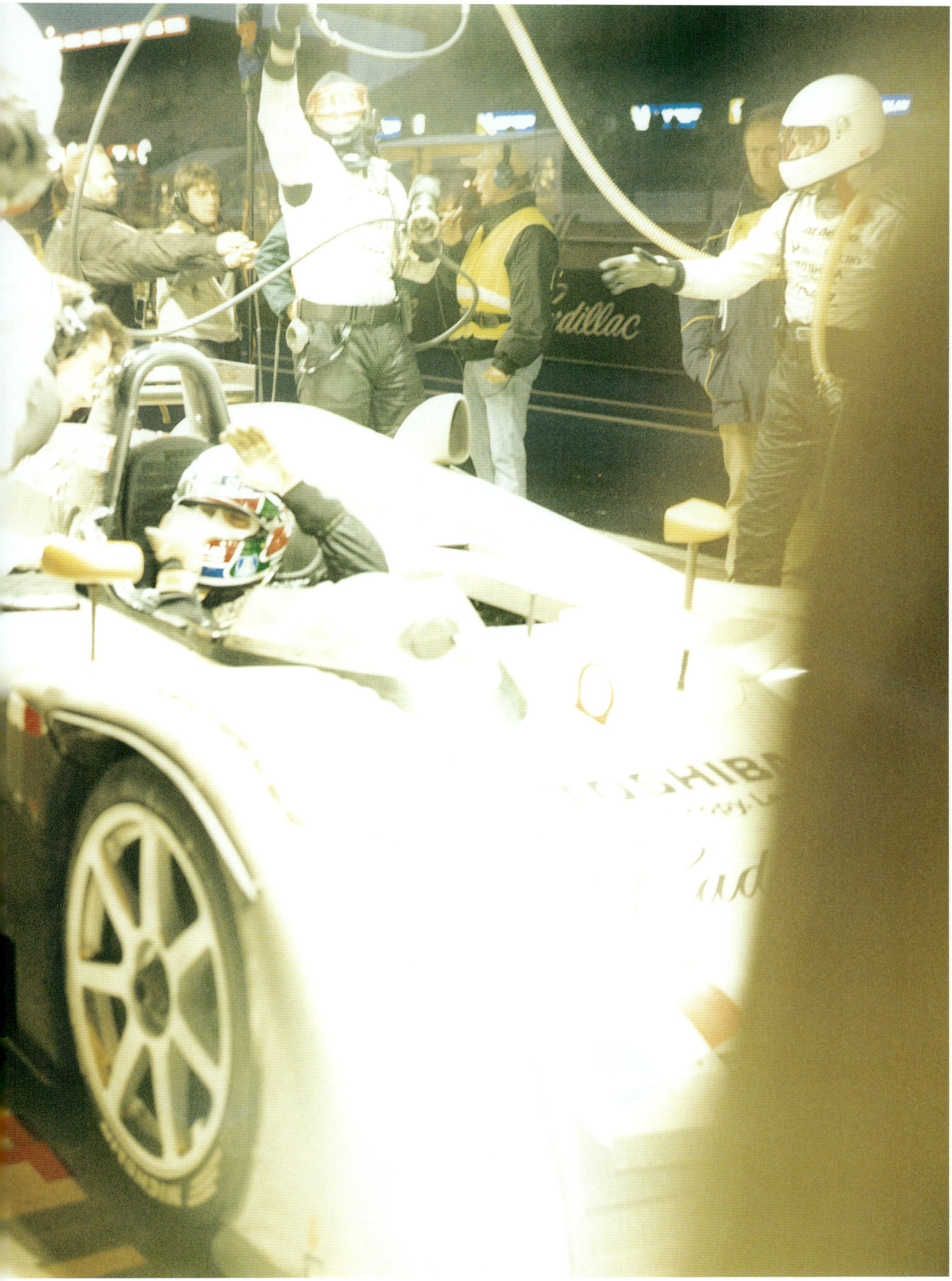

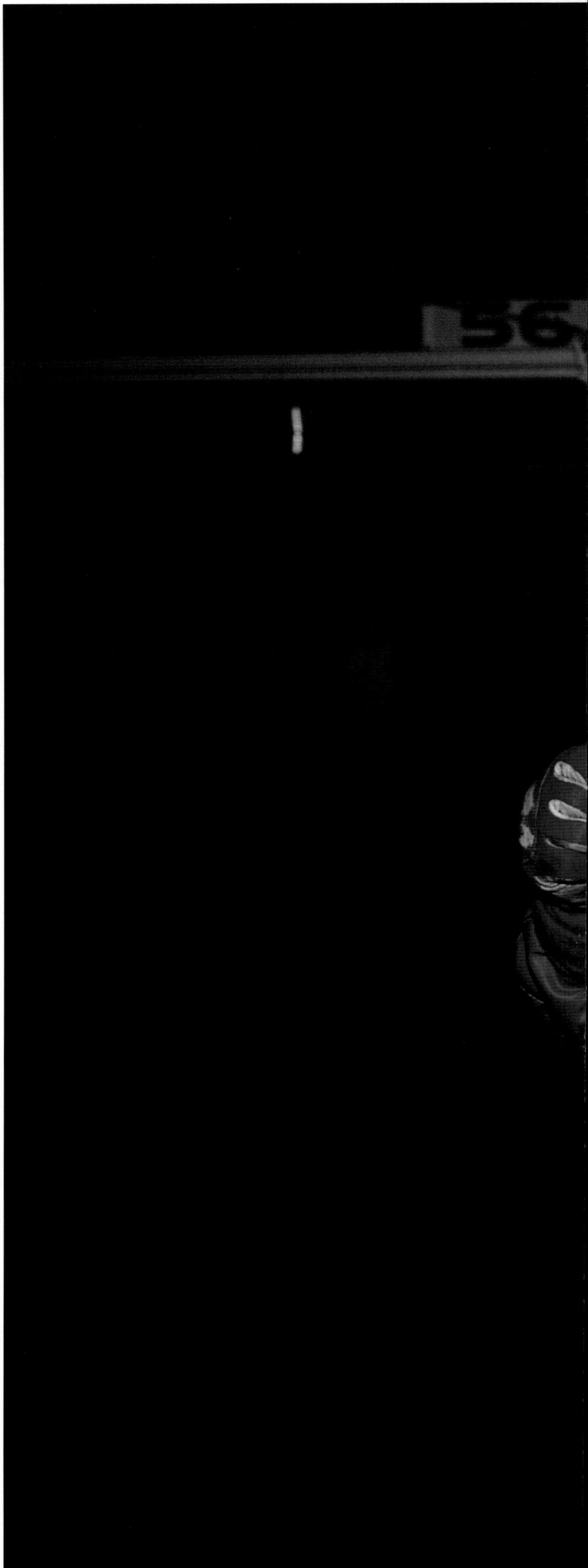
56

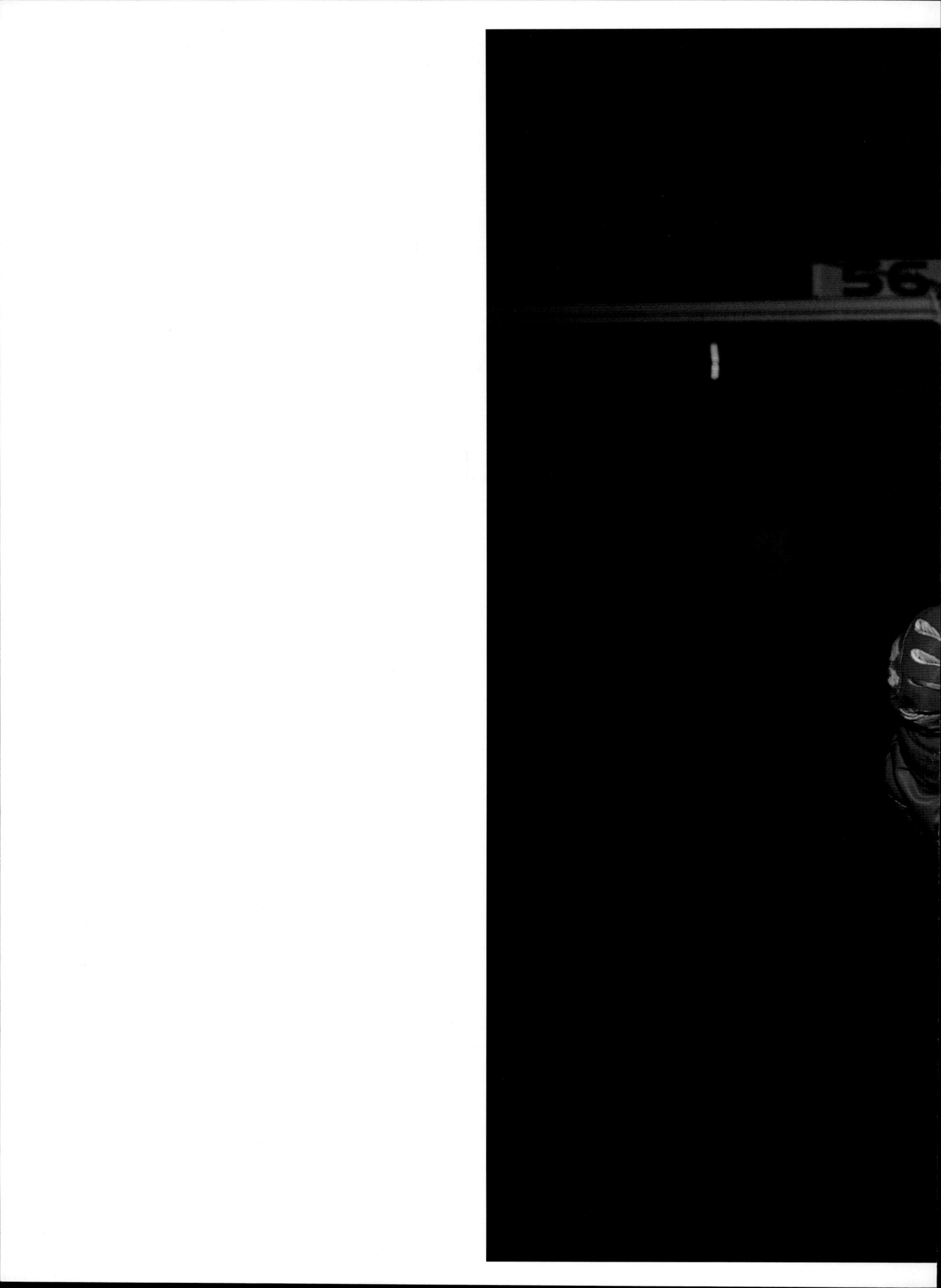

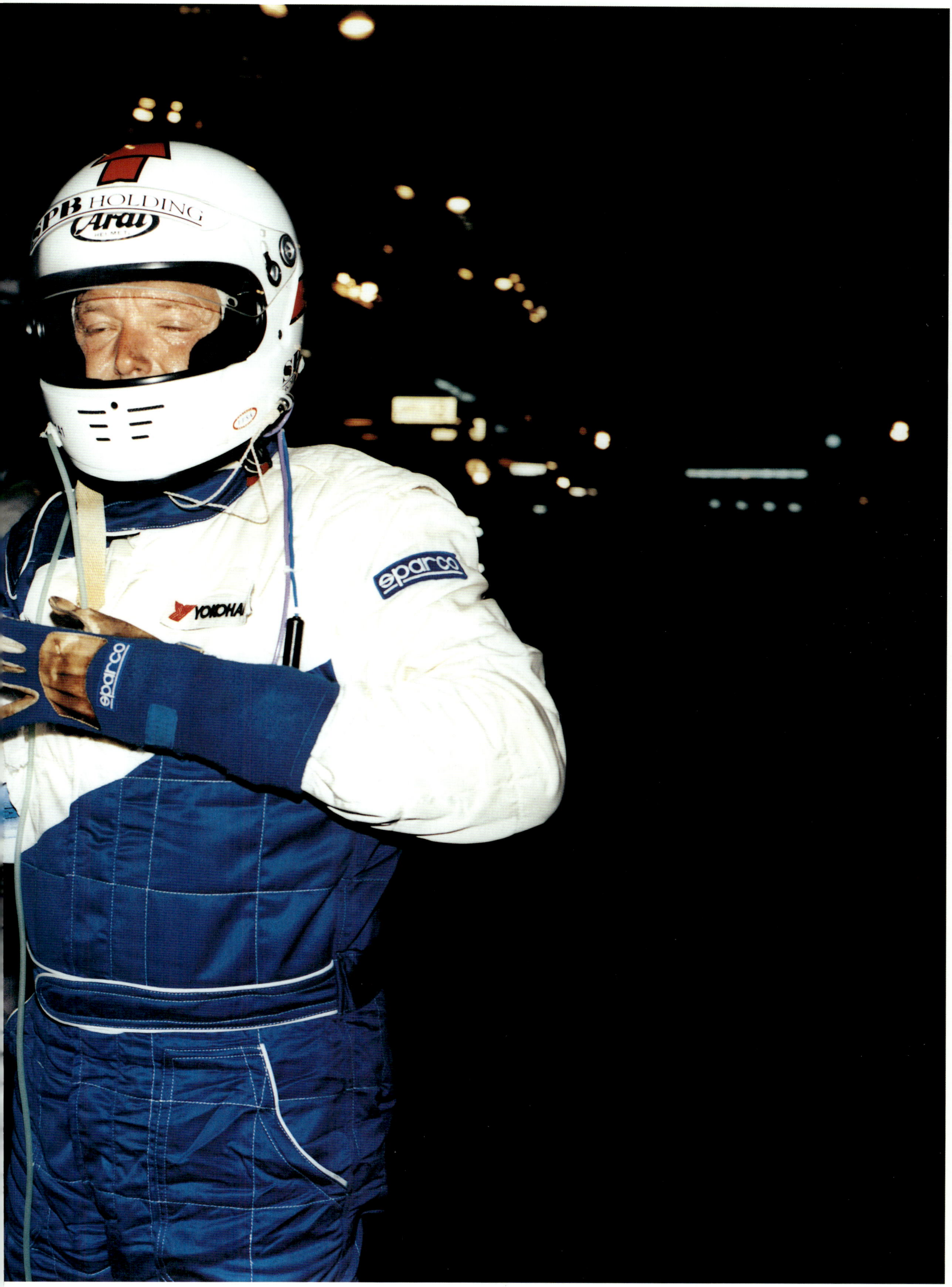
SPB HOLDING
Arai
sparco
YOKOHA
sparco

ILLUSTRATION YORGO TLOUPAS

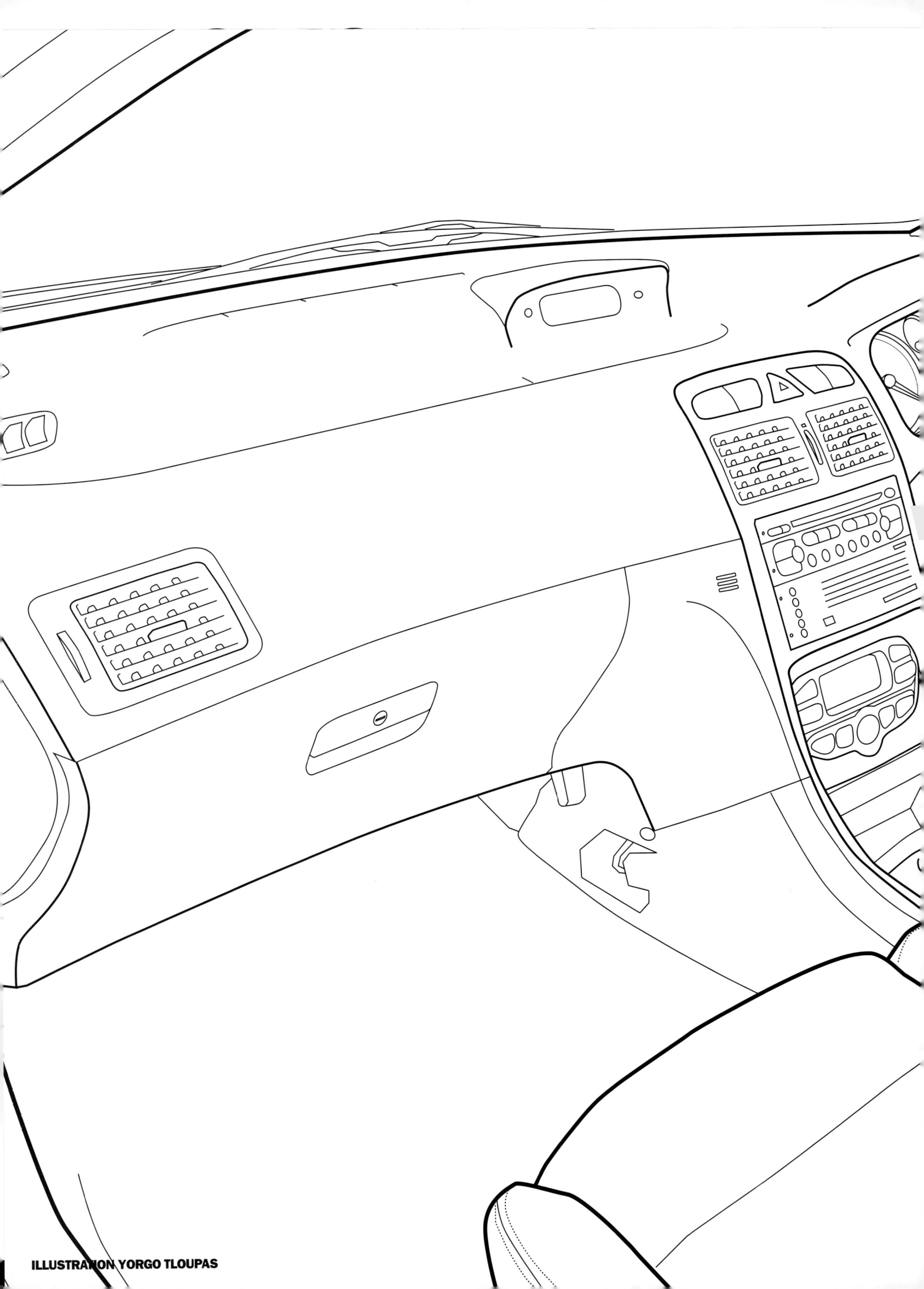

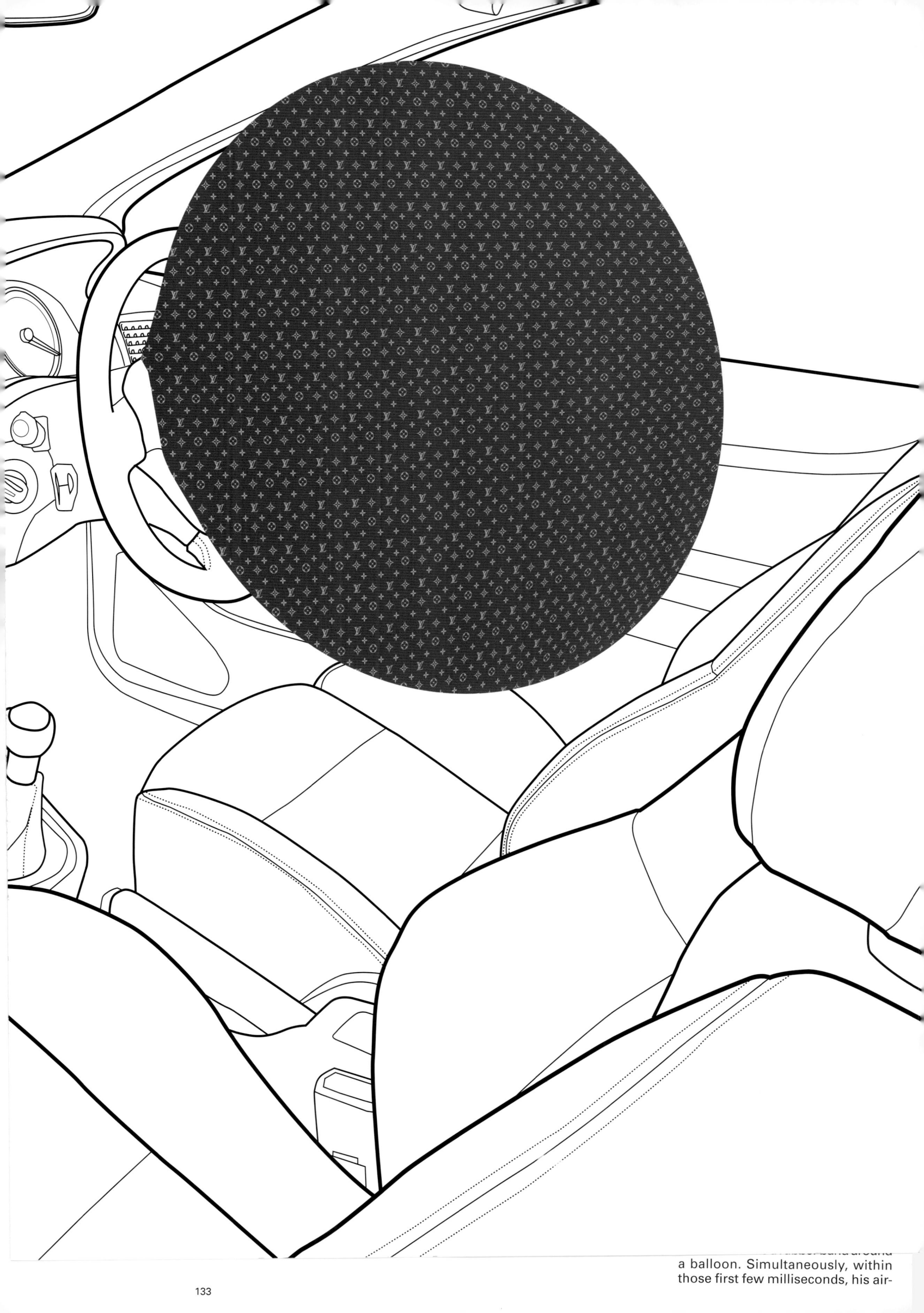

a balloon. Simultaneously, within
those first few milliseconds, his air-

This is not to suggest, of course, that Haddon's crusade is responsible for

bag exploded and rose to meet him at more than a 100mph. 40 to 50 milliseconds after impact, it had enveloped his face, neck, and upper chest. A fraction of a second later, the bag deflated. Capoferri was thrown back against his seat. Total time elapsed: 100 milliseconds. Would Capoferri have lived without an airbag? Probably. He would have stretched his seat belt so far that his head would have hit the steering wheel. But his belts would have slowed him down enough that he might only have broken his nose or cut his forehead or suffered a mild concussion. The other way around, however, with an airbag but not a seatbelt, his fate would have been much more uncertain. In the absence of seatbelts, airbags work best when one car hits another squarely, so that the driver pitches forward directly into the path of the oncoming bag. But Capoferri hit Day at a slight angle. The front-passenger side of the Aerostar sustained more damage than the driver's side, which means that without his belts holding him in place he would have been thrown away from the airbag off to the side, toward the rearview mirror or perhaps even the front-passenger "A" pillar. Capoferri's airbag protected him only because he was wearing his seatbelt. Car-crash statistics show this to be the rule. Wearing a seatbelt cuts your chances of dying in an accident by 43%. If you add the protection of an airbag, your fatality risk is cut by 47%. But an airbag by itself reduces the risk of dying in an accident by just 13%. That the effectiveness of an airbag depended on the use of a seatbelt was a concept that the Haddonites, in those early days, never properly understood. They wanted the airbag to replace the seatbelt when in fact it was capable only of supplementing it, and they clung to that belief, even in the face of mounting evidence to the contrary. Don Huelke, a longtime safety researcher at the University of Michigan, remembers being on an NHTSA advisory committee in the early '70s, when people at the agency were trying to come up with statistics for the public on the value of airbags:

"Their estimates were that something like 28,000 people a year could be saved by the airbags," he recalls, "and then someone pointed out to them that there weren't that many driver fatalities in frontal crashes in a year. It was kind of like 'Oops.' So the estimates were reduced."

In '77, Claybrook became the head of NHTSA and renewed the push for airbags. The agency's estimate now was that airbags would cut a driver's risk of dying in a crash by 40% - a more modest but still implausible figure. "In '73, there was a study in the open literature, performed at GM, that estimated the airbag would reduce the fatality risk to an unbelted driver by 18%," Leonard Evans says.

He didn't see something he was supposed to see. His mistake is, on "NHTSA had this information and dismissed it. Why? Because it was from the automobile industry."

The truth is that even today it is seatbelts, not airbags, that are providing the most important new safety advances. Had Capoferri been driving a late-model Ford minivan, for example, his seatbelt would have had what is called a pretensioner: a tiny explosive device that would have taken the slack out of the belt just after the moment of impact. Without the pretensioner, Stephen Kozak, an engineer at Ford, explains, "you start to accelerate before you hit the belt. You get the clothesline effect." With it, Capoferri's deceleration would have been a bit more gradual. At the same time, belts are now being designed which cut down on chest compression. Capoferri's chest wall was pushed in two inches, and had he been a much older man, with less resilient bones and cartilage, that two-inch compression might have been enough to fracture three or four ribs. So belts now "pay out" extra webbing after a certain point: as Capoferri stretched forward, his belt would have been lengthened by several inches, relieving the pressure on his chest. The next stage in seatbelt

**WEARING A SEATBELT CUTS YOUR CHANCES OF DYING IN AN ACCIDENT BY 43%. BUT AN AIRBAG BY ITSELF REDUCES THE RISK OF DYING IN AN ACCIDENT BY JUST 13%**

design is probably to offer car buyers the option of what is called a four-point belt - two shoulder belts that run down the chest, like suspenders attached to a lap belt.

Ford showed a four-point prototype at the auto shows this spring, and early estimates are that it might cut fatality risk by another 10% - which would make seatbelts roughly five times more effective in saving lives than airbags by themselves. "The best solution is to provide automatic protection, including airbags, as baseline protection for everyone, with seatbelts as a supplement for those who will use them," Haddon wrote in '84. In putting airbags first and seatbelts second, he had things backward.

ask people, 'Did you see anyone walking across the screen?' They'd

Robert Day suffered a very different kind of accident from Stephen Capoferri's: he was hit from the side, and the physics of a side-impact crash are not nearly so forgiving. Imagine, for instance, that you punched a brick wall as hard as you could. If your fist was bare, you'd break your hand. If you had a glove with two inches of padding, your hand would sting. If you had a glove with six inches of padding, you might not feel much of anything. The more energy absorbing material - the more space you can put between your body and the wall - the better off you are. An automobile accident is no different. Capoferri lived, in part, because he had lots of space between himself and Day's Wagoneer. Cars have steel rails connecting the passenger compartment with the bumper, and each of those rails is engineered with what are called convolutions - accordion-like folds designed to absorb, slowly and evenly, the impact of a collision. Capoferri's van was engineered with 27 inches of crumple room, and at the speed he was travelling he probably used about 21 inches of that. But Day had four inches, no more, between his body and the door, and perhaps another five to six inches in the door itself. Capoferri hit the wall with a boxing glove. Day punched it with his bare hand.

Day's problems were compounded by the fact that he was not wearing his seatbelt. The right-front fender of Capoferri's Aerostar struck his Wagoneer squarely on the driver's door, pushing the Jeep sideways, and if Day had been belted he would have moved with his vehicle, away from the onrushing Aerostar. But he wasn't, and so the Jeep moved out from under him: within 15 milliseconds, the four inches of space between his body and the side of the Jeep was gone. The impact of the Aerostar slammed the driver's door against his ribs and spleen.

Day could easily have been ejected from his vehicle at that point. The impact of Capoferri's van shattered the glass in Day's door, and a Wagoneer, like most SUVs, has a low belt line - meaning that the side windows are so large that with the glass gone there's a hole big enough for an unrestrained body to fly through. This is what it means to be "thrown clear" of a crash, although when that phrase is used in popular literature it is sometimes said as if it were a good thing, when of course to be "thrown clear" of a crash is merely to be thrown into some other hard and even more lethal object, like the pavement or a tree or another car. Day, for whatever reason, was not thrown clear, and in that narrow sense he was lucky. This advantage, however, amounted to little. Day's door was driven into him like a sledgehammer.

ILLUSTRATION YORGO TLOUPAS

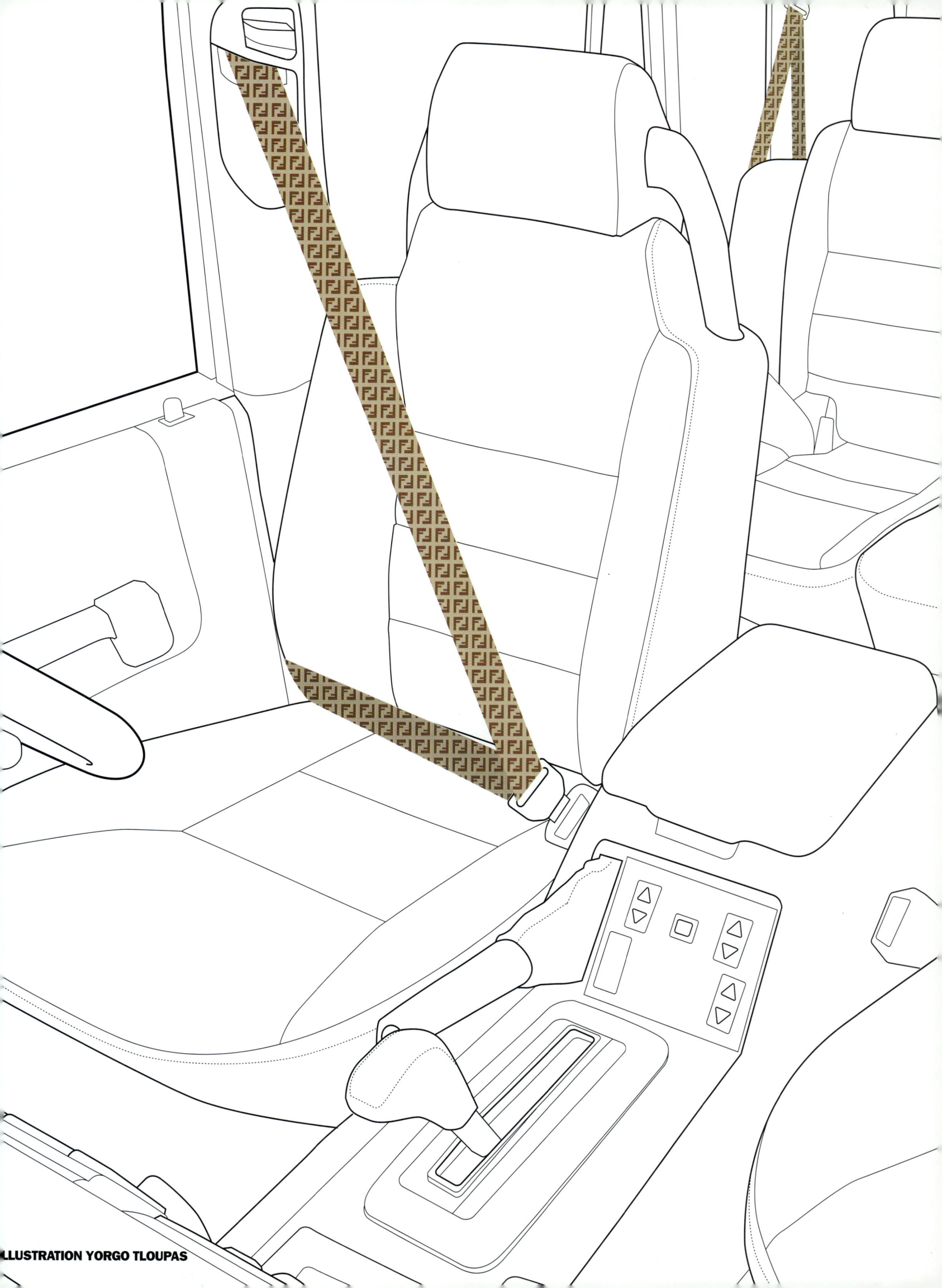

Would a front airbag have saved Robert Day? Not at all. He wasn't moving forward into the steering wheel. He was moving sideways into the door. Some cars now have additional airbags that are intended to protect the head as it hits the top of the door frame in a side-impact crash. But Day didn't die of head injuries. He died of abdominal injuries. Conceivably, a side-impact bag might have offered his abdomen some slight protection. But Day's best chance of surviving the accident would have been to wear his seatbelt. It would have held him in place in those first few milliseconds of impact. It would have preserved some part of the space separating him from the door, diminishing the impact of the Aerostar. Day made two mistakes that morning, then, the second of which was not buckling up. But this is a point on which the Haddonites were in error as well, because the companion to their obsession with airbags was the equally false belief that encouraging drivers to wear their seatbelts was a largely futile endeavour.

In the early '70s, just at the moment when Haddon and Claybrook were pushing hardest for airbags, the Australian state of Victoria passed the world's first mandatory seatbelt legislation. The law was an immediate success. With an aggressive public-education campaign, rates of seatbelt use jumped from 20 to 80%. During the next several years, Canada, New Zealand, Germany, France, and others followed suit. But a similar movement in the United States in the early '70s stalled. James Gregory, who headed the NHTSA during the Ford years, says that if Nader had advocated mandatory belt laws they might have carried the day. But Nader, then at the height of his fame and influence, didn't think that belt laws would work in this country. "You push mandatory belts, you might get a very adverse reaction," Nader says today of his thinking back then. "Mindless reaction. And how many tickets do you give out a day? What about back seats? At what point do you require a seatbelt for small kids? And it's administratively difficult when people cross state lines. That's why I always focussed on the passive. We have a libertarian streak that Europe doesn't have." Richard Peet, a congressional staffer who helped draft legislation in Congress giving states financial incentives to pass belt laws, founded an organisation in the early '70s to promote belt-wearing. "After I did that, some of the people who worked for Nader's organisation went after me, saying that I was selling out the airbag movement," Peet recalls. "That pissed me off. I thought the safety movement was the safety movement and we were all working together for common aims." In *Auto Safety*, a history of auto-safety regulation, John Graham, of the Harvard School of Public Health, writes of Claybrook's time at the NHTSA.

Her lack of aggressive leadership on safety-belt use was a major source of irritation among belt use advocates, auto industry officials, and officials from state safety programs. They saw her pessimistic attitudes as a self-fulfiling prophecy.

One of Claybrook's aides at NHTSA who worked with state agencies acknowledged: "It is fair to say that Claybrook never made a dedicated effort to get mandatory belt-use laws." Another aide offered the following explanation of her philosophy: "Joan didn't do much on mandatory belt use because her primary interests were in vehicle regulation. She was fond of saying 'it is easier to get 20 auto companies to do something than to get 200 million Americans to do something.'" Claybrook says that while at the NHTSA she mailed a letter to all the state governors encouraging them to pass mandatory seatbelt legislation, and "not one governor would help us." It is clear that she had low expectations for her efforts. Even as late as '84, Claybrook was still insisting that trying to encourage seatbelt use was a fool's errand:

"It is not likely that mandatory seat-belt usage laws will be either enacted or found acceptable to the public in large numbers," Claybrook wrote. "There is massive public resistance to adult safety-belt usage." In the very year her words were published, however, a coalition of medical groups finally managed to pass the country's first mandatory seatbelt law, in New York, and the results were dramatic. One state after another soon did likewise, and public opinion about belts underwent what the pollster Gary Lawrence has called "one of the most phenomenal shifts in attitudes ever measured."

Americans, it turned out, did not have a cultural aversion to seatbelts. They just needed some encouragement. "It's not a big Freudian thing whether you buckle up or not," says BJ Campbell, a former safety researcher at the University of North Carolina, who was one of the veterans of the seatbelt movement. "It's just a habit, and either you're in the habit of doing it or you're not."

Today, belt-wearing rates in the United States are just over 70%, and every year they inch up a little more. But if the seatbelt campaign had begun in the '70s, instead of the '80s, the use rate in this country would be higher right now, and in the intervening years an awful lot of car accidents might have turned out differently, including one at the intersection of Egg Harbor Road and Fleming Pike.

## VI. CRASH TEST

William Haddon died in 1985, of kidney disease, aged 58. From the time he left government until his death, he headed an influential research group called the Insurance Institute for Highway Safety.

Joan Claybrook left the NHTSA in 1980 and went on to run Ralph Nader's advocacy group Public Citizen, where she has been a powerful voice on auto-safety ever since. In an interview this spring, Claybrook listed the things that she would do if she were back as the country's traffic-safety czar. "I'd issue a rollover standard, and have a 30mph test for airbags," she said. "Upgrade the seating structure. Integrate the head restraint better. Upgrade the tyre safety standard. Provide much more consumer information. And also do more crash testing, whether it's rollover or offset crash testing and rear-crash testing." The most effective way to reduce automobile fatalities, she went on, would be to focus on rollovers - lowering the centre of gravity in SUVs, strengthening doors and roofs. In the course of outlining her agenda, Claybrook did not once mention the word "seatbelt."

Ralph Nader, for his part, spends a great deal of time speaking at college campuses about political activism. He remains a distinctive figure, tall and slightly stooped, with a bundle of papers under his arm. His interests have widened in recent years, but he is still passionate about his first crusade. "Haddon was all business - never made a joke, didn't tolerate fools easily," Nader said not long ago, when he was asked about the early days. He has a deep, rumbling press conference voice, and speaks in sentence fragments, punctuated with long pauses. "Very dedicated. He influenced us all." The auto-safety campaign, he went on, "was a spectacular success of the federal-government mission. When the regulations were allowed, they worked. And it worked because it deals with technology rather than human behaviour." Nader had just been speaking in Detroit, at Wayne State University, and was on the plane back to Washington, DC. He was folded into his seat, his knees butting up against the tray table in front of him, and from time to time he looked enviously over at the people stretching their legs in the exit row. Did he have any regrets? Yes, he said. He wished that back in '66 he had succeeded in keeping the criminal-penalties provision in the auto-safety bill that Congress passed that summer. "That would have gone right to the executive suite," he said. There were things, he admitted, that had puzzled him over the years. He couldn't believe the strides that had been made against drink driving. "You've got to hand it to MADD. It took me by surprise. The drink-driving culture is deeply embedded. I thought it was too ingrained." And then there was what had happened with seatbelts. "Use rates are up sharply," he said. "They're a lot higher than I thought they would be. I thought it would be very hard to hit 50%. The most unlikely people now buckle up." He shook his head, marvelling. He had always been a belt user, and recommends belts to others, but who knew they would catch on?

Other safety activists, who had seen what had happened to driver behaviour in Europe and Australia in the '70s, weren't so surprised, of course. But Nader was never the kind of activist who had great faith in the people whose lives he was trying to protect. He and the other Haddonites were sworn to a theory that said that the way to prevent typhoid is to chlorinate the water, even though there are clearly instances where chlorine will not do the trick. This is the blindness of ideology. It is what happens when public policy is conducted by those who cannot conceive that human beings will do willingly what is in their own interest. What was the truly poignant thing about Robert Day, after all? Not just that he was a click away from saving his only life but that his son, sitting right next to him, was wearing his seatbelt. In the Days' Jeep Wagoneer, a fight that experts assumed was futile was already half-won.

One day this spring, a team of engineers at Ford conducted a crash test on a 2003 Mercury. This was at Ford's test facility in Dearborn, a long, rectangular white steel structure, bisected by a 550ft runway. Ford crashes as many as two cars a day there, ramming them with specially designed sleds or dragging them down the runway with a cable into a 20ft cube of concrete. Along the side of the track were the twisted hulks of previous experiments: a Ford Focus wagon up on blocks; a mangled BMW SUV that had been crashed out of competitive curiosity, the previous week; a Ford Explorer that looked as though it had been thrown into a blender. In a room at the back, there were 50 or 60 crashtest dummies, propped up on tables and chairs, in a dozen or more configurations - some in Converse sneakers, some in patent-leather shoes, some without feet and legs at all, each one covered with multiple electronic sensors, all designed to measure the kinds of injuries possible in a crash.

The severity of any accident is measured not by the speed of the car at the moment of impact but by what is known as the delta V - the difference between how fast a car is going at the moment of impact and how fast it is moving after the accident. Capoferri's delta V was about 25mph, seven miles per hour higher than the accident average. The delta V of the Mercury test, though, was to be 35mph, which is the equivalent of hitting an identical parked car at 70mph. The occupants were two adult-size dummies in orange shorts. Their faces were covered in wet paint, red above the upper jaw and blue below it, to mark where their faces hit on the airbag. The back seat carried a full cargo of computers and video cameras. A series of yellow lights began flashing. An engineer stood to the side, holding an abort button. Then a bank of stage lights came on, directly above the point of impact.

**A CRASH TEST IS BEAUTIFUL. THE DUMMY RISES MAGICALLY TO MEET THE SWELLING CUSHION, ALWAYS IN SLOW MOTION, THE BANG REPLACED BY MOZART**

16 video cameras began rolling. A voice came over a loudspeaker, counting down: five, four, three... There was a blur as the Mercury swept by - then bang, as the car hit the barrier and the dual front airbags exploded. A plastic light bracket skittered across the floor, and the long warehouse was suddenly still.

It was a moment of extraordinary violence, yet it was also strangely compelling. This was performance art, an abstract and ritualised rendering of reality, given in a concrete-and-steel gallery. The front end of the Mercury was perfectly compressed; the car was 30 inches shorter than it had been a moment before. The windshield was untouched. The "A" pillars and roofline were intact. The passenger cabin was whole. In the dead centre of the deflated airbags, right where they were supposed to be, were perfect blue-and-red paint imprints of the dummies' faces.

But it was only a performance, and that was the hard thing to remember. In the real world, people rarely have perfectly square frontal collisions, sitting ramrod straight and ideally positioned; people rarely have accidents that so perfectly showcase the minor talents of the airbag. A crash test is beautiful. In the sequence we have all seen over and over in automobile commercials, the dummy rises magically to meet the swelling cushion, always in slow motion, the bang replaced by Mozart, and on those theatrical terms the dowdy fabric strips of the seatbelt cannot compete with the billowing folds of the airbag. This is the image that seduced William Haddon when the men from Eaton, Yale showed him the People Saver so many years ago, and the image that warped auto-safety for 20 long years. But real accidents are seldom like this. They are ugly and complicated, shaped by the messy geometries of the everyday world and by the infinite variety of human frailty. A man looks away from the road at the wrong time. He does not see what he ought to see. Another man does not have time to react. The two cars collide, but at a slight angle. There is a 270 degree spin. There is skidding and banging. A belt presses deep into one man's chest - and that saves his life. The other man's unrestrained body smashes against the car door - and that kills him.

"They left pretty early, about eight, nine in the morning," Susan Day, Robert Day's widow, recalls. "I was at home when the hospital called. I went to see my son first. He was pretty much okay, had a lot of bruising. Then they came in and said, 'Your husband didn't make it.'"

Copyright 2001, Malcolm Gladwell

**ROUTES
AND ROADS
TEXT MILAN KUNDERA
PHOTOGRAPHY NICOLAS FAURE**

Road: a strip of ground over which one walks. A route differs from a road not only because it is solely intended for vehicles, but also because it is merely a line that connects one point with another. A route has no meaning in itself; its meaning derives entirely from the two points that it connects. A road is a tribute to space. Every stretch of road has meaning in itself and invites us to stop. A route is the triumphant devaluation of space, which thanks to it has been reduced to a mere obstacle to human movement and a waste of time.

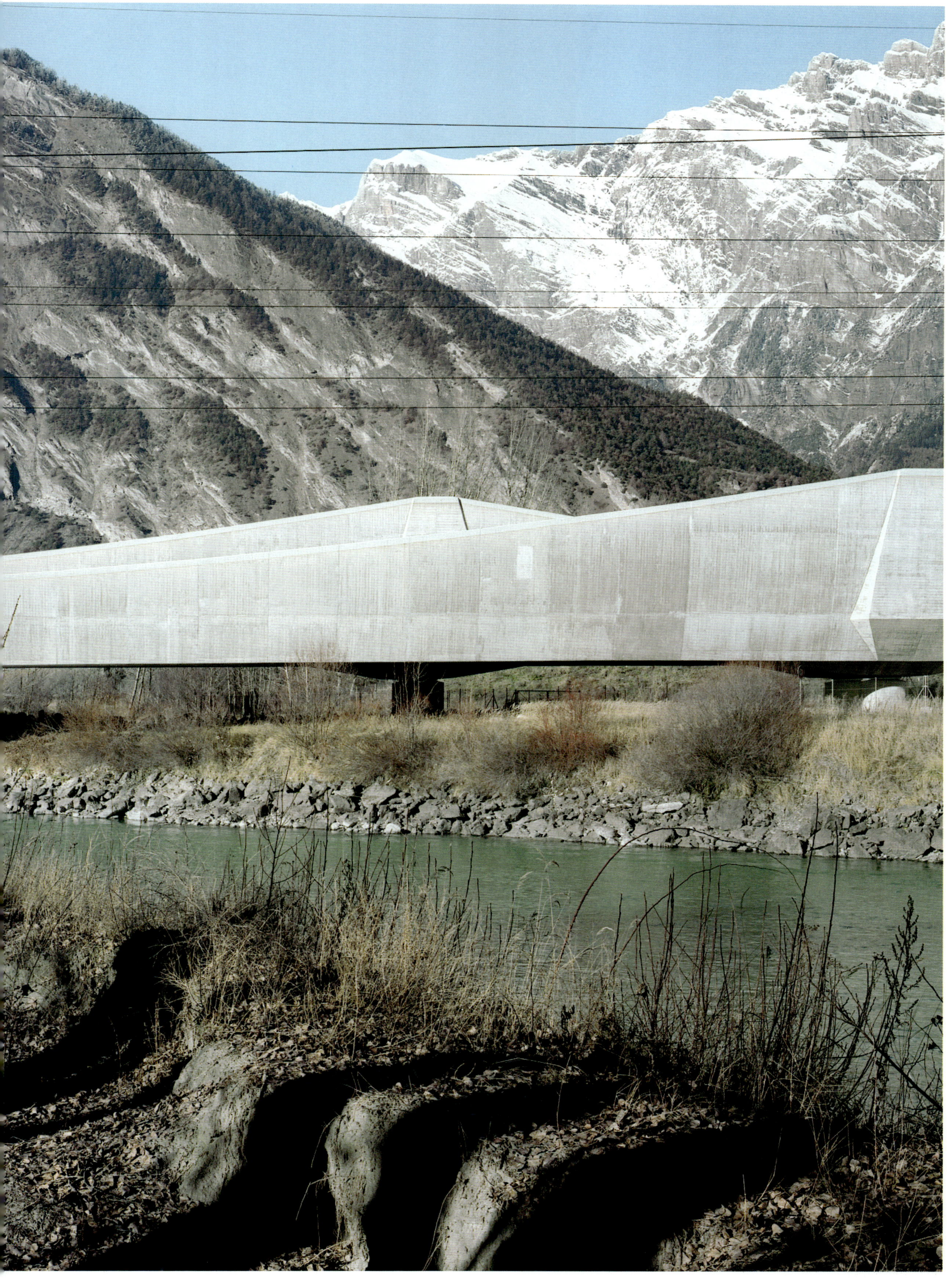

Road and route; these are also two different conceptions of beauty. When Paul says that at a particular place the landscape is beautiful, that means: if you stopped the car at that place, you might see a beautiful fifteenth-century castle surrounded by a park; or a lake reaching far into the distance, with swans floating on its brilliant surface.

Chemin des Viaducs

In the world of routes, a beautiful landscape means: an island of beauty connected by a long line with other islands of beauty.

In the world of roads and paths, beauty is continuous and constantly changing; it tells us at every step: 'Stop!'"

Milan Kundera *Immortality* (Faber & Faber)

Nicolas Faure *Autoland* (Scalo)

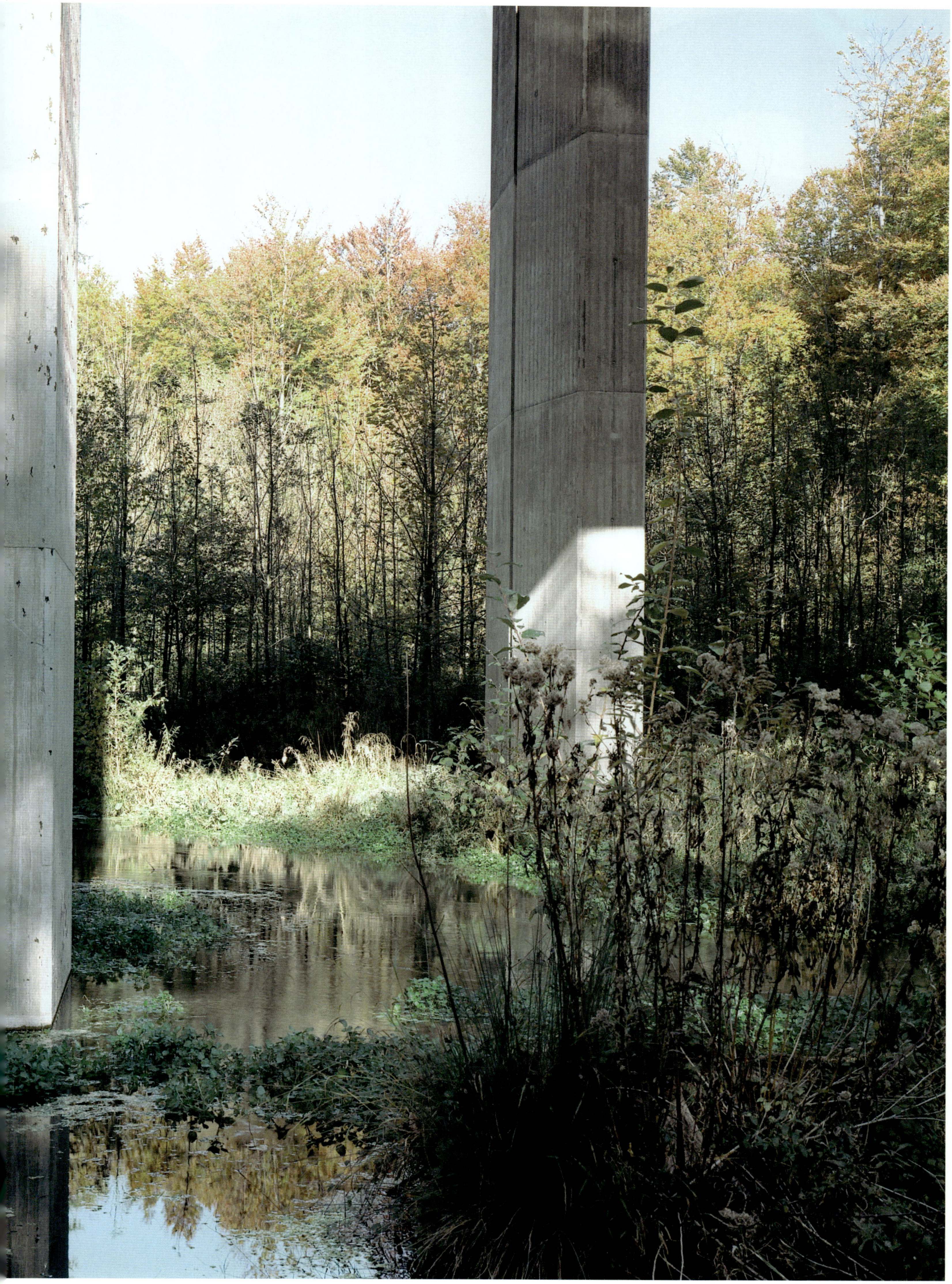

LAGOS
PHOTOGRAPHY BY
BRUNO BARBEY - MAGNUM

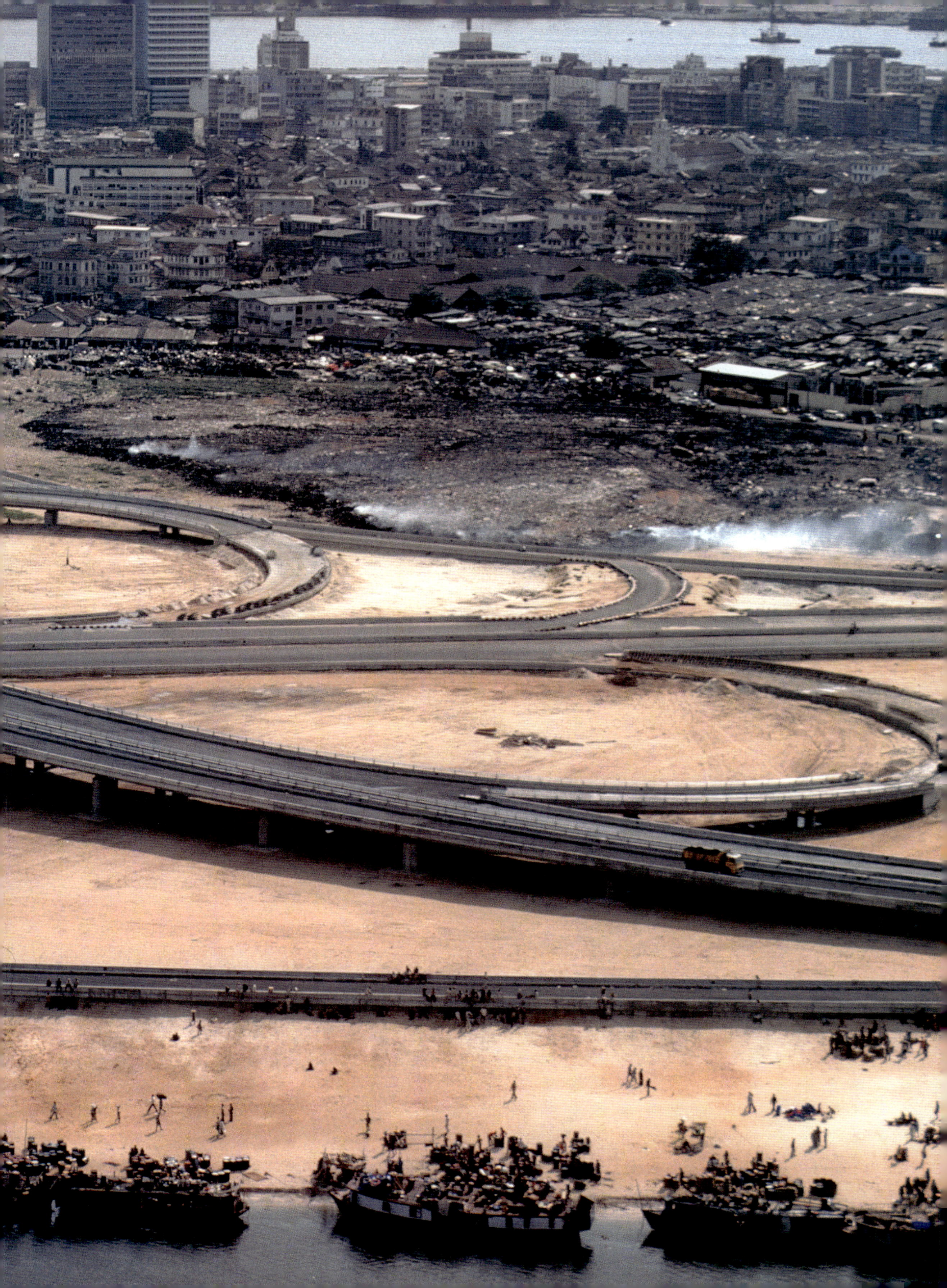

it's taken as a declaration of intent to purchase; expect change from a large note and watch them disappear through the fumes. Buying from them is a gamble. They have many tricks to up their profit margins - is that a bottle of car cleaning fluid or has it been refilled with washing up liquid? Are those batteries dead? There's no chance of refunds from a go-slow boy. If the traffic is a moving jam, the go-slow boys' job becomes more hazardous; as well as the fumes, angry drivers and the complex and often violent interactions within their own community they also have to cope with moving metal. Drivers pay them scant regard. The engine does not yield even a concessionary amount to the soft fallibility of flesh. Despite the danger, they stand with vacant expressions, like nonchalant matadors waving their wares at bullish drivers.

## II. MOTOR DEY COME

Traffic is not a new problem. Ever since the oil boom of the '70s that brought a flood of cars and road construction projects, Lagos has been plagued by near coronary congestion. Although cars have inspired many lyricists to pen songs about road trips and driving, in Lagos the source of inspiration is not the open road. Whilst Americans were waxing over route 66 and the Californian open-top experience, the famous Nigerian artist Fela Kuti sang of cramped public transport, go-slows and traffic police.
*Vehicles are coming from the north/ Motor dey come from south/ Vehicles are coming from the south/ And policeman no dey for centre/ And there are no policemen in the centre/ Na confusion be dat o o/ That certainly is confusion.*
One famous Lagos landmark in the '70s was an army colonel named Paul Tarfa. Colonel Tarfa was often to be seen standing in the street with his bullwhip-wielding troops, supervising the men unfurling their weapons on terrified drivers. He justified the brutal ritual as a means of resolving the perennial Lagos traffic problem. Challenging the practice, Fela immortalised him in the song "Unknown Soldier". The locals call traffic police "yellow fever" after their uniforms and in reference to the virulence of the tropical disease, but I saw few in action on the city's streets.

We've been stuck on this roundabout for 20 minutes now and it feels like someone is pushing hard on my temples. The fumes course over me, causing a nauseous wave to run down my throat, hit my stomach and bounce back. Sound waves are battering their way in on the other

**COLONEL TARFA WAS OFTEN TO BE SEEN STANDING IN THE STREET WITH HIS BULLWHIP-WIELDING TROOPS, SUPERVISING THE MEN UNFURLING THEIR WEAPONS ON TERRIFIED DRIVERS**

side of my head. The big yellow bus next to me is still pouring out fumes. The driver is using his horn to communicate with another bus driver stuck six cars in front. Unless they have some personal code, which translates the loud, hurtful series of blasts into a meaningful conversation, the act just serves to add more pollution to a refuse tip of noise. Everyone hears but no one is listening. To hear each sound and not try to block it out would surely mean instant insanity. Someone in a nearby car suddenly loses patience. They lay on their horn for a full one minute and 17 seconds (I happen to glance at my watch when they start). Other horns add a constant backing track of peeps, beeps and screams. Someone's car alarm joins the orchestra then finally a five-car police convoy, sirens upping the din, tries to muscle its way through the motoring mayhem. In the end it takes us 37 minutes to drive round an average sized roundabout.
Inexplicably, the road we exit on is virtually car free. As we leave the junction I catch a glimpse of a man standing under the flyover. He's bare-chested and bent over a rough workbench. A carpenter, his concentration does not yield a glance to the anxiety, cacophony and insanity that surrounds him. For him it's just another day at the office, his office a small dark space under a concrete, car-covered roof. His office that also probably doubles as his home.
The streets of Lagos aren't merely about transport. They provide a source of income and shelter to a vast proportion of the people who live in the city. The streets really are alive. Property and land here may not cost that much in international terms but for the vast majority of the people living in Lagos, they are out of reach. Many of these people are as poor as it is possible to get. Walls run in every direction, marking out the precious space that has already been claimed, solid social divides between those that have and those that have not. The people they keep out claim the exterior; rough wood

Photography
Huw Williams

and metal sheet shelters, lean-tos, carpets, cloth, tyres and other merchandise hang on display. The thicker walls are even mined to make cramped living caves, proving that you don't need four walls for a home. Every useable space has its function. Raised highways give shelter for workshops and small factories, floor mats rolled out mark where people sleep below the wheels that run above. Dead spaces in the centre of cloverleaf intersections are resurrected as markets, car parks and industrial yards. Go-slow boys patrol the roads, trestle-table stalls line the carriageways and streets selling food, offering haircuts or larger goods that can't so readily be carried amongst the traffic. Bigger stalls, lean-to shacks and proper shops form the third line in the trading onslaught. Smoke from wood stoves dances with the plumed fumes of the traffic, smells that tickle the nostrils, tantalise the tongue and turn the stomach, fight for attention. Smoked fish, fried fish, dead fish. Whatever the local aroma as you pass, the air has a heavy scent like a steam room filled with tropical plants. Sweet smells, pepper smells, sickly rotting flesh smells. When it rains all these scents are washed into the roads turning puddles a milky coffee colour, obscuring the depths of potholes and slowing traffic still more. Even lorries and buses have to creep forward down the lips of potholes that could easily claim a wheel up to its axle.

Like many cities in underdeveloped countries, basic amenities in Lagos are under enormous pressure. Needs become wants. Electricity regularly fails, water is only directly supplied to the privileged sections of society that can afford a house with plumbing and everyone else must make do with communal standpipes, if they can find one that works. The same is true of sewerage.

Even if something is working today, there's no way of telling whether it will be tomorrow. More than a year ago, a fire at the telephone exchange in Ikeja destroyed all lines in the area. It's a very busy residential and industrial area in what by most standards is a busy city, yet the lines are still down.

### III. CALL A FRIEND

Nigeria got its first telephone line in 1886 but more than 60% of Nigerians have never made a call. Lagos has half of all the country's phone lines, but that doesn't necessarily mean you can get a connection - one office I visited had 12 phone lines but only three were working and even those were hit and miss. The mobile phone network is analogue and impossibly expensive to all but the very rich. The Nigerian government has recently auctioned off GSM licences that have been bought by foreign telephone companies and although this offers the promise of improved phone use, it could be a vague promise. The licences were expensive, there have been no tax breaks for the high tech equipment the companies have brought into the country and the price of land in Lagos means building the infrastructure will push costs still higher. In neighbouring Ghana, mobile phones have become almost as ubiquitous as in Europe. For Nigerian people cheap mobile communications are viewed with almost religious expectation, but their perceived life changing potential may be a long time coming. The need for investors to get a return on their massive outlay could mean that the service is still only available to a small section of the population for a while yet.

If the cheap mobiles don't come soon then Lagos has little chance of waking from its traffic nightmare. A lack of working land-lines and the inconsequential number of people with mobiles means that Lagos is a very

**IF THE CHEAP MOBILES DON'T COME SOON THEN LAGOS HAS LITTLE CHANCE OF WAKING FROM ITS TRAFFIC NIGHTMARE AS ALL COMMUNICATION, SOCIAL OR BUSINESS, MUST TAKE PLACE FACE TO FACE**

physical place. All communication, social or business, must take place face to face. Picking up the handset, if you have one, does not necessarily mean you'll get through. If you want to talk to someone you get into a car, onto a moped or board a bus and travel to see them. Then there's no guarantee that they will be there when you arrive, they too may have had to journey to the other side of the city to pass on a message or hold a conversation. Anything you need to do that requires talking to someone else in another part of the city, even if it's only a couple of miles away, might well involve a four hour road trip through some of the worst traffic of any urban area on the face of the planet.

Most trade in Lagos is informal. Small traders and individual hawkers buy and resell anything that might return a profit. Vegetables, fruit and meat from rural Nigeria arrive at huge lorry parks north of the city. A network of traders buy the goods and move them around the city to be sold in shops, stalls or by the go-slow boys. Manufactured goods, local and imported, do the return trip. To physically move the tomatoes, lightbulbs, meat or whatever, a trader will simply gather as much as they can carry and board a bus or taxi. The roads bear the burden in a city where the only option is the road, no matter how crowded. Sometimes the traffic jams are deliberate, local gangs or "area boys" have been known to block roads with spurious breakdowns or repair work just so that the flow is directed through their patch, boosting their income from their shady dealings.

Lagos is dependent on road transport but the fuel the traffic demands is not always available. Petrol shortages are frequent but annoyingly irregular. One resigned Lagos resident described them as: "A thief in the night - they can sneak in at anytime so you can never rest easy."

The recent petrol protests and blockades in the UK caused queues, flared tempers and a near national crisis. But they were a demonstration - people stopped the flow, the flow wasn't stopped. In Lagos and throughout Nigeria petrol has often just not been available. This may seem surprising for a country that is the sixth largest oil producer in the world, pouring out over two million barrels a day but simple equations don't always balance easily. Nigeria has four oil refineries. All are in a poor state of repair and at one point all were out of action at the same time. Even when working at their full capacity, Nigeria still has to import refined fuels from overseas to meet demand. The reasons for this are mired in the complex relationships between the underdeveloped world and the global political economy. It is also down to corruption.

During the military regime it was in the vested interest of some of those in power to ensure that the repairs to the refineries were never completed, so that there was more money to milk from the foreign contractors doing the work. On the streets of Lagos this means that when the pumps run dry the city grinds to a halt. The petrol ceases to propel the cars and fuels the fires of anarchy instead. Queues stretch for miles, people abandon their cars at petrol stations, tempers flare and fights break out. People die. In one incident, a fight at a pump sent petrol from a hose spewing all over the forecourt. It caught fire and killed 20 people including a pregnant woman. There have been other deaths like these. The desire not to be caught short led many cars and vans to be fitted with home-made reserve fuel tanks that promptly exploded when the vehicles were involved in the near-inevitable accidents that occur on the roads of Lagos. At the moment the fuel is flowing, the refineries are being repaired and there have been no queues for months, but now that the pumps are pouring petrol on demand, that demand is soaring up. A year ago 18 million litres per day was bought by Nigerians, at the moment the figure is up to 25 million litres. At that rate, it can't be long before the thief in the night pays his next visit.

In Rem Koolhaas' book, *Mutations*, he and the Harvard Project on the city suggest that the lack of planning and apparent chaos of Lagos means it's difficult to believe that the city functions at all, let alone as well as it does. This in itself he sees as a message for the future, that far from

**JARVIS COCKER**

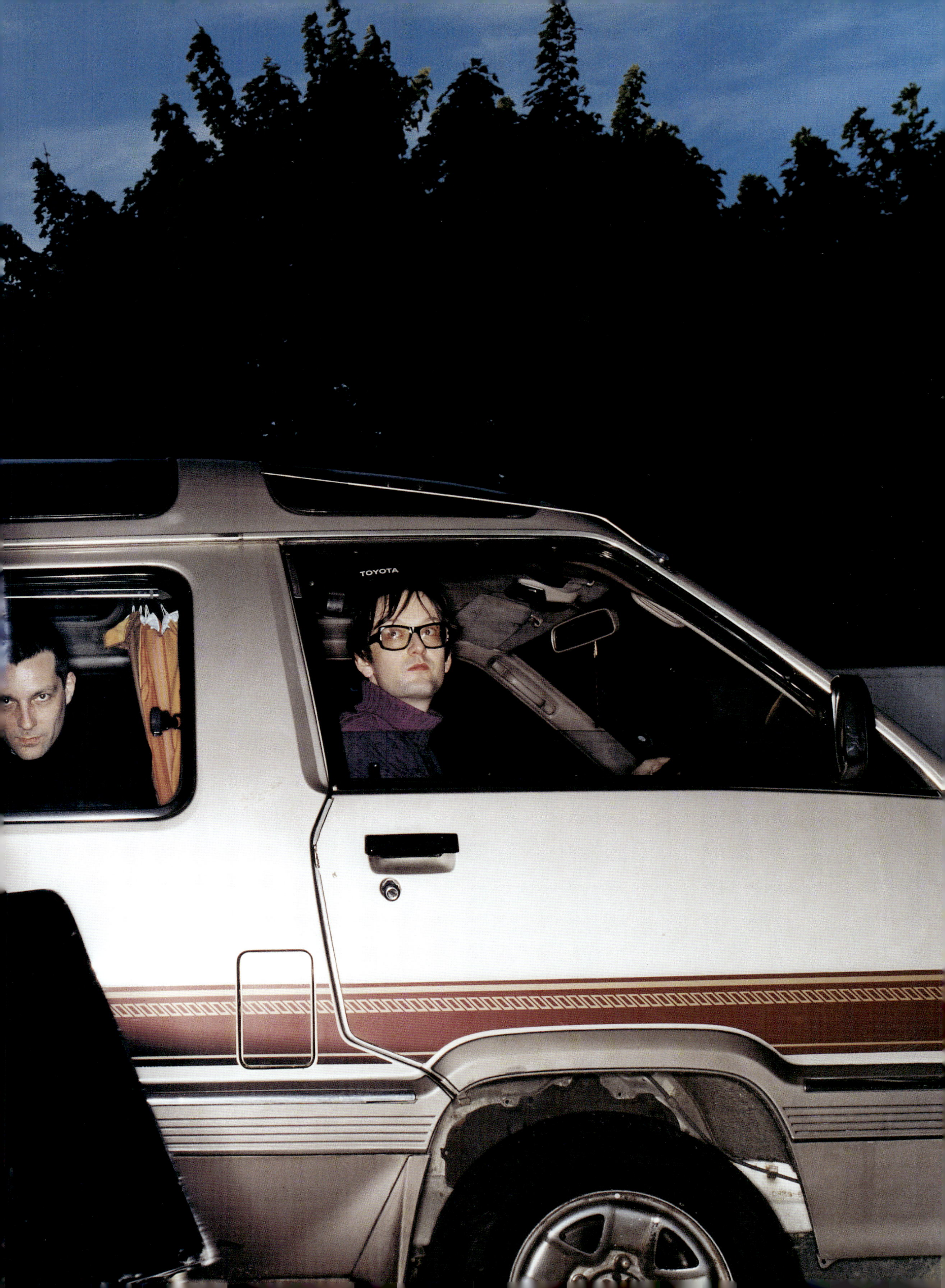
TOYOTA

# JARVIS

**IF YOU BUY INTO THE "CARS AS PENIS EXTENSIONS" THEORY, JARVIS COCKER MUST BE SECURE IN THE KNOWLEDGE HE'S PACKING A FEARSOME AMOUNT OF SHEFFIELD STEEL IN THOSE TROUSERS HE DROPPED FOR MICHAEL JACKSON.**
**TEXT ROB WAUGH**
**PHOTOGRAPHY RANKIN**

He clearly doesn't feel he needs to augment his natural allocation with a giant petrol-stinking 600bhp substitute. Fact is, Pulp's bard of the bedsit seems to have rarely set foot in a vehicle that can move above walking pace. What he has had is a string of long-term relationships with a collection of Britain's most dreadful vehicles, including the legendarily awful Austin Allegro. As you might expect, Jarvis thinks that being a pop star in a fast car is tacky, ugly, and "a bit Jamiroquai".

But since Pulp leapt into the charts after years of haunting John Peel's playlist, Jarvis has upgraded - to a four-wheel drive Toyota Town Ace. And that's just as unlikely as his Allegro to trouble Porsche drivers revving up for a challenge at the red lights. His most famous former drive, a Hillman Imp that cost only £250, currently resides in cubic form in a greenhouse in Doncaster, next to some tomato plants.

**You've admitted publicly to being a former member of the Hillman Imp fan club...**
There was a Hillman Imp Owner's Society - I'd like to say it wasn't a fan club. It was before we became known, and it was a purely practical thing. The main reason you joined that was you could get hold of spares, and you could get contacts for cheap insurance.
**But you drove a Hillman Imp for quite a long time.**
I owned one, yes, but I didn't buy it as a classic car. You see, I never liked them. It was the only car I could afford when I was at college. Not a bad car in some ways though - it's really simple, so you can understand how it works. I'm not really a mechanic-type person, but I could change a spark plug on the Imp. Plus, it was only £250. It lasted me six years, not bad value.
**And we understand you squeezed a little drop more value out of it once it conked out...?**
Well, I couldn't very well sell it - it was a death-trap really. And because I'd had it for so many years, I couldn't bear to just take it to the scrapyard. I wouldn't have got any money for it anyway. I had it crushed up into

## MAKE LOVE NOT WAR - SEE DRIVER FOR DETAILS

a cube, and then we had a competition in our fan club magazine for somebody to win it. I wanted to go to the scrapyard and press the button, you know, but I think we were on tour or something at the time. I wanted to have that full drama, maybe have the funeral march playing or something like that. But it wasn't to be. But at least it went to a good home.
**So where is it now?**
Well, this was three years ago, so I don't know if it's still there. It ended up in some girl's garden in Doncaster. It was occupying a thing that her dad had built to protect tomatoes from severe weather. I think all the tomatoes had died, but at least it was protected from the rain. But you know, she might have gone off us now, she might be into Usher or somebody. She might have got rid of it, because although it was quite a small car, it made quite a big cube.
**And what have you been driving since the cubing of the Imp?**
I've been driving a Toyota Town Ace Super Extra for the past two years. It's a people carrier, but it also has four wheel drive. But to be honest with you, the major selling point is that it has a fridge in the front between the two seats. Well, it's not just a fridge actually, it's got an ice maker, and it can also keep things warm, it's got a hot air blower. So if you've been to get a take away meal or whatever, you can keep it warm until you get home.
**So you didn't buy it with high speeds in mind?**
Well, I do floor it, but you have to floor it just to keep up with the other cars.
**Must be ideal for London then...**
Actually, although it's called Town Ace, if you use it for getting around in London it's a real pain. I really got it for excursions outside town. I don't know if I've mentioned this - ha, I sound like a salesman - but it's got these glass panels in the roof, so if you go to a safari park that's brilliant because you can see the giraffes looming over. And when the monkeys all climb on top of the car, you can really see 'em. Although it's slightly obscene because you can see their arseholes.
**So you only really use the car when you're packing a Thermos?**
Oh, I'm fully kitted up. I've even got one of those little compasses that you stick on the windshield. It's always falling off, but I like it. I used to have a stick-on thermometer, that told you how hot it was inside the car - really useful. I do like my accessories. I used to like car stickers a lot - you know, like Make Love Not War - See Driver For Details. My Father Said I'd Inherit An Estate - And This Is It. All those kind of things - I mourn the passing of those.

**Proper Sunday driving kit. So you don't use the motor to get around in London?**
If I'm just going for general getting around in London, I'll use the bicycle. I have to admit sometimes I do use the van for non-excursion things, but generally I try and keep it for weekends away or for special trips. Obviously occasionally I walk as well, at the moment especially, since the Town Ace is currently awaiting a verdict on whether it's going to live or not. I used it to drive up to my cousin's wedding, and the fan belt broke on the motorway. I set off from this wedding at midday, and I arrived at 10pm. The first AA man that they sent out strained his arm trying to undo some bolts. I had to get a taxi to Sheffield from Leicester. The van is still in Leicester being looked at. That weren't so good.

**You know how to pick them. What's the worst car you've ever owned?**
Well, the first car I ever owned was a VW Passat, which the guitarist in our group sold me. It broke down two weeks later, and that caused a little bit of friction. After that I had an Austin Allegro. That lasted quite a long time and then it just broke down. It was stuck outside the flat in Camberwell, and we had a party one weekend, and we had some games, and I made that the top prize. I said, 'Congratulations, you've won the car,' and gave them the keys for it and everything. They just left it there. I think some gypsies nicked it after a while.

**So you're not tempted by the idea of getting a sportscar now you've hit the big time?**
I've not got that Jamiroquai streak, no. Especially when you're in a band, I think if you're driving around in a red sports car you look a right tool. I used to really like Reliant Scimitars, I think they look really nice. When I see one of those, I stop and have a look. I don't know if I'll ever own one, I just like the look of them. That's about as sporty as I get.

**So it's been civilised little cars all the way. Don't you ever get up to anything antisocial behind the wheel?**
Well, I do like to drive with bare feet as much as possible. In summer it's great - you can really feel the pedal and feel the response of the car. I

## MY FATHER SAID I'D INHERIT AN ESTATE - AND THIS IS IT

don't know whether the passengers like that or not. And I have got three points on my license at the moment - just from those horrible little speed cameras. Also, I'm probably digging myself a hole here, but I actually find eating while driving quite tranquil. Not in a perverted way, but I quite like it. Well I guess when I'm doing that, it's a crime isn't it?

**I think it depends on whether you use cutlery...**
My other worst habit is fiddling with the radio when I'm supposed to be concentrating on driving. I really hate bad radio reception, and it really bugs me. That possibly makes my passengers slightly worried. I don't know if they find the eating slightly worrying as well. I don't do both at the same time.

**So you don't tend to make up your own Drive Time compilations, then?**
I think the radio is one of the great pleasures of driving. When the right song comes on at just the right time. I don't like listening to tapes because you always know what's coming next. With the radio, you obviously get a lot of crap, but when the right song comes on and you're travelling with the right people - it's quite a special thing. That's the best bit about driving.

**So what's been your worst driving moment?**
Well, I had one that was kind of bad, but in the end turned out to be kind of inspirational. When we used to rehearse up in Sheffield, and I still had the Imp, I left the rehearsal one night and it ran out of petrol. We used to rehearse in quite a dangerous part of Sheffield, so I tried to push it off the road, and I got it about half off the road. And then this car stopped with all these kids in it, aged about 15 and 16, and so I thought, 'Well they've nicked the car, obviously,' and I thought ,'Oh dear, I'm going to get beaten up here.' Well, it all turned out all right in the end, because they thought I was a bit of an idiot, and they said 'What's wrong?' and I said, 'Oh, I've run out of petrol.' They said, 'Get in the car.' So I ended up in this nicked Ford Orion, zooming around, and they took me to this petrol station to get some petrol. So it just shows you. People say joyriders are terrible, but they were very helpful to me. We had a song called "Joyriders" on *His'n'Hers*, which was kind of directly inspired by that.

**Lastly, just to check whether you're in touch or not - how much for a litre of diesel?**
Well, that depends where you're going, but if you're lucky, you can get a litre of diesel for about 77.9 pence. You'll pay more on the motorway.

# ZAHA HADID

161

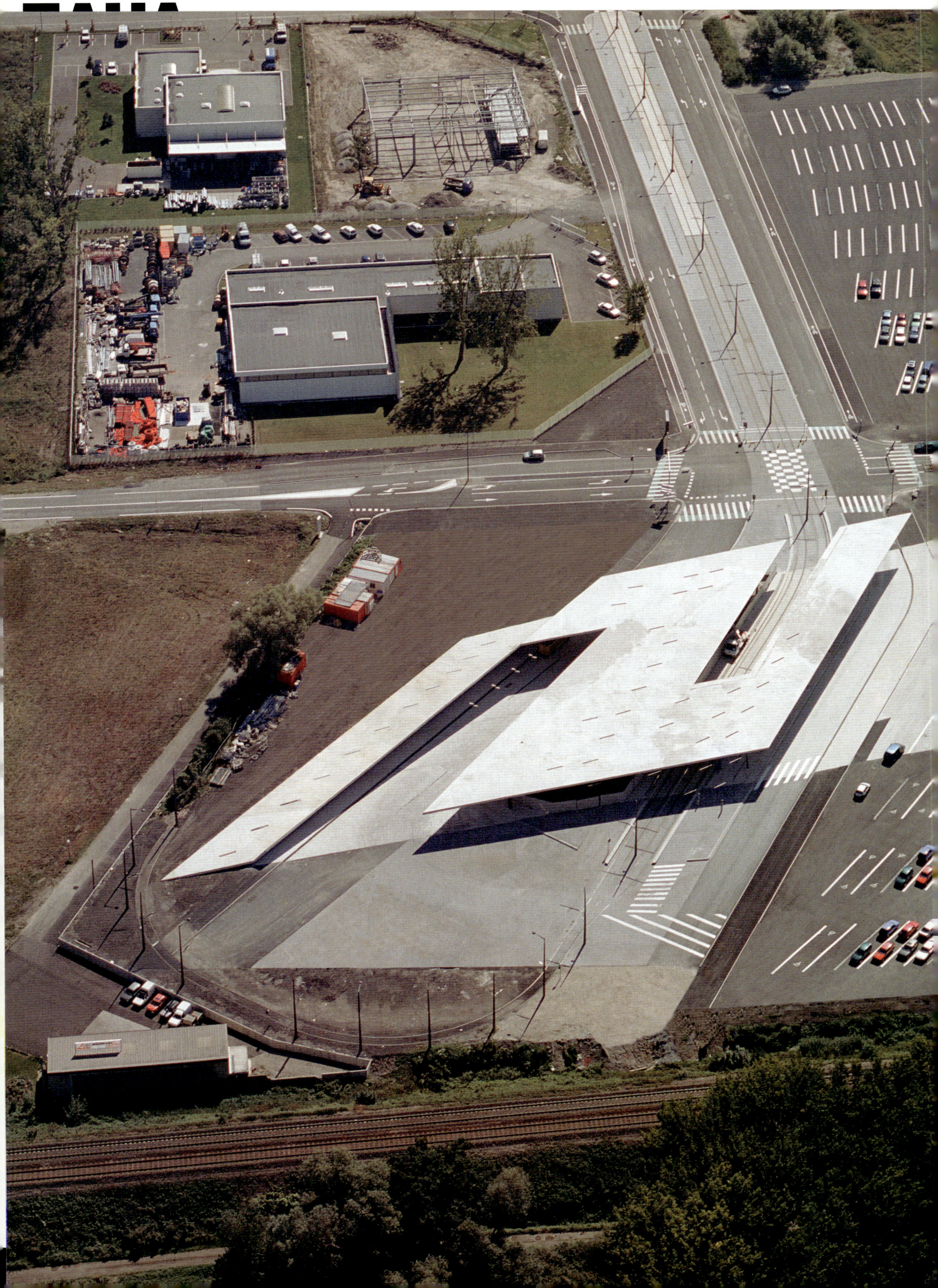

across the street, at oblique angles. They come out from one place and fork out, can go above or below."

For the Third Bridge Crossing in Abu Dhabi, Deputy Prime Minister Sheik Sultan bin Zayed Al Nahayan invited Hadid to design a symbolic gateway from the mainland to Abu Dhabi island. Hadid's concept is of a structural wave propelling across the creek, "They didn't want a suspension bridge. So we looked at the topography, the landscape and the dunes, and that is how it started. So the bridge starts at zero then slowly, gently goes up and comes down again."

Just as natural topography and landscape influence the form and organisation of Hadid's buildings, so do streetscapes and the urban grid. At the Cincinnati Arts Center, what Hadid calls the "urban carpet" - the urban fabric and street grid of Cincinnati - enters and generates the building; an access ramp starts as a gentle slope on the pavement flows up through the entrance hall and zigzags vertically through the building. The exhibition spaces that float over the lobby space, interlock like a three-dimensional jigsaw puzzle, made up of solids and voids. Several weeks on the Holloway Road designing the footbridge reinforced to Hadid the strained relationship between London and cars. "In the last few years people have had more money, more cars, they are trying to show off with them. And look how much retail has been happening here in London the last five years, and all this needs servicing. So all of this traffic has been piling up and nobody has thought about how to release it, it's insane. The government has not improved public transport or parking, they have made it much worse. They have to invent ways to deal with it, with public transport, underground car parking, inner ring roads." She concedes that New York and Tokyo are just as bad. "I was in New York three months ago and it was the worst traffic I have seen in years. It is a big problem because now there is a lot of building work going on, delivery vans for building materials,

*Left*: Aerial view of the Strasbourg tram station. Photography Roger Rothan
*Opening spread portrait*: Make-up Ayami using MAC

scaffolding, skips. Tokyo is a nightmare. You fly for 12 hours to get to Tokyo and then it'll take you three hours sometimes to get from the airport to the city. By the time you arrive you are in a coma." Does she do any sketching in the car? "No." Or read? "No." Or listen to music? "Sometimes. Driving is just a means to an end, to get from A to B."

If pushed, she admits to pleasurable memories of driving. "I used to like driving all over London late at night, over the river and back. Years ago we drove around Berlin for a whole day from east to west, which was really fantastic fun, and I spent a whole day recently driving in California, Los Angeles and San Francisco, which I really enjoyed. I

**I DON'T THINK PEOPLE ARE BORN INTELLIGENT OR STUPID BUT THERE ARE SOME PEOPLE WHO NEVER LISTEN, SO THEY NEVER LEARN ANYTHING**

went around San Francisco with my friend in a battery car, an electric-type car, and you can park them, charge them and use a credit card to pay for them, great idea. They charge up while they are parked. And you just rent them. And they had no sound, very quiet, so it was great going down these hills in San Francisco with no sound."

She confesses to a passing interest in car design. "I was interested three or four years ago how the whole car design changed, because I do watch them on the street. That is when I realised the economy was improving because you began to see a lot of new cars. They went from very boxy to very bulbous, like the new S-type Jaguars and the new Lotus and Audis. They became very blobby." She may soon take a more active interest in cars, as she has been shortlisted to design a "Car World" visitor centre for BMW in Munich. The concept will be similar to Volkswagen's Autostadt at Wolfsburg, a manufacturing facility combined with a £280m theme park, set among 25 hectares of landscaped gardens and lakes. Autostadt includes a car museum, a Ritz Carlton hotel, cafes, restaurants and pavilions dedicated to VW subsidiaries, designed by architects from all over Europe. Hadid was suitably impressed on a tour of Autostadt, which is near the site where she is designing the Science Museum: "Yes, its quite weird, it's quite nice. You start in a 1km-long corridor where you see the entire production line, assembly and all, it is unbelievable, there are these special boxes, like a little train, which drive you around the place. Then the Ritz Carlton is pretty good there, but it is strange listening to this esoteric music and watching this power station, totally surreal. Quite bizarre."

Is she is comfortable with the idea of car brands using signature architecture to seduce potential buyers with a lifestyle vision?

"I think it is okay. I mean in Germany they are into their cars in a big way. Have you ever been on a German motorway? You are sitting there on the autobahn and the surface is so beautifully made, there is nothing, it is like gliding. There is no speed limit in Germany. You can go 200mph. You can get to Frankfurt from Wolfsburg in an hour, two hours."

An anxious member of her staff whispering news of trouble with the Smart Car jolts her out of this wistful automotive reverie. Hadid throws up her hands and rolls her eyes. "He [the driver] forgot to put petrol in it. He thinks it drives itself. He says, 'I've got things on my mind,' and I say, 'Well you've got a job, why don't you think about that?' But he is one of those people who gave up thinking a long time ago. I don't think people are born intelligent or stupid but there are some people who never listen, so they never learn anything." Her exasperation is charming, and revealing. For Hadid, architecture is an all-consuming passion about which she never stops thinking. Her mind is seething with new dimensions, intersections of land and structure, light and space. She lives, sleeps, breathes her work and has no time for slackers in any walk of life. Let's hope Zaha's run of success lasts, for the greater beauty and dynamism of our cityscapes, and for the calmer nerves of the diligent young designers in her office.

*Below and right:*
Strasbourg tram station.
Photography Hélène Binet

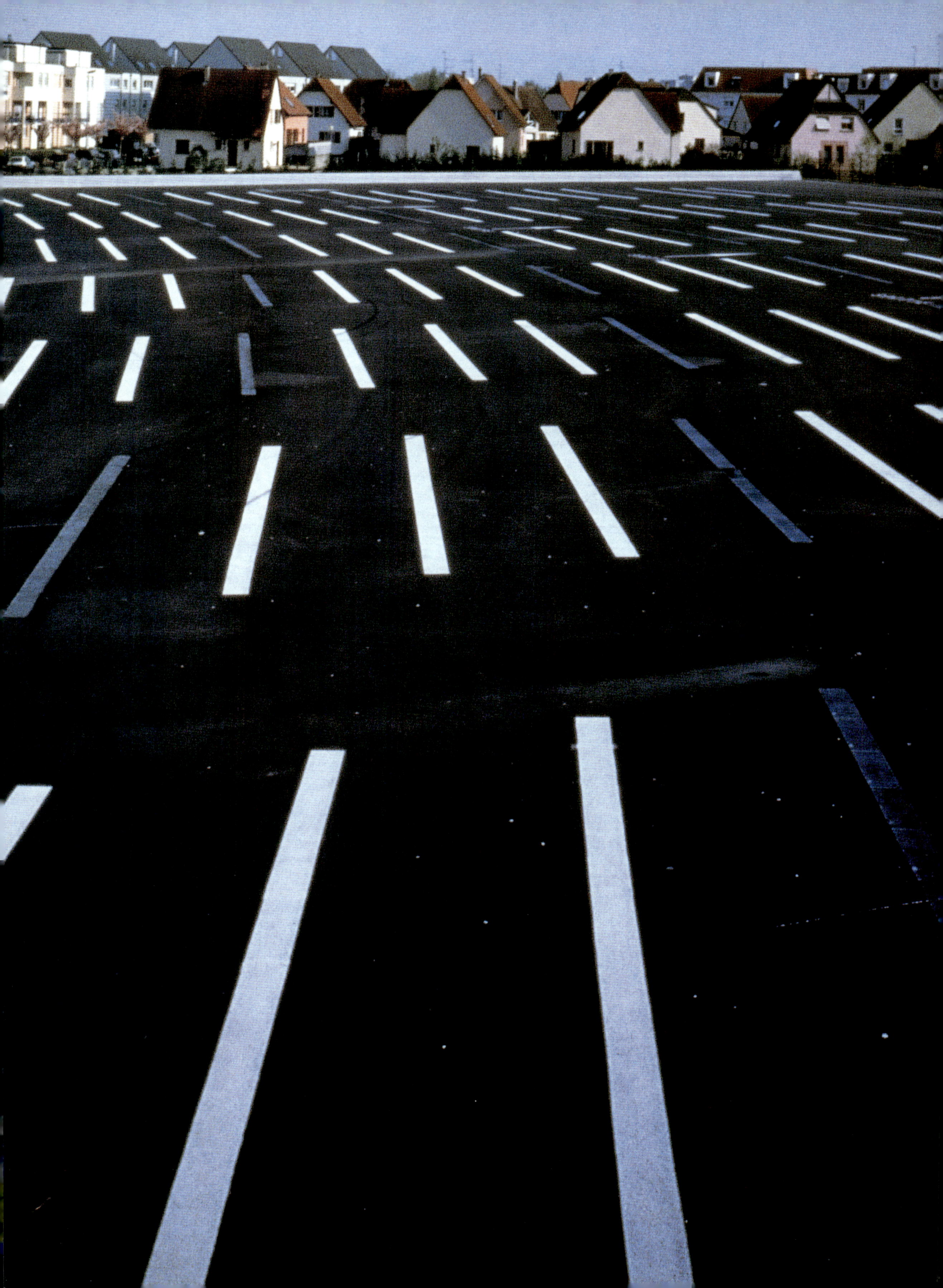

# STIRLING MOSS

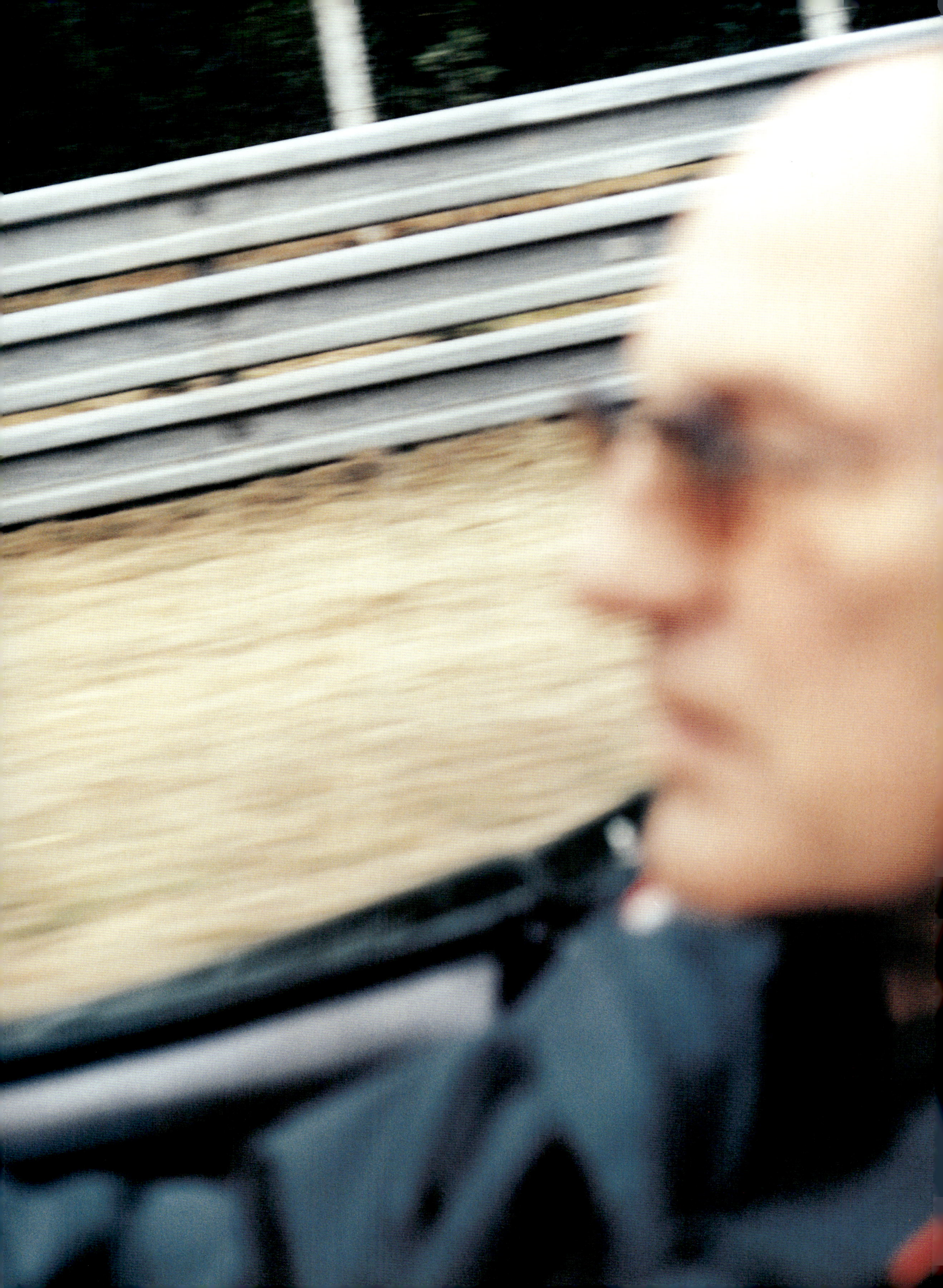

# STIRLING

**WHAT HAPPENS TO RACING DRIVERS WHEN THEY REACH PENSIONABLE AGE? FOR THIS ONE, THE ANSWER IS KEEP ON MOVING.**
**TEXT DAN ROSS**
**PHOTOGRAPHY NEIL MASSEY**

I'm on the phone talking to Stirling Moss, but before I can complete a sentence another call comes through and I'm put on hold. The Beach Boys' "*Something tells me I'm into something good*" replaces the well-spoken voice of the man who embodies the classic period of British motor racing. A national institution, he is the punchline of the traffic policeman's default sardonicism "125mph! Who do you think you are? Stirling-bloody-Moss?" Of course, even in his heyday half a century ago, before racing entered the space age, such a modest speed would mean something was wrong with the engine. As disco-pop favourite "Rock The Boat" by The Hues Corporation comes on, the phone clicks a few times, and an impatient Sir Stirling (he was knighted last year) comes back on the line to instruct me to call him back in a month, and then the line goes dead. Reassuringly, catching up with Stirling Moss still requires skill.

When I eventually manage to do so, it is in France, the day before the Le Mans 24-hour race. Jaguar are commemorating their first victory at the annual race half a century earlier by hosting a heritage event, and he was fulfiling his now honed role as guest of honour. He had led the victorious team in '51, but his own C-type, one of three of the gorgeously low slung racers competing, had bowed out due to mechanical failure, a common occurrence then, as now.

Stirling Moss started making a name for himself by winning his first race in '48 at the age of 18. A subsequent career of some 500 outings mixed numerous near-wins borne with sporting humility alongside equally abundant crowd-pleasing victories. At a time when many racers were wealthy hobbyists, he became one of the first true professionals, setting standards for personal fitness and pay. Known for his versatility, agility and flair but also for his command of racing's more obscure rules and regulations, he always competed fairly, but with an absolute, unreserved determination. It is this wholehearted participation, perhaps more than his record, that won him the accolade of greatest driver ever in his homeland. To this day, Stirling always raises his hand when he passes somebody on the track, a genius blend of grace and assertion. The wave lets the competitor know that they've not only been out-driven, but out-classed. His professional racing days ended with a near-fatal crash at Goodwood in '62. Now an ambassador for the sport, he is used to entertaining crowds, journalists, motoring professionals and enthusiasts with stories and spins down memory lane. It's a dismally wet weekend, and the open-top C-type has just done a circuit in a torrential downpour. We climb in (no doors) and a '51-era mechanic, wiping down the car, says, "They brought it out the factory especially for you, Sir." It's a scene reminiscent of an RAF engineer talking to a Spitfire pilot about to take off in a government-

## OUT OF THE WAY, ROADHOG!

spun war film. Seeing the cliché of bonhomie between the good honest mechanic and the heroic driver enacted is unexpectedly touching. Sir Stirling is the archetypal populist peer and patriot in a country that likes to think of itself as embodied by the qualities with which he is associated. Driving round the drizzly track in the model he once raced at 150mph, scores of British spectators cheer, and the famous arm is raised. At one point, two men streak past, naked, to the cheers of the same crowd. We pass a group of kids, aged between perhaps eight and 11, and they too start to shout. As Stirling raises his arm, one of them raises a super-soaker water pistol back. Shooting a long stream of tight-packed water at his face, it catches him off guard. I feel instinctively protective - he is, after all, a man in his 70s - and he's driving the car I'm in, a car without seatbelts, invented long before the airbag. But an instant later, he has regained his composure. "Out of the way, road hog!" he shouts, out of earshot, at a bicycle wobbling around the centre of the road ahead. Stirling doesn't let anything slow him down.

**How are you finding it today?**
It's fairly tiring. Quite a lot of rushing around. But the circuit is interesting. It is not as nice as I remember the old one, but then the old circuit would not be acceptable to these faster cars, so that's just the way it goes.

**What about the event in general?**
Other than the fact that I have no idea where I am, and I keep going to places that I thought I knew, which are now something else. I think it's incredible, I mean the amount of people around, the way the organisation works is quite surprising.

**...and the atmosphere?**
It's always been like this. There was always a lot of buzz.

**People running naked in the road...**
I must say that was the first time I've seen that. Pity it was guys and not girls. It doesn't surprise me except it is *bloody* cold.

**How do you spend your time these days?**
I spend my year doing promotions and PR appearances. Personal appearances here, or Australia for instance. I go there for the Grand Prix to assist on promotions on television or radio or meeting people and lectures and talks - anything they pay me for. I'm a sort of an international prostitute really, I suppose. If I like the product, I'll go.

**Is that a tradition?**
Well, no, the point is that I've got to make a living. When I was racing, although I was the highest paid driver in the world, and I was doing 57 races a year, I mean my total gross income was £32,700, which in today's money is over half a million, but by the time I paid my expenses and so on, I paid tax on £8,000, which in today's money is about £100,000, which was good money. But if I was racing now... I mean Michael Schumacher does 16 races a year and takes about $70 million. So it's reasonable that doing 57 and winning about half of them, I'd have made quite a lot of money. But that isn't the way it was.

**Do you feel you were born 50 years too early?**
No. I would not swap my time for now. No way. I mean I just wouldn't.

**How do you feel it's different now?**
Now, a driver doesn't respect another driver for his ability, but for the money he earns. It's totally different. The world's different. When I was brought up you behaved in a certain way and now you don't. I mean, now people buy jeans that have got slits in them

because it's fashionable. It's all very different now.
**Do you think your own outlook presaged the current approach to maximising income?**
See, I'm very lucky because I'm glad to say my name has a value when I go and do these things, therefore I'm able to enjoy myself and run the life I enjoy taking part in. If I hadn't made the name then I'd have to work for a living.
(*At this point, Stirling pauses to consider what this would have been like following his crash-enforced retirement.*)
I mean, it would've been a hell of a shock. (*Laughs*) It's just that because drivers are still very difficult to get hold of... I mean if you want to rent a driver for a day, for whatever, it's going to cost you tens of thousands, and you're not going to get them... therefore, I can fill in those gaps so it's very good. And now particularly with this sort of heritage stuff - like Jaguar here and so on - it's wonderful, because they run it very efficiently and they are nice people. And it gives me the opportunity of driving the most beautiful cars in the world as far as I'm concerned. I mean I have no wish to jump in an Audi - I'd like to try the Audi but it wouldn't be my pleasure like it would today with the Jag.
**What do you think of the new Jaguar X-type?**
I'm hoping to try one tomorrow. I haven't tried it yet. I'm thinking of getting one [Moss currently drives a Mercedes 500SL and a Piaggio scooter]. I'm holding back on my decision until I've tried the whole lot.
**So what do you do apart from racing appearances these days?**
I'm in property. I have houses and apartments I've bought and modified, and I rent them out.
**Do you go round to collect the rent yourself?**
No, I have a company that collects the rent - they do nothing else. But it's very much hands on. I mean if anything goes wrong, if a washing machine doesn't work or something, I will go round to the property and see if I can mend it.
**How do your tenants appreciate you doing that?**
I think they're quite surprised, some of them. I write my own leases on my word processor, and I check on the inventory quite often, things like that. And when they leave, I go round to check because I know I've got to get builders or decorators to come in and refurbish the place. So I'm very much hands on.
**How does that compare in terms of buzz to racing?**
It's amazing. When I go to a place on my scooter to look at a washing machine, if I'm able to put it right and go away, I get the same buzz I would being in pole position. (*Laughs*) I think, well, I've saved myself 70 quid which thankfully I can afford, but I feel great for it, you know.
**What do you think that says about the way that society puts certain experiences up on a pedestal as if they are incomparable?**
I mean, it's to each his own really.

**WHEN I GO TO A PLACE ON MY SCOOTER TO LOOK AT A WASHING MACHINE, IF I'M ABLE TO PUT IT RIGHT AND GO AWAY, I GET THE SAME BUZZ I WOULD BEING IN POLE POSITION**

**But if you can get the same buzz out of an everyday...**
Yes, but you see, you can't. I think if I hadn't raced I wouldn't get the same buzz. If I'd been a plumber and I'd fixed the washing machine I'd have got no buzz at all in terms of satisfaction. But because I'm a world famous racing driver, I feel like it's an achievement. It's an enormous achievement. And the same way, if I go along to negotiate a deal with somebody, if I'm able to negotiate a good contract the way I want it, and if the person I'm selling my time to is happy, then I feel a great satisfaction in that.

As Sir Stirling talks, he inserts: "I mean", "Well", and "You see", so as to keep talking constantly, like an engine ticking over. He starts talking, then spots a clearer line of attack, and powers through unfazed by the rapid verbal application of brakes, accelerating to his point. The cadence of his voice gives further expression to a restless nature. He speaks freely and directly, and careers across lanes of engagement and gear shifts of temperament to slip deftly from personable raconteur to corporate spokesman, international icon to unreconstructed patriot.

**Where do you live?**
I live in London W1. Mayfair, right by Hyde Park Corner.
**Nice area?**
Oh yeah. I couldn't live anywhere but the centre of the world. I like the buzz.
**Do you think London's the centre of the world?**
Oh absolutely, absolutely. Beats the world at everything. There are other places I enjoy going to, and there are lots of things wrong with England. I mean the thought of the Euro, and all this joining of the EC to me is appalling.
**Why is that?**
Because I'm terribly pro-English. I mean the fact the cars aren't painted green I think is awful. I think we've done so much to contribute to the world and now they're going to take away our sovereignty. I personally am very pro the royal family. I won't say this particular royal family, but the idea of having royals to me is miles better than having a dictator or whatever you want to call it.
**People don't seem to want that sort of hierarchy anymore.**
I don't think they do. I think I'm out of step in some ways, I must agree. But the thought of England being a republic is to me very upsetting. But then as you get older, you don't like to see change. Change is something you don't understand.
**In the '50s, your preference was always to drive English cars.**
Yes, I've always been very much a loyalist, and very proud to be English and win with an English car. That's always been terribly important to me. We've always led the way in style and many other things - music and god knows what else.
**What kind of music do you like?**
I like '50s, '60s. I like blues. I like rhythm. I like things that you can sing with a lyric. I don't like these things that go "la la la, di di di."
**What do you listen to when you're driving?**
I listen to Melody FM because I enjoy that. Or I like some of the jazz ones. I'm not mad for heavy rock stuff. You see I remember when I was a kid and you could whisper in the girl's ear. Nowadays you go to a dance...
**And you have to shout, so it's not as romantic?**
No. Romance isn't around now so much as it was.

**JUTTA
KLEINSCHMIDT**

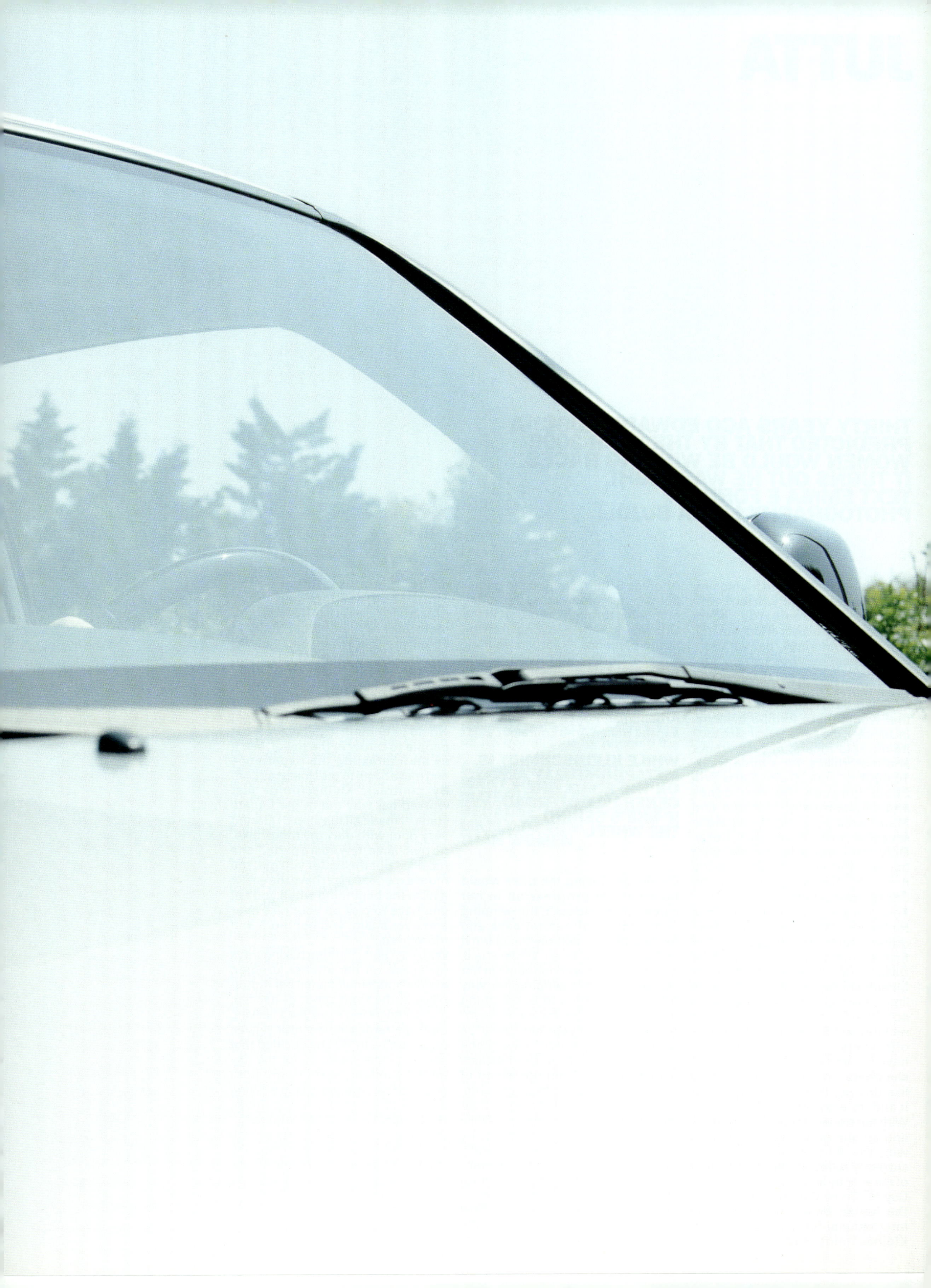

**MARC NEWSON**

CHILWORTH STREET W2
CITY OF WESTMINSTER
DEVONSHIRE TERRACE W2
CITY OF WESTMINSTER

# MARC

**ADDING A RADICAL CAR CONCEPT TO HIS PORTFOLIO OF LUXURY INTERIORS AND LIMITED EDITIONS, MARC NEWSON'S VISION COULD BE ON THE ROAD SOONER THAN YOU THINK**
INTERVIEW YORGO TLOUPAS
PHOTOGRAPHY EWEN SPENCER

Marc Newson's work is stamped with Duplo simplicity, solid functionality, and a technical sophistication, the trademarks that have made him a cult designer. The versatile Australian designer's smooth, organic curves and bold primary colours have been applied to a staggering range of limited edition projects and mass market products including bathroomware, lighting, furniture, watches, the interior of a Falcon private jet, a bicycle, and countless interiors for ultra-chic restaurants and shops. After studio-hopping from Syndey to Tokyo to Paris, Newson is now living and working in London where he's currently crafting the interior and livery of a new airline, a camera for a Japanese company and a residential development. However, probably his most exciting design to date is the Ford 021C concept car.

Ford's Vice President of Design, J Mays, singled out Newson to conceive a car for the millennium Tokyo Motor Show, that would excite the imagination and tap into the consciousness of a younger generation of potential Ford fantastics. The result is an extraordinary vehicle, the meeting of a kindergarten line drawing and a retro-futuristic urban car, it is Newson's creation from the long single lights at each end to the tread on the custom-made Pirelli tyres. Named after the pantone reference for the original brilliant mandarin colour of the car's carbon fibre shell, the boxy shape plays host to a spacious interior which includes swivel chairs, doors that open out like a wardrobe and a boot that slides out like a drawer. It's a special car that clearly merits the high fashion Prada luggage which was tailor-made for it.

The dapper designer talked to Intersection at his immaculately decorated green and orange West London apartment.

**Why have so few major 20th century designers, apart from Raymond Loewy, designed a car?**
It's bizarre. Well I did a car. I think Starck had some experience with Renault or some car company. It was really a study, nothing ever really happened, but he did that motorcycle for Aprillia. I don't know, I think the car companies have just become... It's certainly not the fault of the designers, I think it's more the fault of car companies that they've become increasingly conservative and they've become really out of touch with the culture.

**Corbusier did design a concept car, but it was a prototype and it never got produced. These relationships seem to be style exercises. Car-only designers remain in the shadow.**
It's a different type of design, a much more institutional way of working. Car designers study in car design schools and they only study car design. I'm sure they're not obliged to know anything about fashion or painting or architecture. They're not even obliged to know anything about the world of design. So it's a very insular world and of course a lot of these designers, they get jobs with car companies and they have to go live in Detroit or Frankfurt or Hiroshima or some shitty place. It's a strange industry.

**So it's quite good for the inertia of the car industry that people like you are able to make a mark on it.**
Yes, it's great to have that opportunity but I also think that car companies have become so introspective and self-referential that they've never even thought to ask other people. They just assume that nobody knows anything about cars. It's a very arrogant industry as well.

**Did you feel you could help things evolve, or was it a completely closed world?**

The car industry's view is one thing but the public's is another. I found that when I did my project with Ford that the public was incredibly receptive, certainly the public that is exposed to what I do. You can say it's a very marginal group of people but the point is when I'm designing something, I'm coming from a completely different view. I'm attacking the problem from the opposite direction than typical car design would, which can only help to have different perspectives on automobile industry and culture. I am an absolute car fanatic. I'm obsessed with cars as much as car designers are obsessed with cars, so I do have some knowledge about car culture.

**So what are the most striking differences in approach between you and regular car designers? When designing this car were your thought processes very different?**
I think every aspect of the way I work is quite different from car designers. On an individual level to a corporate level. In every stage it's a completely different way of working. We're much smaller, I can do anything I want. People engage me to do what I do best and I design things myself. Cars are designed by committee you know.

**How much of what you had in mind in the beginning appeared in the finished car?**
As you pointed out, this kind of thing hasn't really happened before, this kind of collaboration between a designer and automotive company, especially a company like Ford which is amongst the biggest. But working with J Mays, he really understood that the whole point of this exercise was that I should be given as much freedom as possible otherwise it would be like sabotaging the whole project... I had complete freedom. But having said that there were obviously a lot of constraints. There were strict parameters to work within, but I never really considered that those parameters were unrealistic or inhibiting. That was just the framework you had to work within. You need that. I'm also quite practical in the way I approach things so it's helpful.

1
Ford 021C
(In lime version)

2
Aston Martin DB4
(Current car)

3
Citroën DS
(A favourite)

4
Fiat 124 coupé
(First car)

5
Lamborghini Miura
(Currently being purchased)

Illustrations by Yorgo Tloupas

**Is there any chance of it being produced at one time or another.**
To be honest it hasn't really been ruled out yet, it's still in the process of being studied for feasibility, so I can't really say yes or no, just maybe.

**Would you drive it?**
I definitely would have one, oh yes, absolutely. Me and all my friends.

**How would you react if someone was to buy one and customise it?**
I would find it really amusing. And one of the things I really wanted to do was - I had those ideas of making modifications myself, of doing big flared wheel arches, of turning it into a rally car. You know you could really change the character of the car. To the purist I can imagine it could be quite irritating. I like cheesy things, I like the irreverence of that kind of modification. No, if it ever got to the point where it got so mainstream to do those modifications I would be really happy because it would mean the car had reached - permeated - every level of society.

**Is this car the 'ultimate' designer achievement in the sense that it's a mass production object, but at the same time a status symbol. Is it on a level above furniture?**
In a sense I really think that it is. Certainly I think it's the most important project I've worked on. A plane's a one off, and the interiors and parameters you work with are very restrictive. With the car I really had an opportunity to do every single thing right down to the tyre grip and if that were to go into production, it would have a life of its own after me, then that's the ultimate kind of achievement somehow. And especially to do it with an object with as much cultural significance as a car. I feel that culturally in terms of the 20th century it's one of the most important objects. And if we're talking furniture or design in general, a car incorporates every other type of design I do; from furniture to products to lights to engineering. You name it, it's all in there somehow.

**What was your first car?**
My first car was a Fiat 124, it was a piece of shit. It went really well but it was kind of a disaster - I abandoned it in the end.

**Its shape isn't that far from the 021C.**
In a way I guess it's true. It's got a very naïve profile. You're right. Even in terms of size; it was tiny. Although I didn't have that car for very long - I graduated quickly to a Citroen DS. They were very popular in Australia. They were actually assembled in Australia until the '70s. They were very popular in rural parts because the suspension could go up and down and they weren't front wheel drive.

**So what cars would you not condemn in terms of design, what carmakers are going in the right direction at the moment, if any?**
I think the automotive industry is really in... it maybe getting a little better right now, but personally I don't think it's been in a worse situation. In the last year or two it seems Audi have been doing pretty interesting things. I mean Audi has had an exceptional ten years. But it's certainly not typical of the industry. I think Ford is starting to come up with some interesting things and the new Aston Martins are looking pretty good.

**It seems like the designing of a nice car is reserved for sports cars, and then for the rest of the range they just forget about making a beautiful car with sexy shapes. That's why I think it's interesting that the 021C is not a sports car at all, but it's very slick.**
It's an interesting point. You can really divide the world into super sports cars and everything else. Of course if someone said to me, 'You have to buy a new car, what would you buy?' it would be an Aston Martin or Ferrari. Of course it doesn't take a genius to figure that out, they shouldn't really be included in the equation. We should really be talking about the mass market. In which case I wouldn't know what to choose. I guess at the end of the day that's one of the best things about it.

**Why do car designers still use those terrible felt-pen sketches?**
That is one of my pet hates as well. When I was working amongst a lot of car designers in the thick of the car industry, I was more or less living in the car factory and you see that stuff day in day out. It's become the common language of communication amongst car designers, it's like the point of entry. If you can't do that sketch you can't even get a job. One of the problems with that is that it has nothing to do with design but everything to do with the way you present an idea even if the idea is shit. I can't do that, I'm absolutely unable to because I was never taught how to do it. They must spend inordinate amounts of training to do car sketches like that.

**I've been taught to do that. It was awful, very strict...**
And it's also the style of drawing. Those very bold lines and everything is completely exaggerated like the size of the wheels, ridiculously large and things are completely disproportionate - don't think I could look at another one of those drawings. One of the things I will not do is present my ideas like that, I do it in a much more restrained way, perhaps it's an older style of drawing like they did in the '40s and '50s. It's much more refined.

**What are you doing right now?**
It's difficult to actually talk about it right now but I will say my collaboration with Ford is to continue and that our experience so far has been really great with the 021C. In particular, working with J Mays, we have a great relationship, and it's developing into future projects. But we'll see - you'll be the first to know.

# TODD TERRY
# "LITTLE" LOUIE VEGA

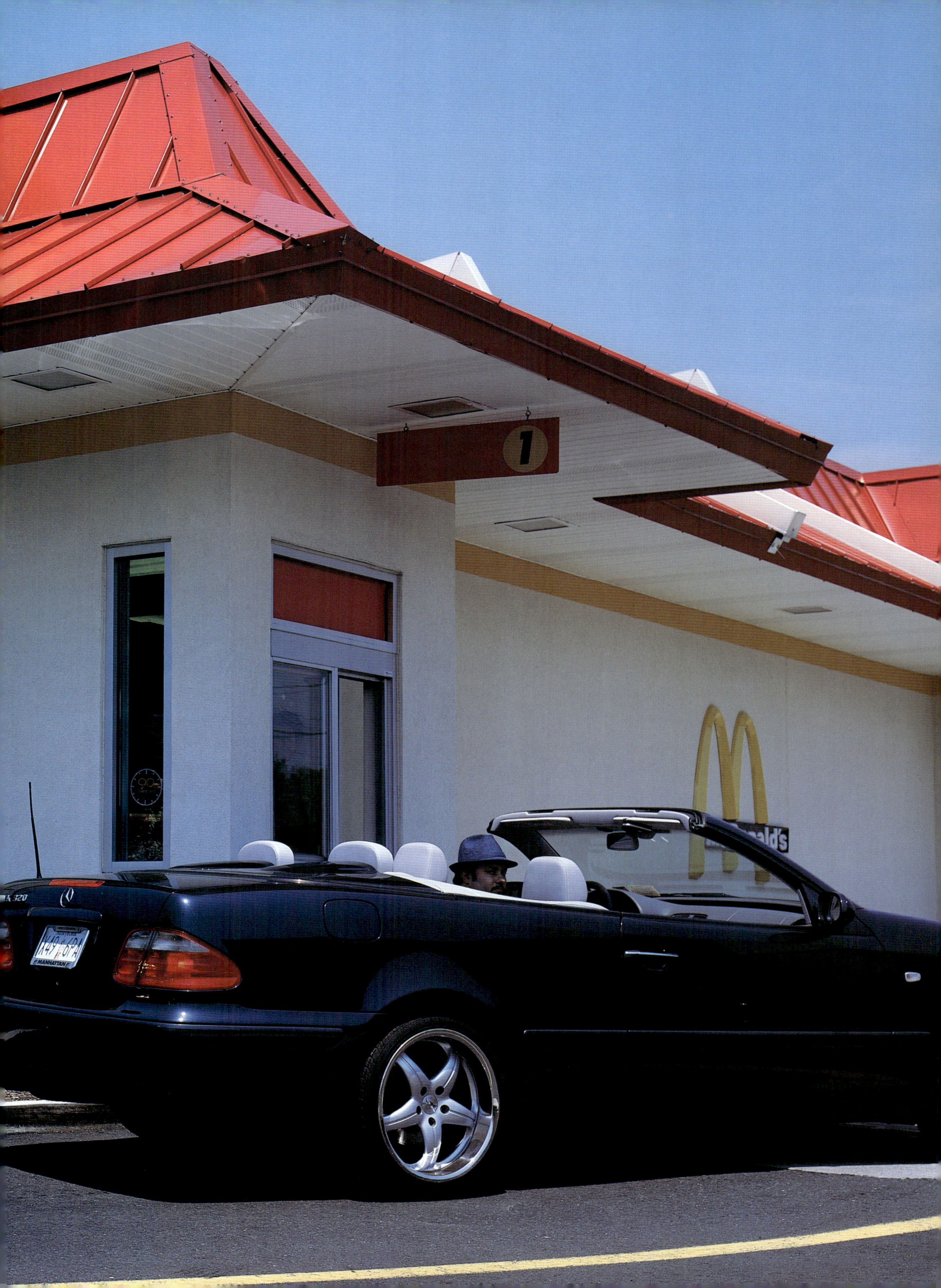
1

# TODD & LOUIE

**TWO OF THE BEST CUSTOMERS AT RAYCO'S IN NEW JERSEY SHARE A STAKE IN HOUSE MUSIC AS WELL AS A PENCHANT FOR ALLOY RIMS.**

TEXT JOSEPH PATEL
PHOTOGRAPHY RISHAD MISTRI

American music culture is not quite the melting pot you might think it would be. Even in a nightlife Mecca like New York City, artists are rather self-contained and you rarely see club DJs and, say, rappers sharing a drink together. There are, though, three things that will unequivocally unite this diaspora: money, women and... well... cars. These playthings are properly pimped, tricked and decorated to reflect their owners' conceit. The shinier the car, the bigger the rep. It's a common libation shared by even the most fledgling street-savvy star. Which is why a rapper like Jadakiss from New York's Ruff Ryders crew - himself the proud owner of a new BMW X5 SUV - couldn't tell you a single track produced by legendary New York house DJ Todd Terry, but could certainly describe in detail Terry's 2001 blue GMC Suburban truck with 22" rims, or "dubs". Motor vehicles like these are extensions of ego and identity in NYC, as elsewhere.

So here we are today just 15 minutes beyond the George Washington Bridge in Little Ferry, New Jersey, a small industrial suburb of Manhattan that is home to the Rayco Rim Shop. From the outside, Rayco is a nondescript storefront with a narrow parking lot adjacent to a local McDonalds. Rayco's is a favourite hotspot of Terry - an avid collector of cars since he was old enough to drive without sitting on someone else's lap - as well as hip-hoppers (Funkmaster Flex, Ruff Ryders), basketballers (Stephon Marbury) and American footballers (the New York Giants).

Todd Terry is a lasting icon of New York's mid and late '80s house music scene. Chicago was certainly house's capital but, by infusing the suavity of disco in its uptempo jiggle, Terry pioneered the distinctive New York sound, creating some of the biggest hits in clubland. He also helped develop the hip-house fusion and revitalised the flagging career of pop group Everything But The Girl.

Initially, Todd was hoping to hang out today with his friends "Little" Louie Vega and Kenny "Dope" Gonzalez, the duo collectively known as Masters At Work. His history is inextricably linked with Vega and Gonzalez. In

Todd Terry at Rayco's Rim Shop, New Jersey

1987, Terry borrowed the Masters At Work moniker from Gonzales to score one of his biggest singles, "Alright, Alright". A year later, Terry introduced the two up and coming New York DJ/producers to each other, and - both of Puerto Rican heritage, loving the same music old and new - they discovered they had plenty in common. If Terry was an influential force for dance music in the '80s, Vega and Gonzales' collaboration as Masters At Work came to shape how dance music moved forward in the '90s. Their mix of Latin, jazz and disco-style beats was infectious, their trademark giving popstars from Debbie Gibson to Madonna a whole new identity with a dance audience. Masters At Work's many side projects include NuYorican Soul, a super-project fusing Latin and house that included contributions from musical heroes including Tito Puente, Roy Ayers and George Benson.

Terry met us at Rayco, eager to show off his GMC truck. It's one of at least eight cars he owns at any one time. Vega, who only keeps two cars, joins late, telling us that Gonzales isn't showing up because his car's in the shop. "It'd be like coming to a gun fight without a gun," he muses.

**Todd, describe your ride and what you did to it.**
**Todd Terry:** It's a 2001 Suburban. I've had it for about a year. Got 22" rims on it. Got a Billy grill on it, which is the hottest grill you can get. The Z-9 lights, that's really hype. Nobody really has them. I special ordered them. Really, it's the rims that make it hot. (*Pointing to the side of the truck*) Here's my lucky nick. Each car I have gets a lucky scratch and I leave it. I figure, why fix it, you know?
**What about the inside?**
**TT:** Inside, I didn't do nothing. Everything is standard.
**No video screens or PlayStations?**
**TT:** Naw, this is my hang-out, family car. I'm not gonna put TV screens in the back for somebody else, unless I'm sitting back there (*Laughs*). I'm not getting TVs for nobody else, that shit is crazy. My kids got enough toys to play with. They don't need nothing.
**Who does this impress more, you or someone else?**
**TT:** This is a like a street thing, you know. Ride around the neighbourhood. A truck with rims is more impressive than a car with rims, though.
**So are rims like dick size? The bigger the better?**
**TT:** Naw, you gotta find the ones that fit. Like the only reason I put 22s on my car is because they fit. Look how big the wheels are - 17s or 18s would've looked stupid. Some cars, you wonder, 'Why'd you have to go with 20s? 18s would've looked just as good, if not better.' My Benz CL600, I had 20s on there and I cracked two rims. They were Lowenhards, $1,500 a piece. That's $3,000 for one pothole. (*Laughs*)
**What other cars do you have?**
**TT:** My Benz I got rid of, and then what I did was trade in my [Mercedes Benz] CL600 and my '99 Bentley for a 2001 Bentley. So I have that and a 360 Ferrari Modena. It's in the shop now, though.
**I didn't think you were living like that with no pop hits!**
**TT:** (*Laughs*) Well, you know. Then I got a '70 Mustang Coup. Then I got a '70 Mustang convertible, blue with cream. I've always been a car fanatic. I keep them in my house here in Jersey and I have another house in Long Island.
**Do you remember your first car?**
**TT:** The first car I ever had was a '76 Cutlass Supreme, white with black interior. I never had any money to hook it up with anything, but that was the car back in the days. Then I got a Camaro I bought off one of my friends for like $2,500. It took me a while to pay him. I was paying him like $200 at a time. After that my next car was a Benz. From there I had Benz, Jaguar, BMWs. I must have had like, 35 cars.
**What do the ladies think of the truck?**
**TT:** Yeah, you know, it's always a head-turner. (*Laughs*) If my girlfriend doesn't catch me. It is definitely a head-turner. You pull up with this truck and, you know, girls like the trucks. They like cars but a truck says something about a motherfucker.

> **THAT'S THE THING WITH NEW YORK, MAN. YOU CAN'T HAVE BEAUTIFUL RIMS AND A LOW PROFILE - ONE POTHOLE AND IT'S ALL GONE**

**But guys pull up too.**
**TT:** Every guy that pulls up to me is like, 'Yo, those 22s? Regular Suburban?' The rims and the grill make the car look so different. Drive it down any block and people are like, 'What the fuck is that?'

(*"Little" Louie Vega joins us*)

**Louie, tell me about this convertible you have.**
**Little Louie Vega:** The [Mercedes Benz CLK] 320. It's a '98 and I got it at the end of '97 I think.
**You're not like Todd then, trading in your cars every year?**
**LL:** No, I keep them for a few years. I was a BMW man before, but I turned Merc with this convertible.
**They say once you've had Merc…**
**LL:** (*Laughs*) It's a great car.
**And your rims?**
**LL:** These are Anteras, 18s. I hurt them bad. That's the thing with New York, man. You can't have beautiful rims and a low profile - one pothole and it's all gone.
**What other cars do you have?**
**LL:** I've got a Land Rover. I used to have the Defender 90. I traded it in. I got a family now so I'm thinking family car. I'm getting rid of this one in July and I'm getting a [Mercedes Benz] 500. I'm gonna have my child in the back seat. That's why I'm switching cars, he don't fit in here. It's a great car, it's a convertible and it's a lot of fun. But when you have a family, it's a little crampy. You need to go a little bigger.
**That's it, those two?**
**LL:** That's it. Todd's the one with the cars. He's got tons of cars, and he's been through a lot of cars as well. I went over to Todd's place and he's got a Bentley over there, he's got that beautiful truck over there. He's got a Merc. He's got room for them, too. You've got to have big garages to fit all the cars.
**So Todd, give me a quick critique of my man's car here.**
**TT:** CLK320, he's got Anteras on there. Louie breaks like ten rims a year (*Laughs*). He breaks BMW rims, which is like impossible. I don't know how he does it.
**LL:** I went through seven of those BMW rims. And that one's got a dent on there. (*Points to right side, back*)
**TT:** Yeah, I see that already. Damn. See, Louie decides to hit the potholes. He just hits it. He's listening to music, so he doesn't care about nothing else when he's listening to music. So if he hears a good record, he's just dancing, dancing, dancing - blaaawh - but he's still going, dancing, dancing.
**When you drive, what do you listen to? Todd says his truck is strictly hip hop, no house.**
**LL:** I listen to other people's stuff. Anything from jazz, soul to Latin music. I listen to some other DJs who give me stuff. I love listening to lounge CDs as well. It's a combination of different things. It depends on what mood I'm in. When Missy's album came out, that was on all the time.
**What do you think of Todd's truck?**
**LL:** I love that truck. I saw it for the first time when we were working on a remix for Todd. I'd never seen it before and I was blown away. It was looking real neat. It's slamming.
**TT:** It's just the rims, that's what they're into. It's a regular Suburban.
**LL:** It's amazing what a set of rims can do. He put rims on that car and it changed the whole thing. If you see that truck regularly, it's a day and night thing. It makes me want to buy a truck like that. (*Laughs*)
**Now you've both got families so you're getting trucks.**
**TT:** You gotta have a truck.
**LL:** (*Laughs*) Kids.
**TT:** The girl and the kids man. You got no other choice. You have to grow up.
**What kind of car does Kenny drive?**
**LL:** What's Kenny got?
**TT:** The 500.
**LL:** Kenny's got the (Mercedes Benz CL) 500 coupe.
**Do you get competitive with your cars at all?**
**LL:** No, we have fun with them, you know. It's more like, 'Yo, that car is dope.' Somebody always gets a newer car, you know, especially this guy over here. (*Laughs, pointing to Todd*) And we couldn't get competitive with Todd over there, with his car show.
**TT:** I'm car crazy. I need help.

# SYLVIE FLEURY

SHE-DEVILS
ON WHEELS

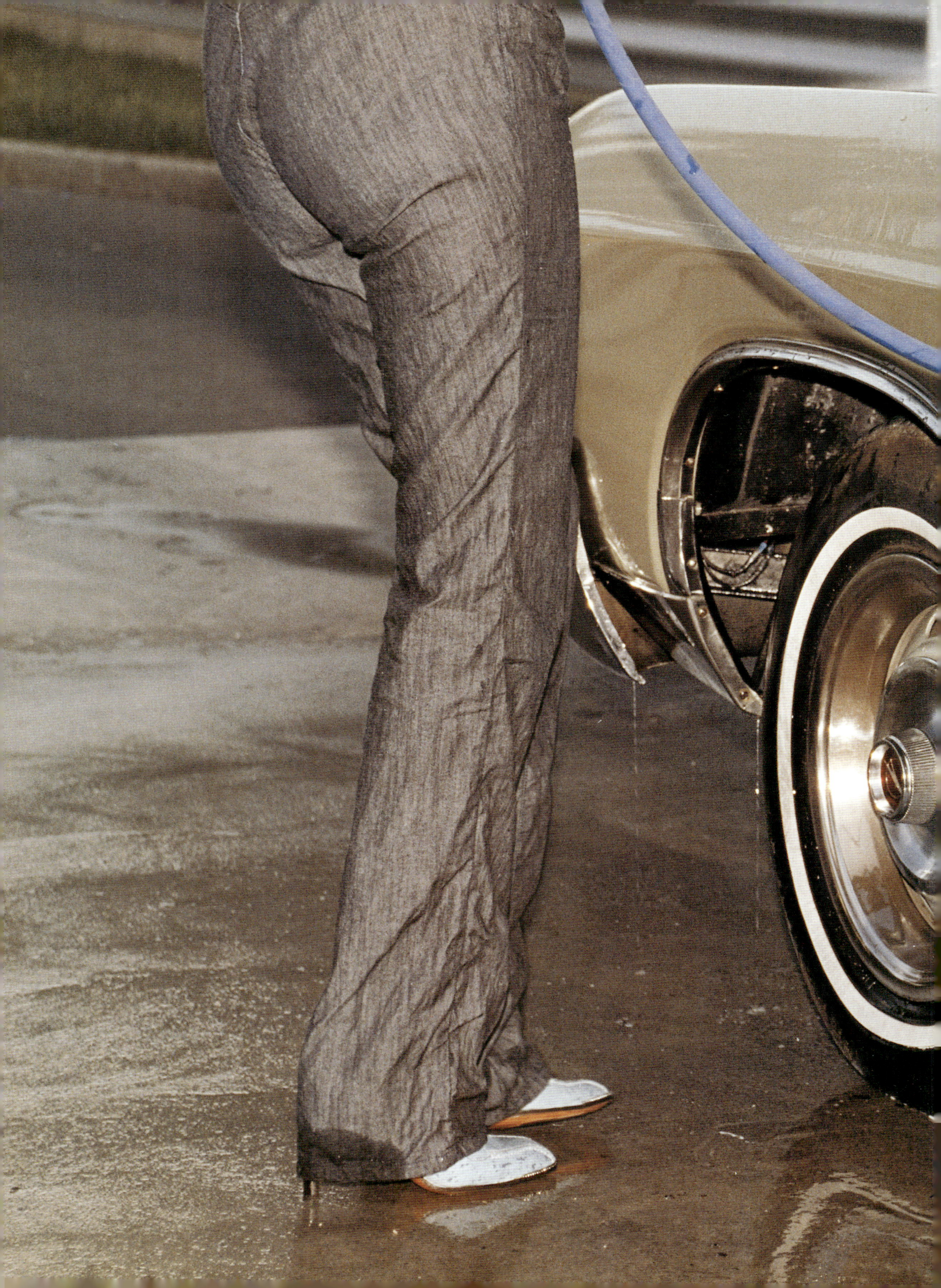

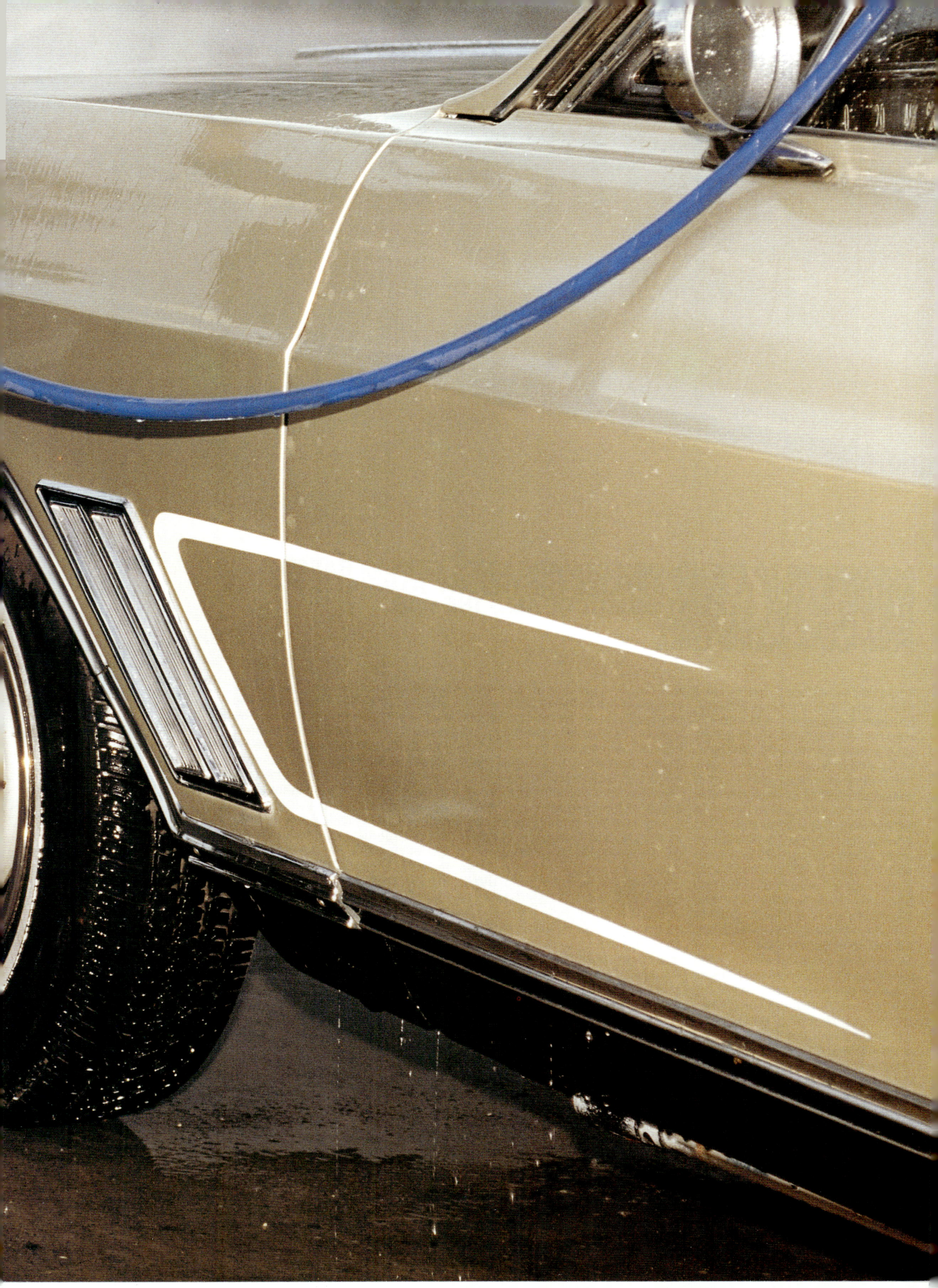

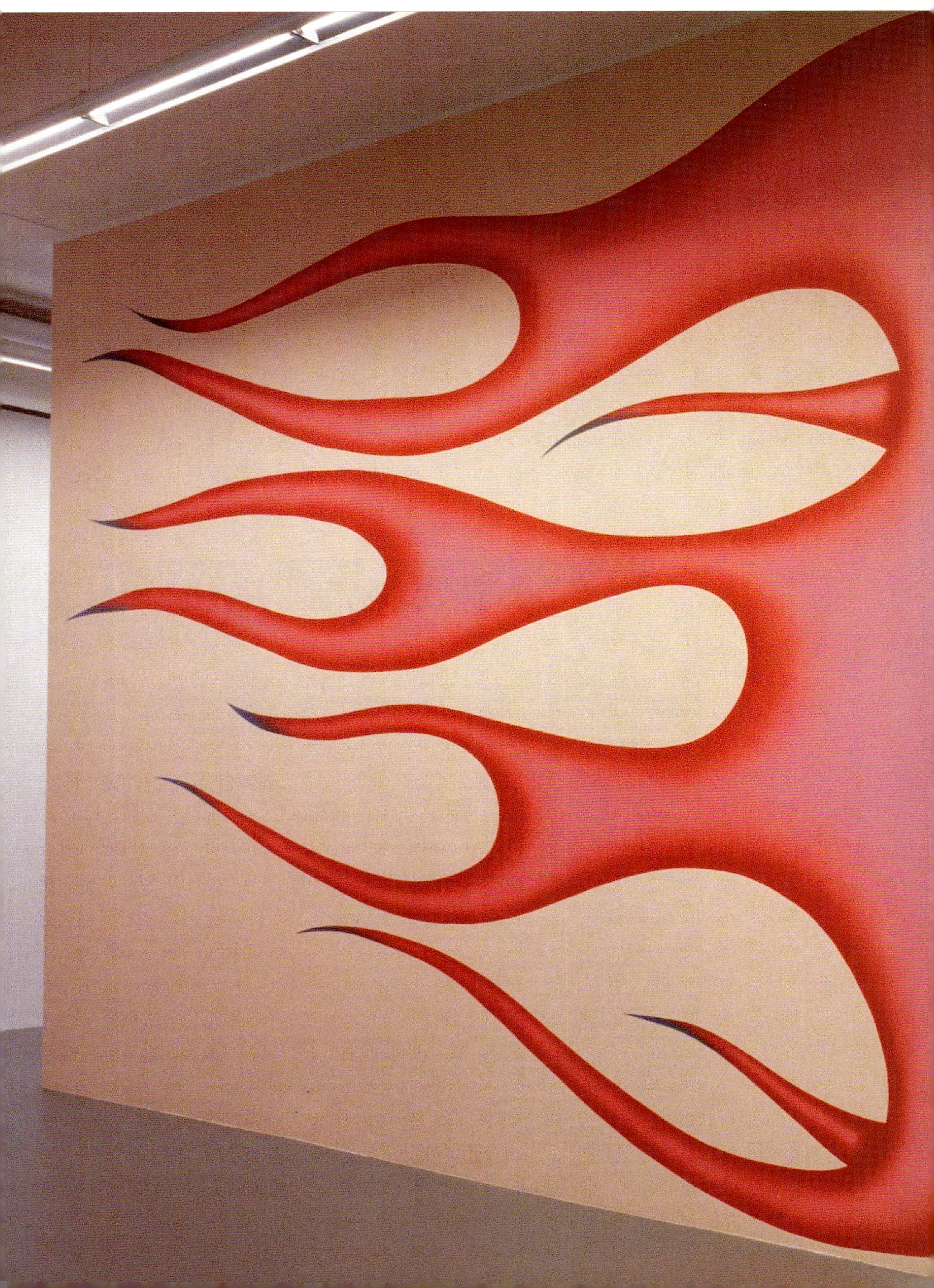

Sylvie Fleury
*Flames*, 1998
Wallpainting, dimensions adaptable
*Hot Heels* installation view,
Migros museum für gegenwartskunst, 1998/1999
courtesy Galerie Hauser & Wirth & Presenhuber, Zürich

Sylvie Fleury
*Skin Crime2 (Givenchy 601)*, 1997
compressed car, enamel
*Sylvie Fleury/John Armleder* installation view,
Kunstmuseum, St. Gall, CH, 2000
courtesy Galerie Hauser & Wirth & Presenhuber, Zürich

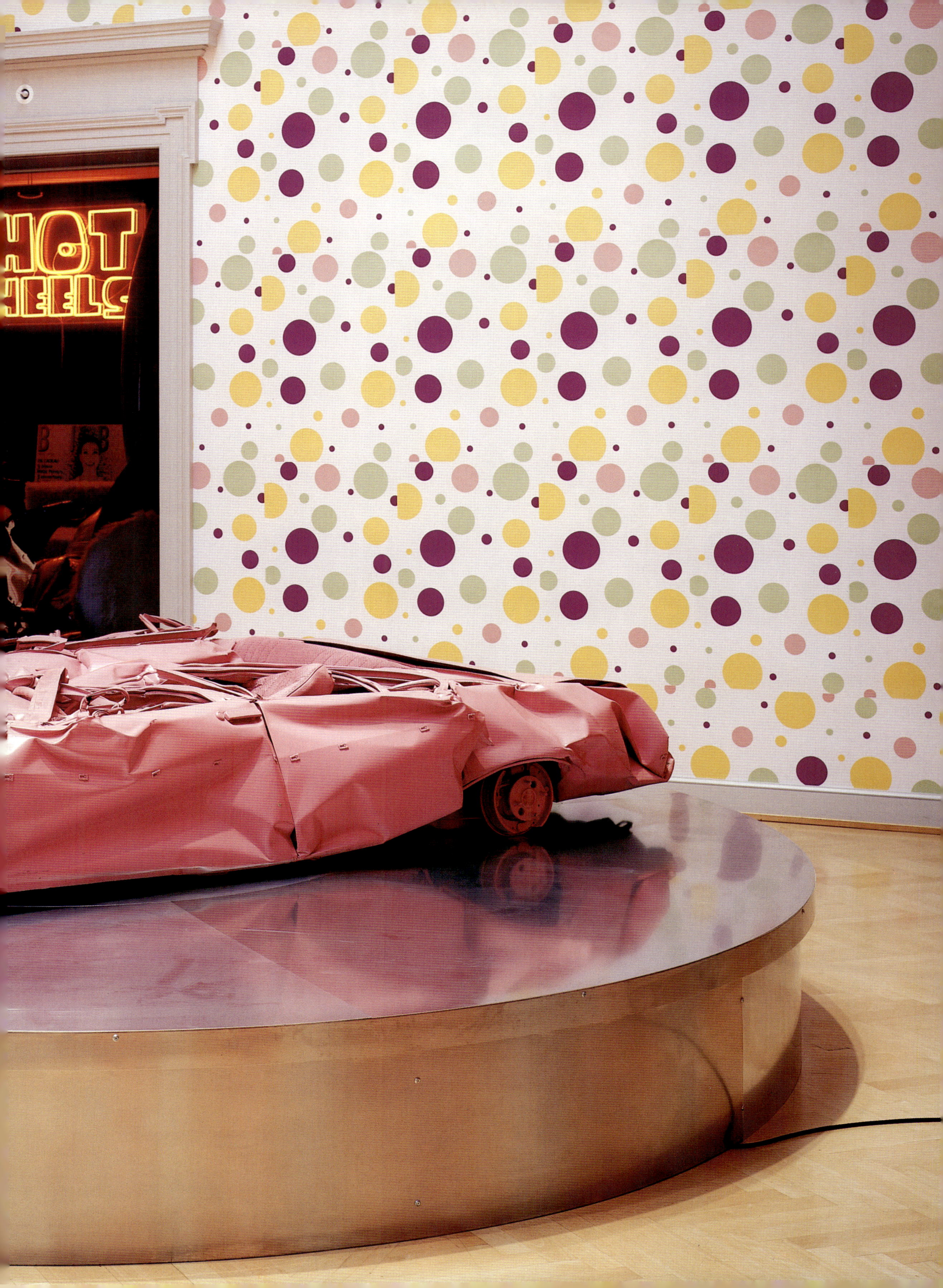
HOT

# THE END OF THE ROAD FOR ONE MAN

The saying goes, when you die you can't take it with you. Yet a tradition has developed on the coast of Ghana over the past 50 years that may have found a loophole in this concept.

Ghanaian fantasy coffins are luminous sculpted containers. The surreal, painted objects depict symbols that reflect an individuals' aspirations or role in life. The coffins often represent status symbol cars, but can range from oversized guns and mobile phones to giant trainers to immense animals.

The tradition began in Teshie, outside of Ghana's capital Accra, half a century ago. Coffin-maker Kane Kwei created a coffin in the shape of a plane for his deceased grandmother, who lived near an airbase. The coffin reflected her life and the worldly things that surrounded her, a trend that spread throughout Ghana. In a country with high mortality rates, death is nonetheless a huge deal and a cause for celebration not remorse.

The relationship between these relatively pagan objects and the church can be problematic. Some churches condemn them completely or only allow Bible-shaped coffins, giving a whole new meaning to dipping into a good book.

Although in Ghana the objects are intensely personal, they are now seen as art objects in their own right in the western world. The coffins are being commissioned and purchased by galleries - the British Museum, for example, has four coffins in the entrance to its new African Galleries. In a world where possession and status are the main driving forces in life, these are fascinating reflections of social appetites.

Green Mercedes and Batmobile carved by
Theophilus Nii Anum Sowah
White Mercedes carved by Paa Willie
Photography Denis Nervig
Courtesy of Ernie Wolfe Gallery, Los Angeles

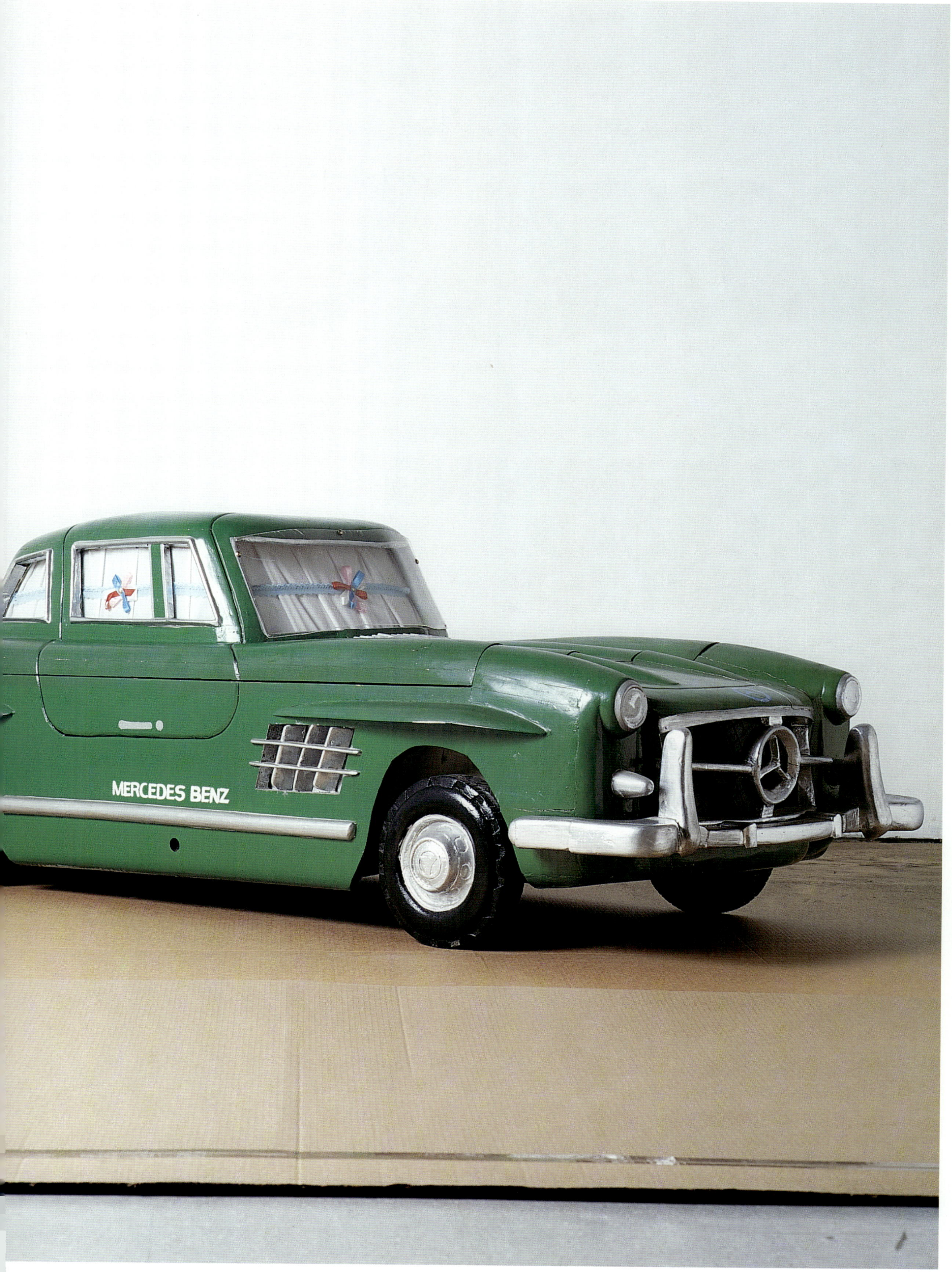
MERCEDES BENZ

# IS THE BEGINNING OF THE ROAD FOR ANOTHER

There's something utterly beguiling about the disturbing form of a family saloon or burnt-out transit van that is wholly absent in their forecourt perfection - in the same way Iggy Pop will always look better Ronan Keating. It's when these dusted, rusted and twisted shells receive further hits to the body, however, that they really begin to live again.

Graffiti writers - always on the lookout for new surfaces to coat - are latching on to snapped axles and beaten panels in the same way they did the sides of trains, shop shutters and civic walls. Just as vultures pick over carrion, graffiti writers like Nylon from Brighton find abandoned four-doors make for good eats.

"The cars are like little gifts to us - they're just like a good street hit. When you've finished it looks rough and ready, like that's where it belongs. This big old piece of junk is like a natural canvas and that's what we like to paint," he enthuses. For Nylon, there is another reason this method of getting fame from his name (or tag) sits so well. "I embrace them because they literally represent the name of my crew - Street Trash Punks. These cars are great big bits of street trash that have got to be smashed and crushed in a breaker's yard and that is where our name belongs."

Yet while writers have discovered there's much fun to be had decorating deceased diesels, local councils in the UK, responsible for removing them, find them a financial pain. At £500 a pop to lift them from the road and with dozens disposed of every week, the cost soon begins to mount up.

The obvious explanation may be to blame the mounting junk on an increase in joyriding. But, less obviously, world peace and environmental legislation are in fact more to blame than delinquent 14-year-olds. According to salvage experts, the price of scrap metal has plummeted due to a drastic drop in demand from its main buyers - global car and military vehicle manufacturers. With a flood of cheap imports from eastern Europe bringing down prices even further, plus higher taxes on landfill sites to encourage the recycling of non-steel car parts, profit from vehicle salvage is being eroded on all fronts. Thus today Mr and Mrs two-point-four eschew the breakers' yard (traditional home of the Rottweiller and its stained-vested, beer-gutted owner who is likely to charge for the privilege of taking their car away) for the quiet side road. Until governments work out a way to either penalise owners who dump, or provide incentives for them to remove the cars themselves, you can look forward to seeing a lot more abandoned cars on the street. Dumped by joe public, then daubed with smash and grab graphology, at least then the scrap-in-waiting can briefly become public art. Council-collected after being freshly painted, it then gets morphed into something new once again.

Text Ephraim Webber and Guy Bird
Photography Yorgo Tloupas

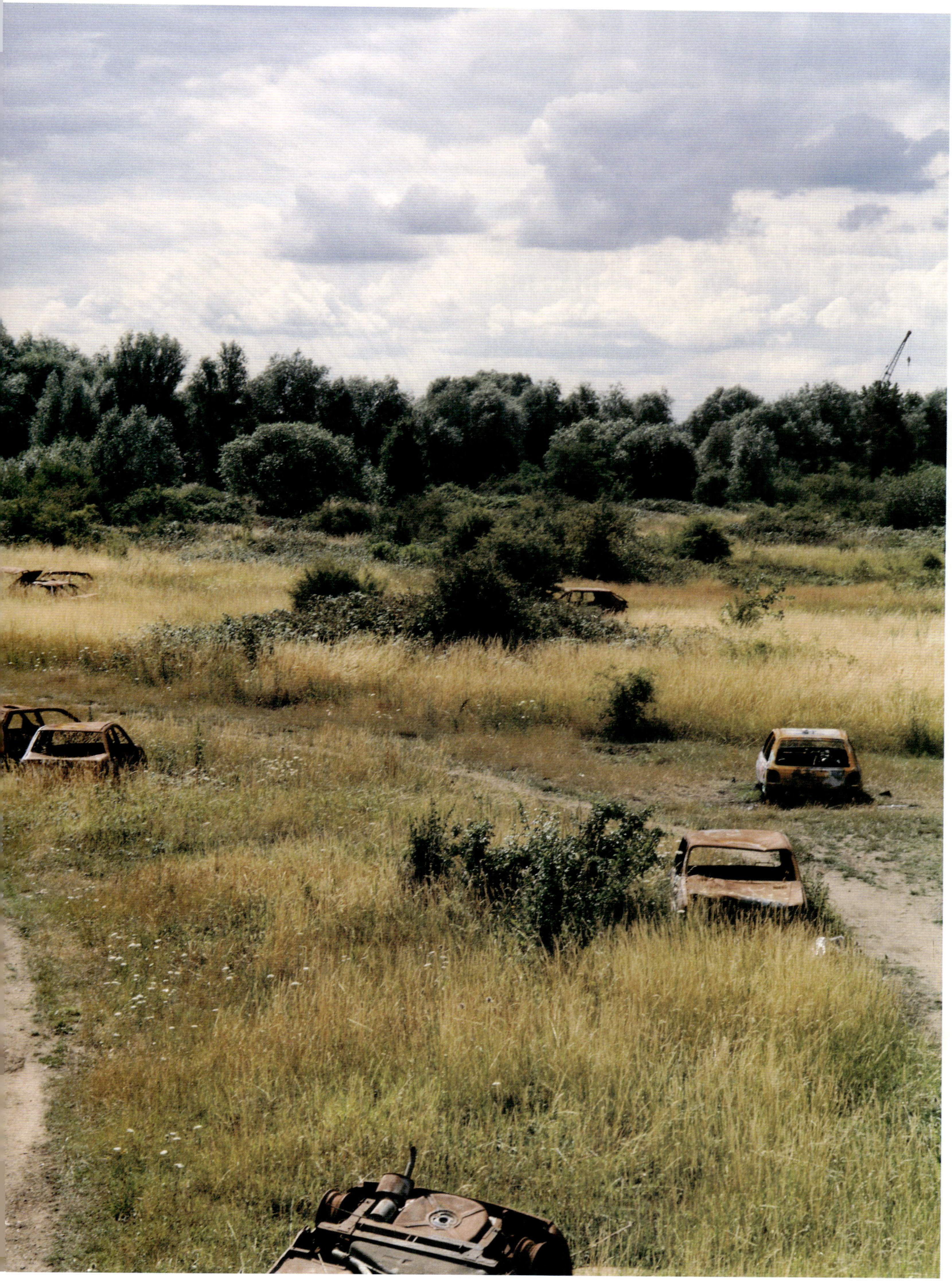

Sens between Champigny-sur-Yonne and Villeneuve-la-Guyard. The car, which wasn't travelling especially quickly according to the survivors, swerved for no apparent reason. It skidded on the damp surface, hit a tree, rebounded, then came to rest on another tree 13m further on. Camus was thrown back through the rear window where he broke his neck and fractured his skull. He died instantly. Gallimard - thrown against the rigid spear-like steering column - was bleeding profusely and died six days later of a brain haemorrhage in a Paris hospital. It took police two hours to free Camus' body from the wreckage.

His wife was found shocked but relatively unscathed, as was her daughter Anne who had come to rest in a muddy field 20m from the car. The dog disappeared, never to be seen again. In the instrument panel, thrown nine metres along from the car's final resting place, was the clock which had stopped at 13.54.

Witnesses were interviewed and the crash scene analysed. Jean Daninos, patron of the company that built the Facel Vega car, was haunted by the idea that the cause of the crash might have been a failure in his car. He sent down his own expert, the former racing driver Lance Macklin, to weigh-up the scene.

"The one thing Lance was terribly good at was reading an accident," said Macklins' wife Shelagh, who had accompanied him. "We went to where this accident had occurred and he said 'It's quite obvious... it was a car failure...'"

Certainly the surviving women reported that they felt something give way underneath the car just before the impact.

"It upset Daninos dreadfully," Shelagh remembered. "He was so upset about that. He said, 'I can't sleep at night thinking about it if it was my fault, a technical fault...'"

Publicly, the finger continued to be pointed even more insistently at Gallimard - despite the fact that he had now died and couldn't answer back. Or perhaps because of it.

The press implied that his tyres were dangerously worn, that one had burst at 90mph, that Gallimard had hit the brakes at just the wrong moment, that he was ill and had

## CAMUS WOULD SAY "NOW, WE ARE NOT IN A HURRY"

fainted at the wheel, that perhaps he had consumed too much at lunchtime and was tired... They had their victim - Camus - and now they needed a culprit to make some kind of sense of his death.

A former tutor of Gallimard, Rene Etiemble, stepped into the fray in his defence. He pointed out the car's tyres were actually new, that Gallimard was in good heath and that Camus had made many trips in the car, because he was confident in Michel's driving. "Only with Michel," Camus had said. "With him, I am never frightened."

Rene Etiemble suspected that the car, not the driver, was at fault and began to assemble a dossier against the company, who were evasive despite the private anguish of Jean Daninos.

Ultimately though, the Gallimard family didn't want a fuss and acquiesced to the court's decision, nearly three years later in April '63, that Gallimard had been driving too quickly on worn tyres and that no responsibility lay with Facel Vega.

On that foggy afternoon in January 1960, Albert Camus - novelist, and reluctant philosopher - died in a mundane car crash, a victim of chance and "the tender indifference of the world" which was the guiding principle of his work. The bitter philosophical irony would not have been lost on this second-youngest ever Nobel Prize winner, a white French Algerian who had once called Sartre a friend, played in goal for his national football team and helped the resistance during the war.

He didn't like cars and hated speed. Whenever possible, he would take a train. If he did drive his old Citroën, it was very carefully - his friends ridiculed him because he drove so slowly. On many occasions Camus had said to his friends, "There can be nothing more scandalous than the death of a child, nothing more absurd than to die in a car accident."

# THE PASSENGER

**TEXT
EMMA FORREST**

It's a ten-hour drive back to New York from Ohio. I look over at him and make a cute face and, for the first tenth of the journey, he makes a cute face back. After that we only look at each other when we stop at gas stations for cheetos, slurpees, ding-dongs and other flammable foods. I am no longer cute and neither is the scenery through which we plod, keeping step with my mood like the radio on a 4am cab ride. Pennsylvania is our nemesis, a big, bad, boring stretch that takes up half the trip and has nothing to offer but a backdrop for bickering.

I have a scarf around my head but this isn't an open top car. There is soda debris rattling around my feet. Every couple of minutes I check my reflection in the mirror above my head. It is like opening a fridge door over and over to see if there's anything new there. I stretch my feet up on the dashboard and it isn't sexy at all. We have been so close this week and now, with the way I bend and bow my legs, he is an underpaid captain, rigid with concentration, and I am a passenger squeezed into coach and we both feel lonely.

"Do you want to hear Tom Waits again?" "No," he says quietly and calmly, as though he were a negotiator in a hostage situation and me and Tom Waits were the kidnappers. He doesn't want to hear anything. He just wants to drive.

The American myth is supposed to ingrain in its citizens the unshakeable belief in "a manifest destiny": this land belongs to all of us, from sea to shining sea. It is the American way to traverse as much of it as we can, hence the hymns of Steinbeck and Springsteen. The immigrant Russians and Poles who invented Hollywood travelled from New York to California to fulfil that dream and the dream repaid them in kind. If you are any kind of American, you are supposed to want to hit the highways at every opportunity. To do anything less would be turning down a great gift. I am not any kind of American: I am the passenger.

Not having a drivers licence never mattered when I lived in London. As much as everyone complained about it, the Underground got me comprehensively from A to B. I even had a dream that the Underground was an interactive board game, guarded by celebrities who would either help or hinder my journey through their magical powers. Paul Newman was the benevolent guardian of the District line.

Living in Manhattan, I can get away with it. I love walking, and the way the streets are numbered rather than named is like a cheer-leading squad: "Keep going, keep going!" And I do, arriving home with snow up to my knees in winter and strange, calf-splash sunburn in July. There are many like me. Although they can drive if they need to, they choose not to since driving in New York, with its enraged bike messengers and incessant traffic jams, is the apotheosis of manifest destiny.

In LA, where there is no public transport, and cabs, which usually cost a minimum of $30 wherever you're going, can't be hailed on the street, it is a different story. People are horrified. It affects friendships. They start off wanting to protect me and come to resent me. Lifts to my meetings melt into unreturned phone calls and friend-ships fizzle out.

I have a secret though: I love Bruce Springsteen. Madly. Hopefully. The way other people love Bob Dylan. I wish I could drive so that I could hear him over a car stereo - in his natural habitat. Is there anything more pathetic than a Springsteen fan who doesn't know how to drive? "You could learn," people tell me all the time. But I couldn't.

I can't cook. I can't clear a table. I stand dumbly and say, "Is there anything I can do?" and the host always says no because they know that there isn't. I can't ride a bicycle, not on a busy road, because I don't understand when I'm allowed to turn and what the cars behind me are up to. I still have no idea what I should do were, God forbid, the driver to collapse at the wheel. And there's something soothing about that. There is nothing I can do. It's out of my hands. There are passengers who can busy themselves reading maps, but they are not true passengers. I can do nothing but be transported.

As we enter New Jersey it rains, really rains, and one by one cars begin to pull over at the side. But he thinks that is too dangerous, so we just try to get through it. I start to shake a little. I squint my eyes, as though the slick road were a slasher film, more watchable with less to see. If I'm going to be killed, I don't want to know. Which is how come he's the driver and I'm the passenger. The rain eases up and he smiles at me, cute. I flip open the overhead mirror one last time. I'm good at this.

# MY OTHER CAR IS A GIANT ROBOT

Straight out of a *Transformers* cartoon, the Robocar is the work of Brazilian-based special effects company Marc Produções.

It took owner Olésio da Silva and sons Marco Aurélio and Marcus Vinícius nine months and US$70,000 to create this singular machine. Disbelief is invariably the first reaction towards Robocar, quickly followed by slack-jawed wonder as the awesome spectacle of transformation unfolds. The lights dim, a faint heartbeat barely discernible through 5,000 watts of music.

Powered by an electromechanical system synchronised with the sound, light and smoke effects, as the beast metamorphosises its heartbeat grows in intensity. Five minutes is all it takes for the family-friendly Kia to become an imposing metal colossus, its heartbeat now thudding in one's ears. After reaching full extension, Robocar tilts its head and speaks to the crowd in a crisp, digitised voice. The show is sinisterly entertaining, creating the impression that the machine could probably take over the world if the thought ever crossed its non-existent mind. Which is, in essence, Robocar's mission in life. Conceived in Brazil as a marketing tool, its roster of appearances so far includes auto shows, raves and children's birthday parties. Turning robotics from a hobby into his profession fulfilled a lifelong dream for da Silva, formerly a television special effects technician. After a slow start (Brazilian demand for recreational robots being rather limited), the financial and technical success of Robocar has kept the dream alive, and its cult status on the internet has spread his company's name around the world. Marc Produções has moved on to other cybernetic creations, such as a car that opens like a flower, splaying into six parts to reveal its innards. But Robocar is still Brazil's leading car-robot combo, a life-sized cartoon toy with automatic transmission and global ambition. Now all we need to figure out is if Robocar belongs to the righteous Autobot clan or the evil Decepticons…

Text Thomaz Autran

*"Try giving me a ticket now"*
(Robocar)

*"The best bit was when it turned into a robot"*
(10-year-old boy)

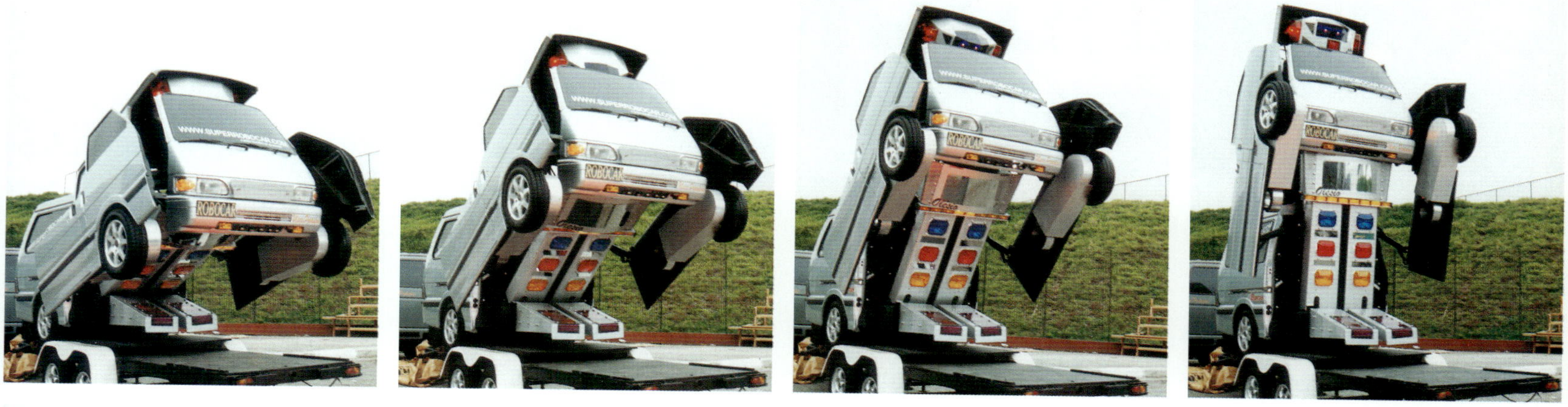

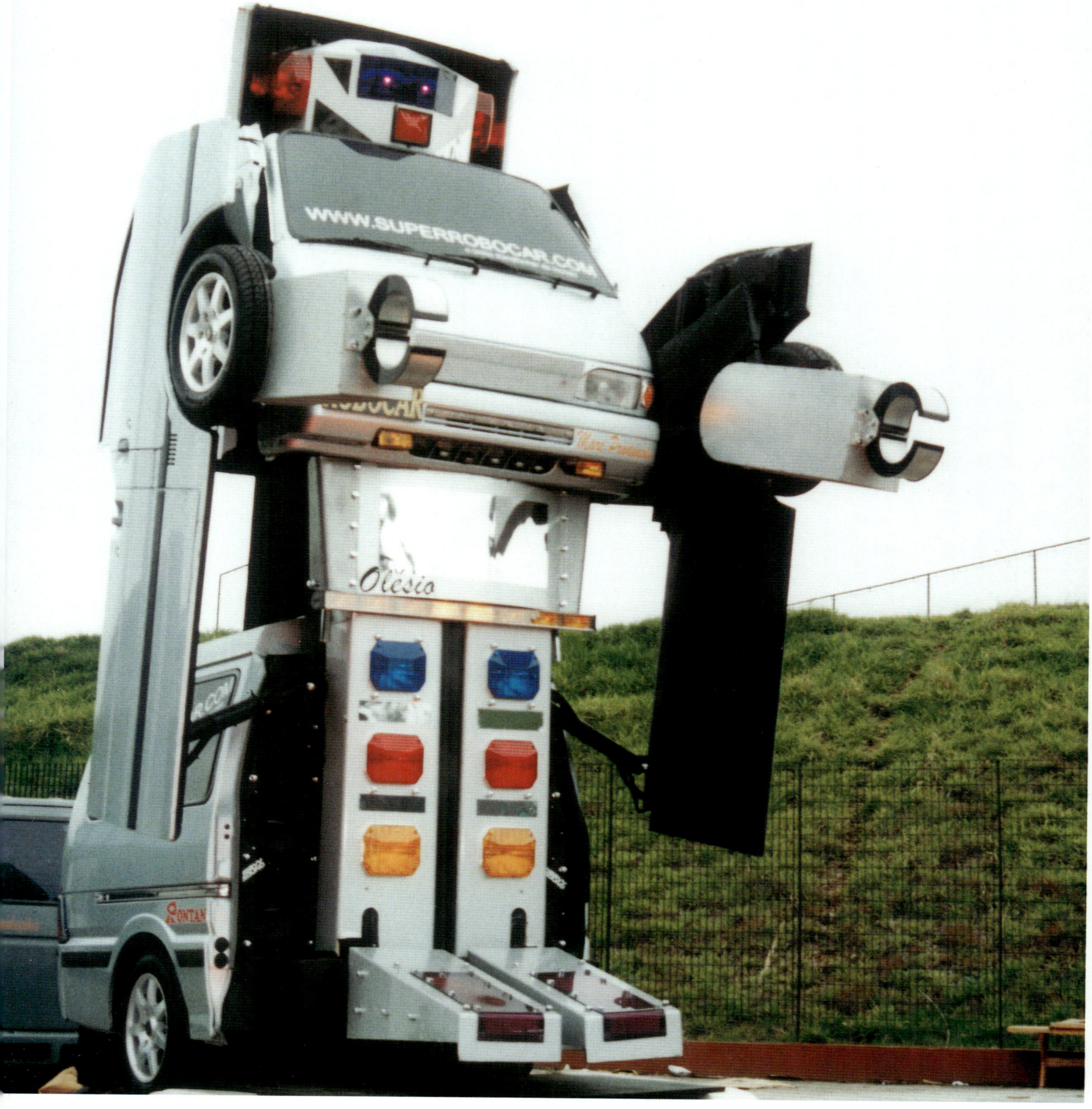
WWW.SUPERROBOCAR.COM
Olésio

# CONTRIBUTORS

**John Arlidge** interviewed Chris Bangle, BMW's head of design. John is on the staff of *The Observer* newspaper, and also writes for *Esquire* and *Arena* magazines and the trends forecasting journal *Viewpoint* / **Lizzie Bailey** investigated the feasibility of flying cars and the future of their land-bound equivalents. Based in London, the American technophile writes for *Wallpaper*, *Wired*, *The Sunday Times* and *Red* / **Hannah Baldock** interviewed Zaha Hadid. Hannah is an architectural journalist, writing for *Building*, *RIBA Journal* and *The Guardian* / **Guy Bird** has a background editing graffiti magazine *Graphotism* and car magazines such as *Business Car*. He is Deputy Editor of *Intersection*, but deputised Jill Evans to test drive a Hummer / **Martin Buckley** is Editor at Large of *Classic Cars*, and is currently writing a book on the Facel Vega. He told us the tale of Albert Camus and the vintage car / **Matt Carroll** is a freelancer writing for *GQ*, *AutoSport* and *FHM Bionic*. He took a look at cars in Britain's garage music scene / **Uma Jones** is a Welsh-born, Hollywood-based pseudonym for a well-known car journalist who wishes to remain anonymous. She went back to the future for a closer look at retro / British born, New York based **Emma Forrest** started her column as The Passenger. Emma writes for *The Saturday Telegraph* magazine, *Arena*, *Interview* and *Harpers Bazaar*. Her new novel, *Thin Skin* will be published by Bloomsbury in spring 2002 / **Emma E Forrest** is Interviews Editor of *Intersection*. She is also edits *Dazed & Confused*'s online magazine www.confused.co.uk, and has written for *Time Magazine*, *The Independent on Sunday*, *Seven* and *Nylon*. Emma interviewed girl racer Jutta Kleinschmidt / **Francesca Gavin** who interviewed artist Sylvie Fleury is the international agenda editor at *Time Out, London*, and is a regular contributor to *Dazed & Confused* and *Blueprint* magazine / **Malcolm Gladwell** is author of *The Tipping Point*, and on the staff of *The New Yorker*, where his article on car safety in America first caught our eye / **Joseph Patel** lives in New York and writes for *Vibe*, *The Source*, *URB*, *Rolling Stone*, *Paper*, *Flaunt*, *Vice* and *The Village Voice*. He went shopping for rims with Little Louis Vega and Todd Terry / **Dan Ross** is Editor-in-Chief of *Intersection*, and hopes to be allowed back on the Gumball Rally after abusing his position to cover it at length / **Rob Waugh** took time out from exotic assignments for *Stuff*, *Computer & Video Games*, and *Kitchens, Bedrooms & Bathrooms* to talk to Jarvis Cocker / Better known as E-frame, **Ephraim Webber** is a hip hop and graffiti art journalist, and is Editor of *Graphotism*. He explored the fields by Feltham Young Offenders Institute with Guy Bird for paint-bombed cars / **Huw Williams** has worked as a video editor in war zones for the *BBC*, but now makes documentaries and writes about extreme sports for publications including *The Guardian* and *The Times*. We sent him to a traffic jam in Lagos / Thanks also to **Sean Pillot de Chenecey**, **John Bell**, **Karta Healy**, **Damien Morris**, **Kira Philips**, **Jefferson Hack** and **Kirk Teasdale** for their ideas, advice and support.

**Bruno Barbey** photographed soldiers posing for a souvenir snap next to a burnt-out car in Kuwait whilst covering the Gulf War for *Magnum* / **Cedric Buchet** is a French fashion photographer, whose trademark bleached-out style emerged from editorial work in *Big*, *Self Service* and *Dazed & Confused*, and advertising campaigns for clients such as Prada. He chose a location in Brittany to shoot the cover image / French photographer **Linda Bujoli** showed her love for bodies, shadows and rays of light in French *Vogue* and *CitizenK*, and photographed rally driver Jutta Kleinschmidt in Monaco / **David Burton** took over an underground car park in London for his portraits of UK garage stars, developing an interest in cars and status from his work in *Arena Homme+* / German **Michael Danner** works regularly for *Tank* and *Wallpaper\**, and created a recent ad campaign for Stüssy. He photographed BMW's new X-coupe with its designer, Chris Bangle / French war photographer **Luc Delahaye** documented the conflict in Northern Ireland. Recognition for his work includes first prize World Press Photo Awards in both '93 and '94 / **James Dimmock** shot his "On Reflection" fashion story on the freshly buffed surfaces of sports cars. Past assignments have been for *Spin* and *The Face* / **Nicolas Faure**'s documentary images of the monolithic Swiss highways have been published in the book *Autoland*, a selection of which are accompanied by a passage from Milan Kundera's *Immortality* (Faber & Faber) in "Routes and Roads" / **Christian Frey** is a Berlin-based graphic artist whose "Zero-G Autobahn" imagines a sky-bound highway as part of the story on flying cars / **Frederike Helwig** found the Gumball Rally an exhausting if ultimately refreshing change from her normal fashion and music portrait work for *The Face*, *Nova* and *i-D* / Long Beach-born, LA-based **Daniel Hennessy** drove to Palm Springs in search of bizzare golf buggies, and has previously shot for *Flaunt*, *Soma* and *Gear* / American photographer **Carol Guzy** is a three-time Pulitzer Prize winner. Her documentation of Ghanaian car coffins was originally shot for *The Washington Post*. / **Christian Lesemann** took his signature-style telephoto lens to Monaco to capture the spectacle of the Grand Prix. The self-proclaimed paparazzo has, amongst others, shot for *Big* and *Dazed & Confused* / We asked Swiss-based graphic artist and photographer **Marie Lusa** to shoot the artist Sylvie Fleury. In a happy coincidence, she had just designed Fleury's latest art book, and was more than happy to oblige / **Angelo Di Marco** is an Italian-born illustrator based in France, who has been working for the crime press for the last 30 years, and was delighted to illustrate the misadventures of a nervous driver / **Neil Massey** shoots for *Fader* and *Nylon* in the US, *Sleazenation* and *The Face* in the UK, and has created recent ad campaigns for Boxfresh. We took Neil to Le Mans to photograph the race and Stirling Moss, and to South London to cross the road under the watchful eye of the Lollipop Lady / Lebanese-born **Rishad Mistri** lives in New York, where he shoots regularly for *Flaunt*. He visited Rayco's with Todd Terry and "Little" Louis Vega / **Kristian Ranker** went to Las Vegas for our group test of people who work in casinos. Ad campaigns for G-star and Replay, as well as fashion for *Rank* and *The New York Times* keep him on the road otherwise / **Rankin** is a British photographer, and is co-publisher of *Intersection*, as well as *Dazed & Confused*, *Another Magazine* and his self-styled *Rank*. Rankin photographed Jarvis Cocker / **Patrick Rimond** divides his time between his native France and Osaka, where he developed a taste for Japanese vans / **Ewen Spencer** documented the Hummer test drive. Past credits include American magazine *Details* and *The Face* / **Daniel Stier** moved to London from Germany, and shoots for *Dutch*, *Wallpaper\**, *The Sunday Telegraph*, *The Face* and *Crash*. His portrait of a Ferrari fan illustrates why "They Call Him Enzio" / **Yorgo Tloupas** is Creative Director of *Intersection*, but moonlights as an illustrator (and sometime) photographer throughout the book / **Huw Williams** found taking photographs on the streets of Lagos wasn't popular with the public - he was assaulted twice, but returned intact with a written explanation of the city's complex relationship to traffic. / Since photographer **Jonathan de Villiers** swapped philosophy for fashion, his work has appeared in *Vogue*, *Self Service* and *Big*. Jonathan's portrait of Zaha Hadid with her private London taxi cab accompanies an interview focusing on her recently constructed, magnetically-styled car park. / Glove Story photographer **Camille Vivier** loves cars, but has mostly been shooting fashion for magazines such as *Purple*, *Big*, and the *Libération* supplement in France.

**Images**
Bruno Barbey, Hélène Binet, Cedric Buchet, Linda Bujoli, David Burton, Michael Danner, Luc Delahaye, James Dimmock, Nicolas Faure, Christian Frey, Sylvie Fleury, Frederike Helwig, Daniel Hennessy, Carol Guzy, Christian Lesemann, Marie Lusa, Angelo Di Marco, Neil Massey, Rishad Mistri, Kristian Ranker, Rankin, Patrick Rimond, Roger Rothan, Ewen Spencer, Daniel Stier, Yorgo Tloupas, Huw Williams, Jonathan De Villiers, Camille Vivier

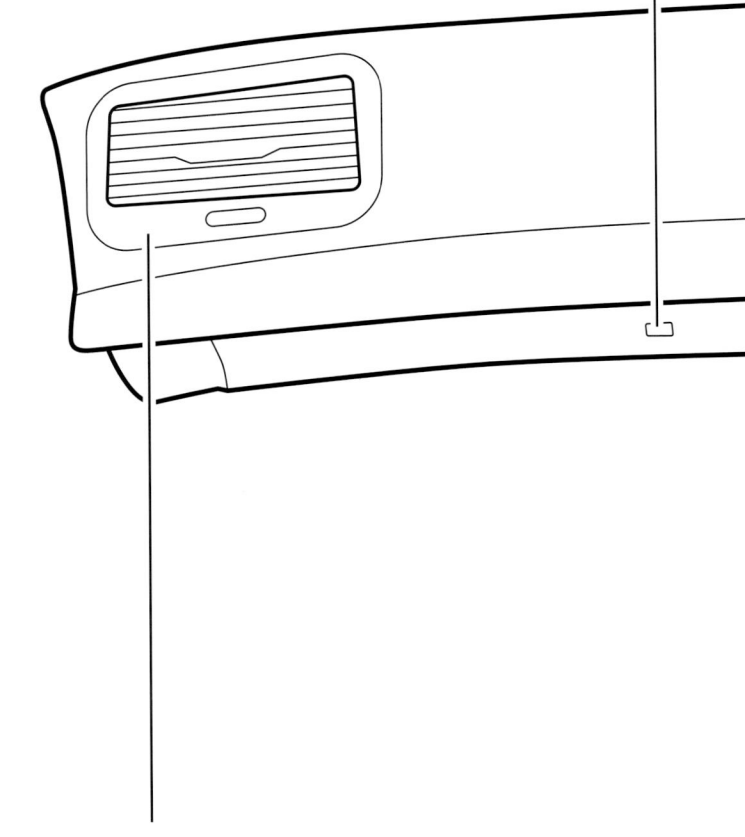

**Text**
John Arlidge, Lizzie Bailey, Hannah Baldock, Guy Bird, Martin Buckley, Chris Campion, Matt Carroll, Paul Flynn, Emma Forrest, Emma E Forrest, Thomaz Garcia, Uma Jones, Fran Gavin, Malcolm Gladwell, Joseph Patel, Dan Ross, Robert Waugh, Ephraim Webber, Huw Williams

**Editor-in-Chief**
Dan Ross

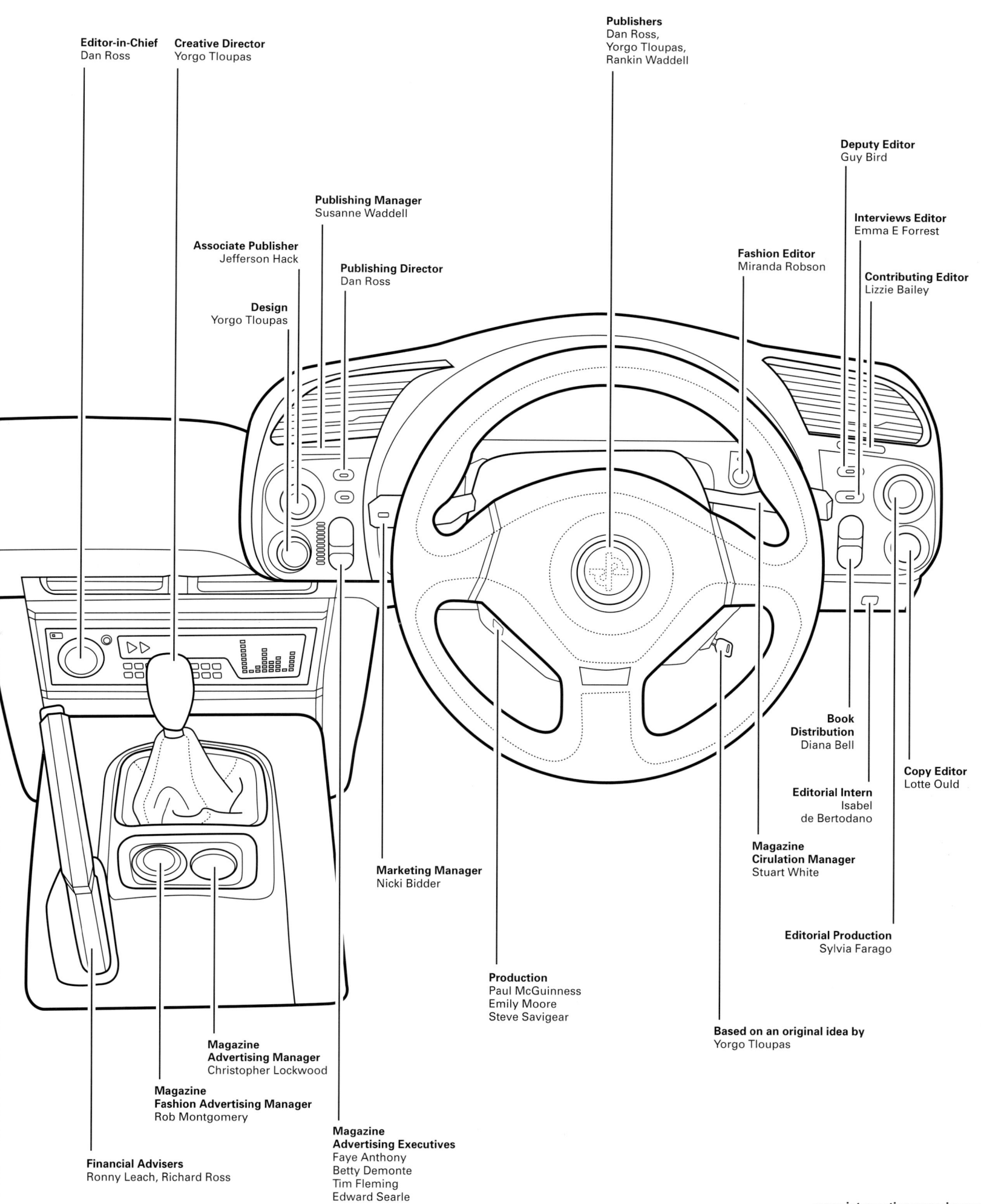

**Creative Director**
Yorgo Tloupas

**Publishers**
Dan Ross,
Yorgo Tloupas,
Rankin Waddell

**Deputy Editor**
Guy Bird

**Interviews Editor**
Emma E Forrest

**Publishing Manager**
Susanne Waddell

**Associate Publisher**
Jefferson Hack

**Fashion Editor**
Miranda Robson

**Contributing Editor**
Lizzie Bailey

**Publishing Director**
Dan Ross

**Design**
Yorgo Tloupas

**Book Distribution**
Diana Bell

**Editorial Intern**
Isabel de Bertodano

**Copy Editor**
Lotte Ould

**Marketing Manager**
Nicki Bidder

**Magazine Cirulation Manager**
Stuart White

**Editorial Production**
Sylvia Farago

**Production**
Paul McGuinness
Emily Moore
Steve Savigear

**Based on an original idea by**
Yorgo Tloupas

**Magazine Advertising Manager**
Christopher Lockwood

**Magazine Fashion Advertising Manager**
Rob Montgomery

**Magazine Advertising Executives**
Faye Anthony
Betty Demonte
Tim Fleming
Edward Searle

**Financial Advisers**
Ronny Leach, Richard Ross

www.intersectionmagazine.com
info@intersectionmagazine.com

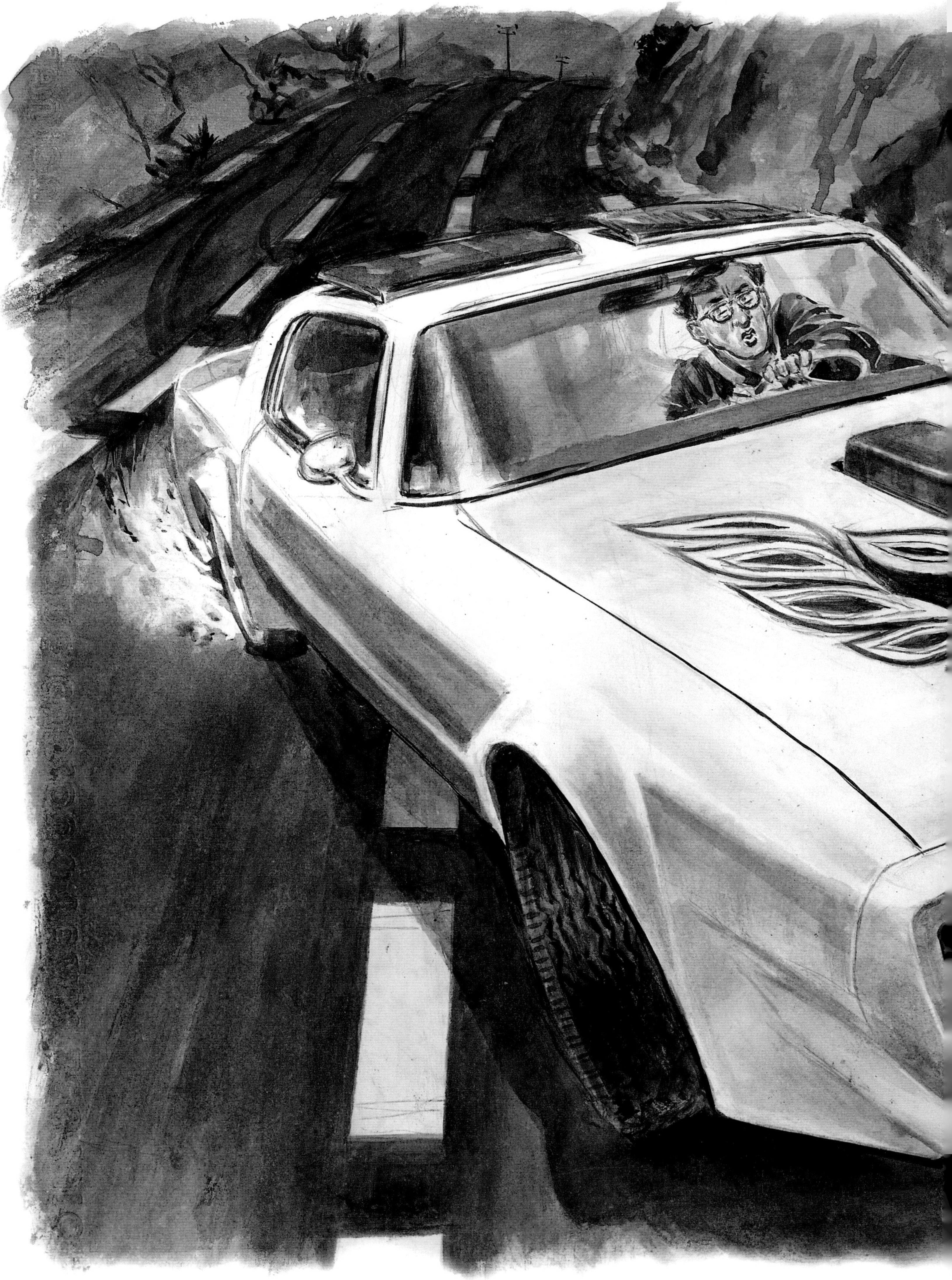

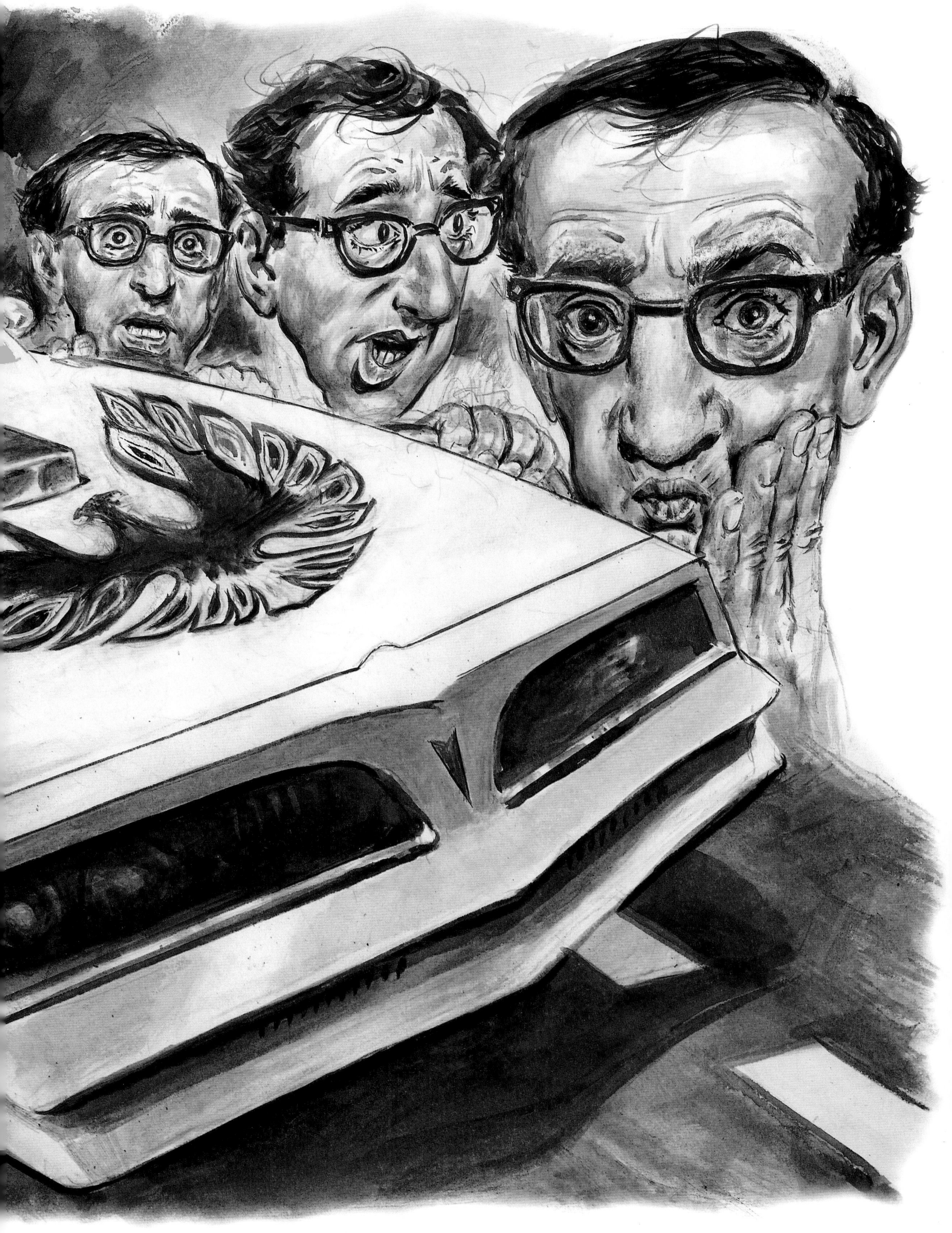

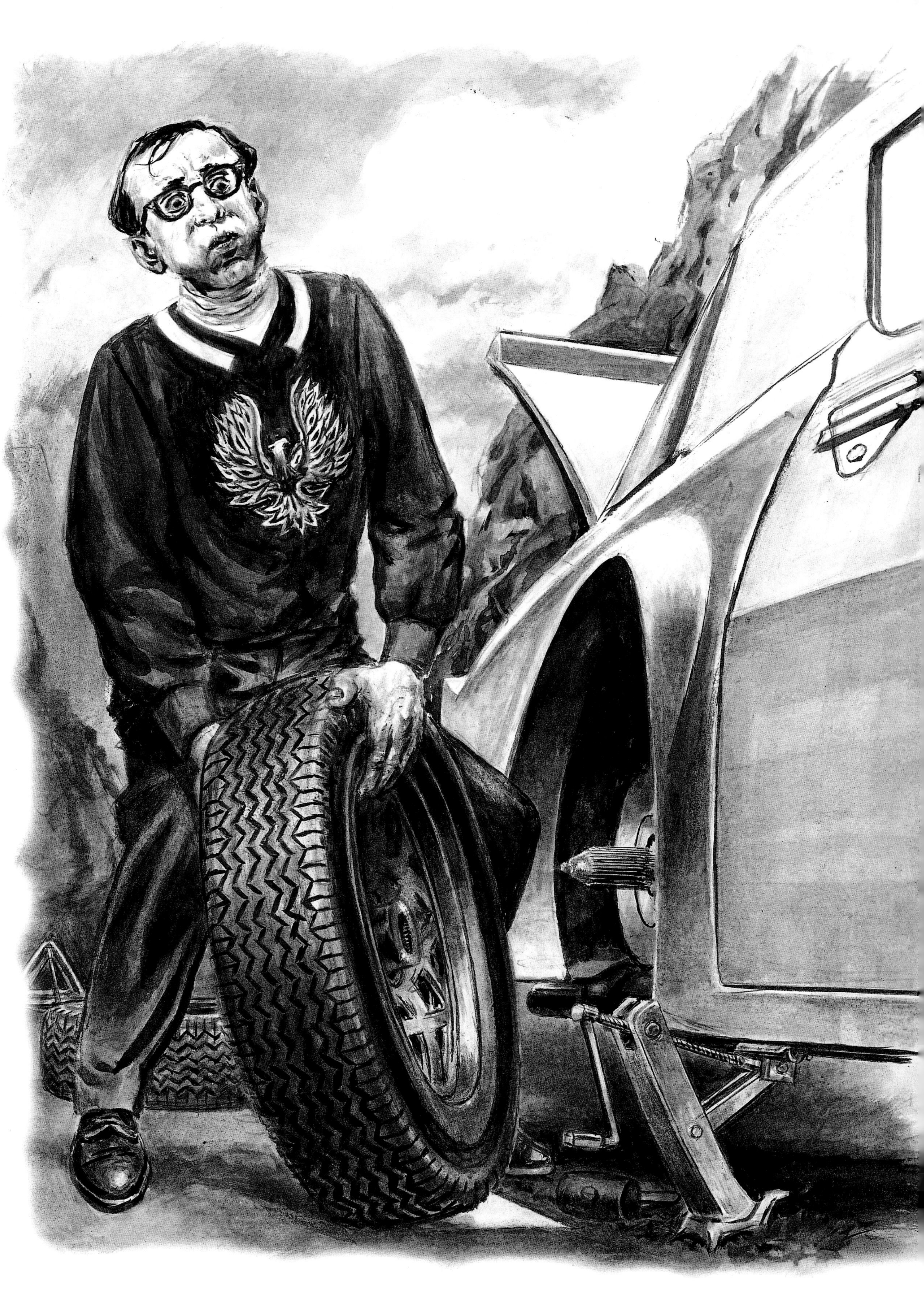

INTERSECTION SUPERACTION SERIES PRESENTS: MANUAL - EPISODE ONE

# THE HIGH SPEED BLOW-OUT

CUSTOMIZED WOOL SWEATER WITH TRIM SKI SWEATER, WOOL TROUSERS AND SHOES ALL BY PAUL SMITH BLACK RIMMED GLASSES BY CUTLER & GROSS WHITE '78 FIREBIRD BY PONTIAC

## ILLUSTRATIONS BY ANGELO DIMARCO

Many thanks to: Emily, Paul, Kirk, Diana, Sarah, Steve and Alex at Vision On; Rachel, Callum, Dave, Suzy, Rupert, Laura and all at Dazed&Confused; Hector and all at Idea Generation; Sandra and the rest of Rankin Photography; Andy, Nick and all at AJD; Omar, Hani, Zeina, Zaid and Imad at the National Press; Alexandre Thumerelle, Michel Mallard and Xavier Favre; Guy, Emma, Sylvia, Miranda, Lotte, Lizzie, Huw, and all those who contributed so generously of their time, ideas and enthusiasm; Rosalyn, Richard, Suzy, Jean and Teresa for their support; and finally, to Rankin and Jefferson for believing in Intersection, even when it was called Le Car.

Retouching The Shoemakers' Elves
Reprographics AJD Colour
Print The National Press, Jordan

Intersection first published in Great Britain in 2001 by Intersection Magazine with production and distribution support from Vision On Publishing Ltd. Both companies can be contacted at :

112-116 Old Street
London EC1V 9BG
T +44 207 336 0766
F +44 207 336 0966
www.intersectionmagazine.com
info@intersectionmagazine.com
www.vobooks.com

All photography © the image-makers listed and/or Intersection Magazine

The right of each image-maker listed to be identified as the author of his or her work has been asserted by him or her in accordance with the Copyright, Designs and Patents Act of 1988. In every instance, all possible attempts have been made to ensure copyright has been respected and protected.

© 2001 Intersection Magazine. All rights reserved.

No part of this publication may be reproduced, stored in retrieval systems, or transmitted in any form or by any means electronic, mechanical, photocopied, recorded or otherwise, without the prior written permission of the copyright owner. The views expressed in Intersection are those of the respective contributors and are not necessarily shared by the magazine or its staff. A CIP catalogue record for this book is available from the British Library.

**Intersection**
ISBN 1903399424

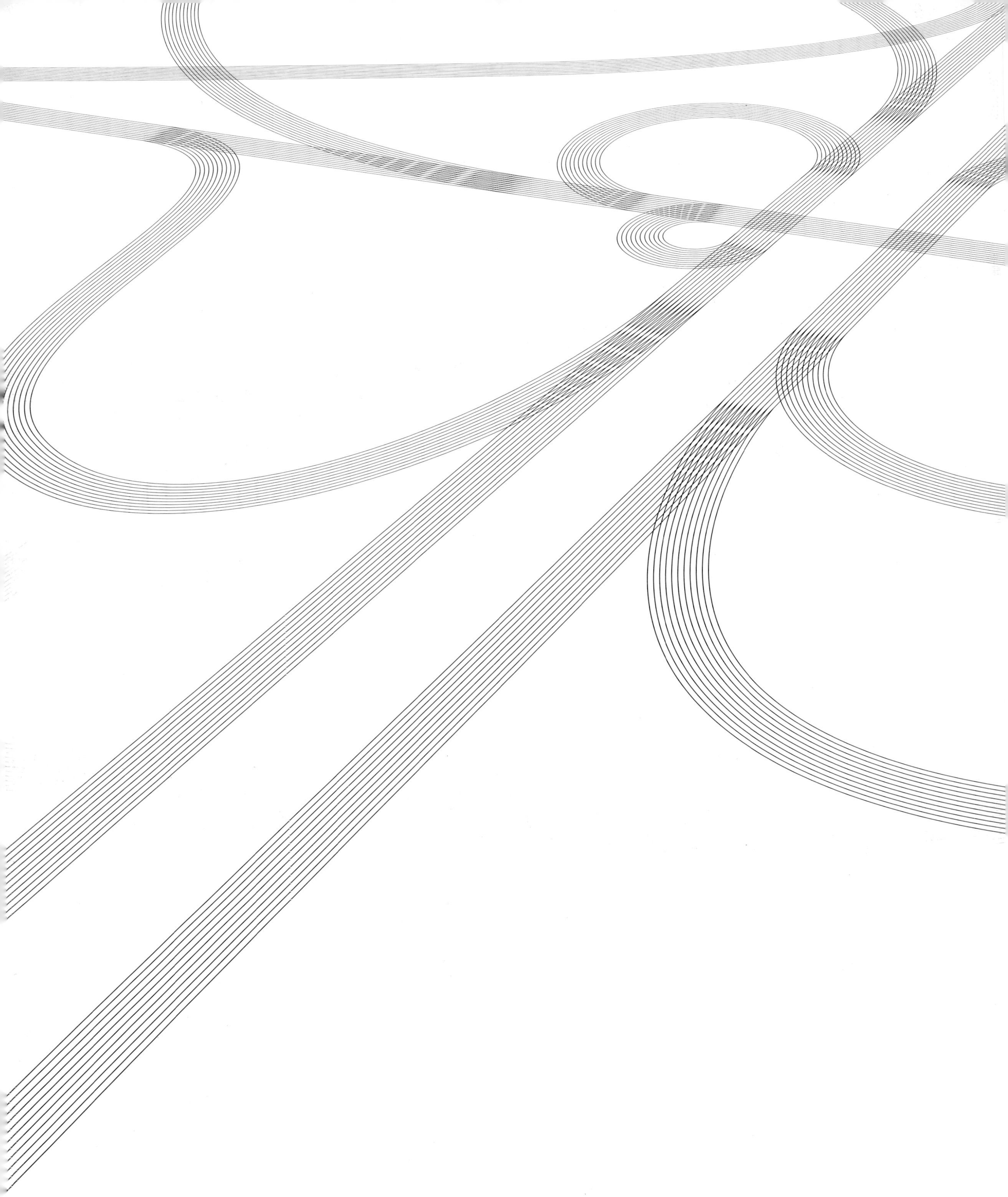